Islamic Economics Series – 19

Essays in
Islamic Economics

D1564377

M. FAHIM KHAN

The Islamic Foundation

ISBN 0 86037 245 6 (HB)
ISBN 0 86037 246 4 (PB)

Published by
The Islamic Foundation,
Markfield Dawah Centre,
Ratby Lane,
Markfield,
Leicester LE67 9RN
United Kingdom

Quran House,
PO Box 30611,
Nairobi,
Kenya

PMB 3193
Kano,
Nigeria

Printed and bound in Great Britain
by The Cromwell Press, Melksham, Wiltshire

Contents

PART I: CONSUMPTION

PART II: BANKING AND FINANCE

PART III: PRODUCTION AND INVESTMENT

PART IV: GROWTH AND DEVELOPMENT

PART V: SOME PUBLIC POLICY ASPECTS

Foreword

It is a great pleasure to write a foreword to this work by Professor Fahim Khan. Over recent years he has been as active as any economist in not only encouraging the development of the Islamic Economics paradigm but in making a serious contribution to research over a broad range of subject areas. This book represents the fruition of these many years of hard work and scholarly endeavour.

The book should be particularly welcome to economists in the Western world who are anxious to understand the economics of Islam and the role of Islamic financial systems, institutions and markets. Its focus is upon macroeconomics; the approach is to develop macroeconomic analysis by adapting Keynesian and neo-classical economics to reflect the principles of economics present in the Holy Qur'ān. As a teaching tool it will be invaluable. Take, for example, the theory of consumer behaviour (Chapter 2) and the macroeconomic consumption function (Chapter 3) which together form Part I of the book. The 'Western' convention is to use indifference curve analysis to describe maximization of consumer's utility. So it is here, with an Islamic perspective of the choice between present and future consumption. This leads into the allocation of resources according to needs identified in Islam, rather than to satisfying wants. The problem becomes not one of maximizing consumer utility using indifference curve analysis, but a 'balancing principle' which takes account of four levels of choice defined within the Islamic framework. Similarly the macroeconomic consumption function is analyzed by reference to conventional wisdom in standard texts in Western literature. There is always therefore a reference point to work to. Here the base is the typical Keynesian income-expenditure approach modified to incorporate consumer behaviour according to Islam.

This book therefore is essentially a very practical work. It makes no pretence to be highly philosophical; it does not, for example, compete with Umer Chapra's *Islam and the Economic Challenge*. Nor does it

Essays in Islamic Economics

want to. Yet it is precisely the kind of book that Western economists have been waiting for because it presents Islamic economics on a level playing field with Keynesian and neo-classical economics and, for this reason, is the vehicle for furthering an understanding, assisting economics teaching and ultimately prompting Western economists to give serious attention to researching the Islamic economics paradigm.

Department of Economics, **John Presley**
Loughborough University Head of Department
3 October 1994

x

Preface

This is a collection of separately written papers; although most have already been published in various places, it was felt that since they together cover the major aspects of an Islamic economy, it would be worthwhile to present them in a single volume. To begin with, these papers may serve as a first reading for students of Islamic economic analysis. There are several books that describe features of an Islamic economy but no one work provides analysis of the major aspects of such an economy in one place. With Islamic economics now recognized as an independent discipline in several universities of the world, this is a serious handicap for both students and teachers. While this collection has no pretensions to being a textbook, it is hoped that the papers in it may be of use as teaching/reading material when economic analysis in an Islamic perspective is the subject of study.

Secondly, the arguments put forward here may stimulate further thought and research on issues of urgent relevance for Islamic economic analysis. While the answers offered may not satisfy the reader at places, the questions raised will provoke him/her to identify gaps, point out methodological flaws, and suggest better ideas or instruments to analyze Islamic economic issues. Thirdly – and this is why these issues are immediately relevant – the arguments put forward may help to brief planners and policy makers in countries like Pakistan, Iran and Sudan which have explicit programmes to develop interest-free economies, and in other Muslim countries that intend to do so. It is vital, in view of various apprehensions being expressed in the literature about the consequences of Islamizing the economy, to offer convincing demonstrations of the viability of Islamic reform, for all major sectors in a contemporary economy. Our analysis shows that the fears of negative consequences are largely groundless, the positive consequences are shown to be both more striking and more logical.

Inevitably, in such a collection of separately written papers, the reader will find a measure of discontinuity between chapters, as well as some unnecessary repetition. The overview provided by the introductory first chapter should offset, at least in part, the discontinuity between chapters,

1

so that the reader has some sense of how the arguments of individual chapters contribute to an analysis of the Islamic economy as a whole.

Two aims were kept in mind when selecting the papers for this volume:

First, to show that an Islamic economy is viable, that it will not face any disorder if it decides to work according to Islamic injunctions.

Second, to show that Islamic economics is as amenable to rigorous theoretical analysis as conventional economics is, not only by way of demonstrating its amenability to predictions and policy control, but also its comparability with the economic paradigms.

The following limitations of this collection, not already mentioned, should be clearly understood.

Firstly, it cannot be said to cover all aspects of an economy. It covers only the broad contours of major aspects, namely, consumption, production, investment, money, finance and banking, and analyzes these with respect only to some topical issues currently bothering researchers and policy makers.

Secondly, it also cannot be said to have discussed and analyzed the implications of all Islamic economic injunctions and teachings. The eradication of interest is the dominant focus of discussion, not least because the eradication of interest is precisely the issue raised when doubts are cast on the viability of an Islamic economy. It seems quite proper that in first attempts to discuss the viability of Islamic economic injunctions, this subject should be the focus of the argument.

Other elements of an Islamic economy, such as the introduction of *zakāh* and other spending in the cause of Allah, reform of the system of property rights (particularly with reference to the economic role of the public sector, the treatment of market failures, etc.), reforms in market practices, and so on, have been discussed but they have not been accorded the prominence accorded to the eradication of interest. Because these elements of an Islamic economy have not so far been seriously pointed to, by anyone, as posing any sort of threat, fuller discussion of them can therefore be left for future study.

A comprehensive account of an Islamic economy in all its philosophical, political and ethical aspects, given the multi-disciplinary nature of such a task, can hardly be done at one go. It will take several steps by several scholars to realize such an aim. This collection is humbly presented as a first step, in the hope that fair and careful academic scrutiny will help in the revisions and extensions necessary before the subsequent steps can be taken.

I am grateful to the Islamic Foundation who agreed to make my manuscript available in presentable form for publication. May I express also my thanks to the Chairman of the Foundation, Professor Khurshid Ahmad, who has contributed so much to the discipline of Islamic economics, not least through the series of books on the subject published by the Foundation.

Jeddah   **M. Fahim Khan**
1 July, 1994
22 Muharram, 1415 H

CHAPTER 1

Introduction:
Overview of an Islamic Economy

The twelve papers in this collection describe and analyze various aspects of an economy committed to operating according to Islamic principles. The discussion is in five parts. Parts I–III focus on micro as well as macro aspects of major elements of the economy, including consumption, production, investment, and finance. Part IV resumes and furthers the preceding discussion to focus, in particular, on the implications for economic development, and how best to exploit the development of an Islamic economy. Finally, Part V reviews in brief some public policy aspects with special reference to Islamizing a contemporary economy.

This introduction, by way of a preliminary overview, may help the reader to place each paper in the overall framework of the economy discussed in the book.

Consumption

Following the conventional approach, we begin with consumption. At micro level the fundamental question is how Islamic teachings affect the consumer's behaviour with respect to allocation of his income.

Needs (not Wants) as Basis for Consumer Behaviour

Chapter 2 points out that needs (rather than wants) will be the distinctive feature determining consumer behaviour in an Islamic perspective. Just as 'satisfying wants' is the ground of the theory of consumer behaviour in the conventional framework, 'fulfilling needs' must be the ground of an Islamic theory of consumer behaviour. Particularly in the context of Islamic norms, needs are more objectively definable than wants. Two principal benefits follow from this.

5

Wants are by nature unlimited. The problem of matching wants with resources is consequently, at best, only manageable; it cannot be resolved. By contrast, needs in an Islamic framework cannot be unlimited. Levels of needs are definable and the economic problem can always be defined in terms of fulfilling needs up to a certain level in view of the available resources. The *Sharī'ah* provides particular guidance on how this can be done.

Secondly, in a society where consumer behaviour is grounded on wants, it is difficult to reconcile private and social interests. Indeed, private interest generated by wants very often conflicts with social needs. It may not be interpersonal comparison of utility that creates this problem, so much as the very philosophy itself of 'satisfying wants'. Even if every individual wants some particular thing, that thing may still not be 'needed' by the society. This conflict largely loses its significance when need is the basis of consumer behaviour, and when the determinants of individual needs are derived from the same source as the determinants of social needs. Many market failures have been identified, in the conventional economic literature, because of the non-convergence of private wants and social needs. An Islamic economy aims at a new market order in which consumer behaviour is motivated to converge individual and social needs. Islam has very specific and forceful teachings intended to develop and educate this motivation.

Following a Middle Path (not Maximization) as a Norm for Consumer Behaviour

Another distinctive feature of consumer behaviour in an Islamic economy is the preference for 'balance' and 'following a middle path', which replaces 'maximization' as the norm. The choice before the Islamic consumer is not how best to maximize his utility but how to balance the fulfilment of his needs. He is induced by the *Sharī'ah* to find a balance between spending for his worldly needs and spending in the cause of Allah; among the former, to find a balance between present and future consumption; and to find a balance among essentials, that which complements the essentials, and that which enhances and improves their quality.

To understand this 'balancing' and 'following a middle path' behaviour requires tools other than those developed in conventional economics for the analysis of maximizing behaviour. Until these tools are developed, the existing tools will be used to show that at least an

Islamic economy is not inconsistent with either the logic or common sense of the prevailing discourse, and that there is nothing to fear for planners and policy makers interested in Islamizing their economies. But what the ultimate benefits for an Islamic consumer may be and what the final economic structure of an Islamic economy, created by such a behaviour may be, can only be properly worked out when the appropriate methodology is in place to do so.

Effect on Aggregate Savings

A negative effect on aggregate savings is one of the principal apprehensions that policy makers may face. It seems common sense to suppose that *zakāh* and other charitable spending (so much encouraged in Islam) simply means transferring resources from those who have more propensity to save to those who have less or none, and then to suppose a consequent decline in aggregate savings with negative effects on economic growth and development. This is an example of how lack of proper tools to analyze an Islamic economy prevents understanding of its true potentials. The above conclusion follows directly from treating *zakāh* as a tax and mechanically working out its implications on savings.

Whether *zakāh* will in fact increase or decrease the propensity to consume, is not a major issue in itself. Various writings to date, whether demonstrating an increased or decreased propensity to consume, indicate only a marginal increase or decrease.[1]

It is, therefore, not worth devoting energy to determining what will happen to the marginal propensity to consume in a Keynesian macro-economic framework. We need to recognize that consumer behaviour in an Islamic framework is different from that in a Keynesian or any other framework, and the differences must be incorporated into the consumption function of an Islamic economy. Islamic economists should now be seeking to identify the building blocks of the Islamic economic system so that an ideal Islamic economy is presented, and compared and evaluated against the Arrow-Debreu type economy. For example, we are still not clear what the Islamic approach to the time value of resources is and whether, with such an approach, general equilibrium will exist, and be unique and stable as the Arrow-Debreu type economy is being proved to be. We must first define our own structure before we can speak of such specific consequences as those on savings or propensities to consume.

Confining ourselves to the MPC in a Keynesian framework takes us nowhere as regards describing the system and the decision making process in an ideal Islamic economy. In an Islamic system, consumer decision making is much more than simply a consumption-income relationship.

Chapter 3 on macro consumption function makes it very clear that it is incorrect to treat *zakāh* as a tax on savings and to work out its effects on the economy as such. *Zakāh* is only the lower limit of a broader concept of *infāq fī sabīl Allāh* (spending in the cause of Allah). Islam teaches Muslims to set aside a part of their resources for such spending, the choice of how much is left open. There is, however, the obligatory minimum of *zakāh* if resources exceed a certain level. *Zakāh* is thus better regarded as a part of consumer behaviour than as a tax. A number of injunctions are quoted in Chapter 3 to substantiate this approach towards *zakāh*. Seen in this perspective, the whole analysis of the impact of *zakāh* changes its direction, the effect on savings no longer remains the immediate force.

Consumer Behaviour and Distribution of Wealth

An important economic implication of Islamic consumer behaviour is that giving to the needy in the society is a normal part of consumer behaviour. Distribution of wealth must be seen as a part of individual choice, as part of an individual's micro economic decisions. The motivation for such spending is the same as for his own consumption. So far no economic theory has made distribution of wealth a conscious outcome of an individual's own economic decision. Competitive markets may take the economy to a pareto optimum point but cannot guarantee that this point will not be the one where there are extreme inequalities of income and wealth. With distribution as a part of individual consumer behaviour, a part of normal self-interest as shaped by Islamic values and laws, there is reason to believe that, while moving towards efficiency, the Islamic economy will take care of wealth distribution as well (without formal state intervention).

Viewing *zakāh* in this perspective, its effects on savings cannot be mechanically determined as for a conventional savings tax. *Zakāh* and other charities may significantly alter the spending allocated for worldly consumption. It is also possible that a need-oriented approach may reduce spending on worldly goods so that consumption is lower than it would be under a want-oriented approach.

8

Islamic Economy

Dynamic Perspective on the Effect of Zakāh on Growth and Employment

As already mentioned, until we develop our own tools to analyze such underlying philosophies, we can apply existing tools and approaches to make it clear that there is no reason for concern if an economy adopts Islamic injunctions. Chapter 3 argues that even if *zakāh* is considered merely as an instrument for transfer of resources, we may not presume a negative effect on aggregate savings, particularly if we see the effects of *zakāh* in a dynamic perspective. A very simple model shows that even if there is some chance of a short-term decline in the aggregate savings level due to Islamization of the economy (particularly of improving such injunctions as *zakāh*), the decline will soon be reversed and the long-term savings and growth path will be higher than in a non-Islamic economy. This results from the income distribution effects of *zakāh*: improvement in the economic conditions of the poor provides them an opportunity to make productive efforts, to improve their income-earning capacity and eventually enter the group of savers. The important underlying argument is that Islamic teachings specifically emphasize that *zakāh* and charities do not generate the type of consequences on work efforts currently reported in the context of negative income taxation. Islam provides sufficient motivation for the able-bodied poor to exert themselves. *Zakāh* only serves as an interim support while they seek and take up opportunities to improve their economic condition. In another article, not included in this collection,[2] a special feature of *zakāh* and charities has been highlighted in this context. Neo-classical economies fail to explain satisfactorily why poor subsistence farmers and poor workers in the informal sector do not avail themselves of credit facilities offered to them to improve their productivity and hence income. The only explanation that the economists offer is that the poor are at that stage of subsistence where they cannot afford to make new experiments. Uncertainties about their ability to increase output with improved methods and to market the increased output, prevent them from making the experiments because, in the event of failure (no matter how improbable) they and their family will face starvation.

> . . . the main motivating force in the peasant's life may be maximization, not of income, but rather of his family's chances of survival. Accordingly when risks and uncertainties are very high, a small farmer may be very reluctant to shift from a traditional technology and crop pattern that over the years he has come to

know and understand, to a new one that promises higher yields but may entail greater risks of crop failure. When sheer survival is at stake, it is more important to avoid [catastrophe in] a bad year than to maximize output in better years.[3]

Zakāh and other spending in the cause of Allah will serve as a major instrument to combat this reluctance to improve methods of production and to take the risk to improve income. This aspect of *zakāh,* with its very positive impact on employment, growth and development in the economy, will more than compensate for any short-term negative effect on aggregate savings resulting from transfer of resources from rich to poor.

Framework for Consumption Function

In an Islamic economy, the consumption function is much more than merely a consumption-income relationship.

Firstly, unlike the Keynesian function, consumer behaviour, in the Islamic framework, is not important simply because it determines savings which in turn determine investment and hence growth. It is important, in the Islamic framework, because it first determines distribution of income and wealth in the economy before it implies savings and hence growth. The primary focus of Chapter 3 is that spending for others in the cause of Allah is a part of consumer behaviour motivated by self-interest in the same way as spending for oneself is. No doubt, the two self-interests are different in nature[4] but the point is that the wealth distribution results from the consumer's economic decision making in the same way as savings do.

This is one of the unique features of the actions of economic agents as consumers that distinguishes an Islamic economy from the Arrow-Debreu type, particularly in the context of the outcome of the system. Self-interest as a motivating force may still guide the system to some competitive equilibrium, but the presence of two different types of self-interest – one of them linked to wealth distribution – may give the outcome a specific dimension absent from the outcome of the Arrow-Debreu type economy. Social justice, for example, may figure as a specific dimension of competitive equilibrium in an Islamic economy. It is in this perspective that the basic issue is addressed in Chapter 3, and focuses on the distinctive contribution of consumer behaviour to wealth distribution. The argument then goes on to the next question, a secondary one – 'Is this improvement in distribution in an Islamic economic system realized at the cost of savings and, in turn, of investment and development?' The answer is 'no', even in a simple Keynesian framework. Munawar Iqbal (2) confirms that any such effect would be extremely marginal or negligible.

Besides the contribution to distribution, the savings implications of consumer behaviour are also important. Again, a Keynesian framework will not reflect the true picture, irrespective of whether the principle of moderation is adequately incorporated into the consumption function. In such a framework, the introduction of *zakāh* (no matter how incorporated) will simply function as a tax disincentive to savings, whereas *zakāh,* if it is indeed such a tax, will in fact be a disincentive only for certain types of channels in which savings are held. Indeed, *zakāh* may be expected to direct savings into channels where they can earn income out of which *zakāh* can be paid. This aspect cannot be (or has not so far been) accounted for in working out a Keynesian type consumption function for an Islamic economy.

Even in modern secular economics, there is a recognition that consumption patterns and therefore, by implication, savings behaviour, are not determined by economic considerations alone. There are other elements, such as maintaining a competitive standard of living, keeping up with others, if only in appearances and outward norms. It is not purely an economic phenomenon.

Consumption and savings behaviour are in reality a function of the cultural values of a society. The whole value system of the society is, of course, more than can be reflected in economic arithmetic. An Islamic economy operating within an Islamic value system would be led in particular directions by that system. Strictly economic calculations cannot be worthwhile and relevant if the totality of the Islamic system is not adequately referred to and accounted for.

Further, we must remember that consumer decision making in an Islamic framework is a process in which at least four stages can be distinguished (Chapter 2). Consumer decisions at each stage have implications for savings as well as for distribution. Even if we intend only to study the former, our efforts are unlikely to be very fruitful unless we can design a consumption function to specifically take account of these four stages of Islamic consumer decision making.

Thirdly, we must, in discussing the savings implication of Islamic consumer behaviour, reflect on the institutional framework within which that behaviour takes place. The capitalist economies offer the market as the institution that caters for consumer needs. In addition they have special institutions to meet some of the needs of those individuals unable to use the market to satisfy their wants. Such institutions will also be needed in an Islamic economy. There will, however, be others, peculiar to an Islamic economy, to oversee certain aspects of consumer behaviour – in particular to assure against gross deviations from Islamic law, against prodigality (*isrāf*), and to assure consistency in the fulfilment of needs at the three levels of *ḍarūriyyāt, ḥājiyyāt* and *taḥsīniyyāt* (details in Chapter 2).

How far an individual consumer will maintain the desirable means between necessities relating to his personal satisfactions and the necessities relating to his *dīn* (religion, faith), *'aql* (reason), *nasl* (posterity); how far he balances his private interests against the needs of the community as a whole (education, health, defence, etc.) – will depend on the non-market institutions by which his behaviour is guided. It follows that the savings pattern in an Islamic economy cannot be realistically described unless such institutions and their operation are clearly envisaged.

Banking and Finance

Before moving from consumption to production, an overview of the Islamic financial system is essential as it is a key element in the production and investment relations in an Islamic economy.

Risk Bearing

Chapter 4 gives a brief overview of the salient features of the Islamic financial system. First, financial capital is entitled to claim a return only through commercially productive activity which involves the possibility of loss, should a loss arise. In no other case is financial capital allowed to claim return. Second, there is no fixed mode of financing. There is complete flexibility to adopt any mode of financing, as long as the basic principle 'no risk, no return' is not violated.

Possibility of Reducing Risk Bearing in Financing

A mode of financing that substantially reduces risk is permissible, one that eliminates risk is not, if a return on finance is claimed. Thus, while there are participatory modes of financing (*muḍārabah* and *mushāra-*

kah) in which the finance-owner risks the full amount and during the entire period of investment, there are other modes (e.g. mark-up based trade financing – currently very much in practice) where it is possible to reduce the risk being carried to a fraction of the total risk of the activity in which investment has been made.

This flexibility, on the one hand very helpful in mobilizing resources for investment, is on the other, a temptation to devise convenient modes of financing which minimize risk. This temptation is all the greater when Islamic financial institutions are obliged to compete with interest-based institutions which obviously enjoy the least risky and more convenient mode of financing.

Significance and Desirability of Mark-up Based Financing

Just this competition with interest-based institutions led most contemporary Islamic banks to resort to mark-up based financing on their asset side. Using the flexibility allowed by *Sharī'ah*, the Islamic banks designed instruments of mark-up based financing which reduced risk to practically zero, and made their dealings competitive in the interest-based financial markets. Though at micro level there is no doubt about the permissibility of such techniques, they cannot be regarded as desirable at economy-wide level. Islamic jurists as well as Islamic economists are almost unanimous that overwhelming use of such modes of financing, practically as an alternative to interest, cannot serve the purpose of *Sharī'ah*. Such modes of financing cannot bring about the substantial changes that Islamization of the economy is supposed to bring about, i.e. reducing concentration of wealth, improving income distribution, reducing poverty, etc. The economy will continue to have the same structure, institutions and outcome as the interest-based system. According to Islamic economists, an economy will not enjoy the full benefits of the Islamic financial system unless it is overwhelmingly based on profit/loss-sharing financing. This conflict in the commercial interests of Islamic banks and the macro-economic interests of the economy is a serious dilemma for policy makers. Chapters 4 to 6 go into the details of the philosophy and economics of the Islamic financial system. Understanding the philosophy of the Islamic financial system (Chapter 4), and analyzing the features (Chapter 5) and economics (Chapter 6) of the various modes of financing, it is not difficult to decide how the financial system should be organized to best suit the needs of a particular economy. The flexibility and variety of modes available enable policy makers in different economies to devise the package best suited to their particular circumstances.

Production and Investment

The eradication, from the economy, of interest in any form, immediately raises in the minds of those trained in neo-classical traditions the following questions:

How will capital be priced as a factor of production?

What will be the time value of money and how will it be determined for the purpose of investment decision making?

How will the demand for investment be determined in the economy?

The pricing of capital is discussed initially in Chapters 5 and 6, where it is argued that the interest rate is irrelevant to price of capital which is determined in fact by its own productivity. Actual rate of return on capital will, therefore, in the Islamic economy, be the basis of the price of capital. While expected rate of return (based on actual rates in the past) may serve as a price for the *ex ante* calculations, the actual payment to capital will be on the basis of actual rate of return as is the case with the most neglected factor of production, namely, entrepreneurship.

Need to Reclassify Factors of Production

This similarity between the pricing of capital and entrepreneurship, which follows from the rejection of the concept of interest, leads to a reopening of the whole question of the classification of factors of production. Chapter 7 goes into the details of the need to reclassify factors of production with reference to the Islamic approach towards factor pricing. The conventional classification is unacceptable in the framework of an interest-free economy which must distinguish fixed assets (or non-malleable capital) from financial (or malleable) capital. In an Islamic framework the former can enjoy fixed, predetermined rent per unit (never as a predetermined percentage of capital value). The latter cannot enjoy a predetermined guaranteed rent and its return is determinable only *ex post*. This distinction is followed through consistently for the other factor of production, namely, human resources. Human resources can work as labour on the basis of predetermined, fixed wage, or for uncertain income determinable only *ex post*. According to this distinction, argued in Chapter 7, production results only from either (a) productivity or (b) entrepreneurship. Productivity means a definite, predetermined capacity to produce more goods and services. Entrepreneurship means the ability to organize a production process and/or bear the risk associated with it. Unlike productivity, the outcome of entrepreneurship cannot be known *ex ante*. Both abilities are essential for production, and production will not result if either is lacking. The inputs that go into any production process will either have productivity characteristics or entrepreneurial characteristics or both.

Factor Rewards as Basis for Reclassification

The factor rewards are determined on the basis of their function in the production process. If some inputs are utilized to benefit from their productivity, they are paid (what in *fiqh* terminology is called) *ujrah* (rent), whether the factor is labour or land, or building or animal, equipment or non-malleable capital. This rent is fixed and predetermined. No distinction is made between wage and rent. If some inputs are subject to risk-bearing responsibility, they receive profit which cannot be predetermined and is known only *ex post*.

Since factors of production are paid according to their function, they need to be classified accordingly. There is no point in defining labour and capital separately if both are paid *ujrah* (rent) on the basis of their productivity. But if one is paid a predetermined *ujrah* for its productivity, and the other is being paid from the actual profit for risk-bearing, it makes sense to distinguish them.

Suggested Classification

For the purpose of economic analysis, the primary classification of factors of production should include only (i) factors which are employed on a *ujrah* (rent) to benefit from their productivity; and (ii) factors which are employed on a profit basis for their entrepreneurial abilities. A further, secondary classification within these categories may also be desirable. Within the *ujrah* (rent) receiving factors, referred to as Hired Factors of Production or HFP, we may include labour, land, buildings, etc. Within the profit-sharing factors, referred to as Entrepreneurial

Factors of Production or EFP, we may include entrepreneurs' financial capital, risk-bearing, human efforts, fixed assets, etc.

This classification on Islamic premises serves two purposes. First, it makes the economic analysis less complex and less confusing compared to conventional economics where the role of capital as a factor of production is confusing and controversial. Second, it enables a more useful analysis with respect to distribution in the economy. For example: how much income in the economy goes to productivity and how much to risk-bearing; how much of the risk-bearing income is due to human and how much to other resources; how much productivity income is due to human labour and how much to fixed capital; how the rent income of fixed capital compares with the project income of risk-bearing capital; and so on. Answers to such questions can help policy makers to plan growth and distribution in the economy better.

Time Value of Money

The need to reclassify factors of production only arises because of the nature of reward that financial capital is entitled to receive. If financial capital were allowed to receive fixed rent, there would be no need to reclassify the factors of production (the conventional classification is probably a way of justifying the payment of a fixed financial capital). Since financial capital is not allowed to earn a fixed rent, the inevitable next question is whether there is a time value of money in the Islamic framework and, if there is, how it is determined so as to enable discounting for the time in the investment decision making process. The question is rather a tricky one. Chapter 8 makes a brief attempt to resolve these questions without going too deeply into the theory of time preference. It is assumed that Islam has nothing against individuals having positive time preference. It is then argued that Islam also has nothing against realizing (pure) time value of money, so long as this value is not realized on the basis of any predetermined rate. It may be realized on the basis of *ex post* outcome of the use of money in an economically productive activity.

How to Calculate Discount Rate

For any exercise that requires some knowledge of (pure) time value of money or rate of pure time preference, it is argued that the actual rate of return paid by Islamic banks in the past will serve. Since Islamic banks minimize risk by diversifying their portfolio, the actual rate of return paid to their depositors allows for a fairly sound estimate of the rate of return they can expect in future from their banks. This expected rate of return, hence, will be proxy for their rate of (pure) time preference, and be based on the past history of actual returns. Chapter 8 also raises the question of why the rate of (pure) time preference should be constant. Simply because interest rate is constant? This is not rational. Pure time preference is an outcome of pure time-related uncertainties which intensify the longer the time frame involved. Hence, rate of pure time preference is assumed to be some function of the time period involved in the project regarding which an investment decision is to be made. This is then matched with the actual practice of Islamic banks which pay a higher rate for a fixed investment deposit for a longer period. With this classification on time value of money and discount rate, it becomes easier to visualize how investment decisions will be made in an Islamic economy.

Supply of Investible Funds

Before coming to the question of determinants (in the absence of interest) of demand for investment in the economy, the question of the supply of investible funds is briefly touched on in Chapter 9. Some writers have pointed out that supply of investible funds may decline because of the adverse effect of elimination of interest on the lender's welfare, and because of the extra cost imposed by the asymmetry of information in profit/loss-sharing. The fallacy of these arguments is briefly explained in Chapters 6 and 9.

Firstly, the fear of reduction in the lender's welfare is a groundless one. Using the same framework as the other writers have used it is shown that there are *a priori* reasons for expecting the elimination of the interest option and introduction of the Profit/Loss-Sharing (PLS) option to improve the lender's welfare, and certainly no *a priori* reasons for expecting it to worsen.

Asymmetry of information was proposed as an explanation for why, if PLS is superior to the interest-based system, it has failed to prevail in a competitive market. But, as our argument shows, this is not at all the correct explanation. There may be a number of reasons for PLS not coming into practice, not least of which is the simultaneous presence of the interest option. Interest is a convenient, less effort-requiring option for both parties, and so drives out PLS on analogy with Gresham's Law

17

of bad money driving out good. Chapters 6 and 9 together show that no adverse effect is likely to occur on supply of investment funds, though the possibility of a favourable effect is very high.

Demand for Investment

The issue of demand for investment has also led to a good deal of confusion among writers on the subject. Chapter 10 discusses two major confusions: firstly, that level of investment will (definitely) rise with the introduction of PLS; and, secondly, that investment demand will become definitely elastic in the PLS-based system. Both these propositions are as baseless as the apprehensions with respect to the supply of investible funds discussed above.

The prediction of rise in investment level is a mechanical consequence of assuming that an interest-free system means zero price of capital. If we formulate a new classical production function entering capital without a definite price attached to it, the maximization of profit exercise is bound to yield the consequences that level of investment will be higher compared to a situation where capital has a definite positive price (rate of interest). As already pointed out, Islam has nothing against positive time preference, it is permissible to realize time value of money (though not at a predetermined rate). It is illogical therefore to assume that opportunity cost of capital is zero and hence marginal productivity of capital can be allowed to go to unity (or rate of return to go to zero), and hence level of investment to be higher. Whether investment level in an Islamic economy will be higher or lower is at best an empirical question which will be answered depending on where the opportunity cost of capital settles in comparison with what it was in the interest-based system. It is rather a general equilibrium question, as elimination of interest does not merely affect demand for investment. It simultaneously affects the supply of capital, the rate of return on capital, the motives for savings, etc., which together will determine a new equilibrium in the capital market which needs to be compared in total with that of the interest-based system. Any conclusion that level of investment is bound to increase in an Islamic economy simply because there is no interest is a very naive conclusion indeed.

Similarly, the conclusion that there will be an infinitely elastic demand for investment under PLS because the one seeking investment has nothing to lose and more to gain from more investment, is based on the quite unrealistic assumptions that (i) the profit-sharing ratio is exogenously given, and remains constant irrespective of supply and demand for investment funds; and (ii) the opportunity cost of capital is zero. As we argue, profit-sharing is related to investment demand as well as investment supply. As soon as we incorporate this relationship, and simultaneously solve the supply, demand and profit-sharing ratio, investment demand no longer remains infinitely elastic.

Following clarification of this misunderstood issue, an alternative view of the nature of demand function in an Islamic perspective is presented in Chapter 10. It is there argued that investment demand can be expressed as a function of the profit-sharing ratio.

Growth and Development

Strategy for Development

Without going too far into how the state can mobilize resources to meet the heavy development requirements of contemporary societies, Chapter 11 suggests a strategy aimed at eliminating poverty hence, at helping the people to meet basic needs, which is low-cost and does not force the state to indulge in heavy borrowing, and which is consistent with (indeed built-in within) the system. The strategy stresses that improving the economic conditions of the poor should be the objective with which to begin. This should be done by motivating all human resources to take up every possible opportunity to contribute to family income. Subsistence and poor families should be given every encouragement for self-employed activity and improved family enterprise. The type of assistance initially needed by such families would imply extremely low capital expenditures. A large programme of promoting self-employment opportunities alongside a parallel programme of incentives to promote the modern formal sector would quickly create competition for labour between the formal and informal sectors. This in turn would put the economy not only on an accelerated growth path but also diminish poverty and unemployment in the economy at an accelerated rate. Chapter 11 argues that this strategy is consistent with the spirit of an Islamic economy and that Islam provides for institutions for the success of such a strategy.

Economists have generally been of the view that people at subsistence level in rural or urban areas are not attracted to improved methods of production or new technologies to improve their income, because the uncertainties involved in realizing such opportunities puts their survival at stake. That fear, together with the problem of how to repay capital in the event of failure, persuade them to stay with the status quo. Chapter 11 explains how, in the Islamic framework, two institutions in particular can help subsistence workers to overcome those fears. Firstly, Islamic financing, especially in the PLS-based modes, does not require any collateral from them, nor puts them in the agonizing difficulty of having to repay the principal with return (no matter how small) in the event of failure to make income. Secondly, Islamic institutions of social insurance (*zakāh*, etc.) will look after their subsistence needs in the event of failure.

Several experiences in the world have shown that provision of cheap capital for self-employment activities for the poor of the population has done wonders in alleviating poverty and unemployment. Experience of Gramin Bank in Bangladesh and ACCION in Latin America are but two examples. It is now only a matter of simply simulating these experiences at economy-wide level with the presence of two institutions (risk-bearing financing and social insurance against starvation) to assess the benefits of the strategy outlined in this chapter.

Macroeconomic Model

Macroeconomic viability of an Islamic economy in a general equilibrium framework is the next issue under discussion. Chapter 12 focuses on whether it will be possible to describe a macroeconomic model for the economy and if so what variables it would include. The argument goes beyond merely specifying the macroeconomic model to address the question of whether the economy would have any built-in mechanism for growth and development, and if so, how we can see it in a macro framework.

The model developed in Chapter 12 is kept simple in order to concentrate on highlighting the elements that would require to be formulated in a non-conventional way because of the absence of interest and the presence of PLS. Since consumption function is described in Chapter 3 (with no explicit role for PLS financing) and investment function is described in Chapter 10, Chapter 12 focuses on the money demand function. A closed economy has been assumed, and government sector not explicitly shown, in order to keep the model simple. The discussion argues the possibility of expressing money demand as a function of the profit-sharing ratio in the economy. The model then shows how this macro framework contributes to economic development.

Macro Model and Development Process

To draw conclusions for development through the income determination macro model, though rare is not unusual. Keynes related a macro model with growth through the concept of full employment equilibrium. The macro economic model of an Islamic economy shows that this relation is further strengthened because of the peculiar nature of investment and money demand functions, and because of the PLS financial system. An important feature of the Islamic economy highlighted in Chapter 12 is that the investment supply raises a simultaneous demand for human resources which in turn motivates the human resources to raise the demand for investment. The sort of rigidities usually blamed for the failure of the Keynesian model do not apply in an economy based on PLS financing.

Development Strategy

An economy based on PLS financing has the potential to accelerate employment and growth provided appropriate development strategies are designed to this end. Development strategy, in fact, requires *a priori* discussion of the economic role of the state in the economy. As already mentioned, this is an area of the subject not included in this collection. Moreover, a specific answer is probably impractical with respect to economic development in the economy. The role of the state in economic development is basically an empirical question. From the early history of Islam, the following can be inferred in the context of economic development.[5]

(a)   The state was concerned with fulfilment of the minimum needs of the members of the society. This concern had an immediate priority in any concept of development.

(b)   Borrowing was done to meet the economic needs of the state but, firstly, the loans were interest free and, secondly, they were primarily meant to meet the subsistence needs of the people.

Islamic Management of Economy

Having described the main features of an Islamic economy, the final question is how to implement and manage such an economy. Since the main focus of the discussion has been on the implications of introducing a PLS-based financial system to replace the interest-based one, the basic question is whether PLS is a practicable option. The argument that PLS cannot prevail in the economy because of the problem of asymmetry of information involved in the PLS-based modes of financing, already touched upon, is answered in detail in Chapter 13. The discussion concludes that PLS will succeed in the economy with all its known benefits only if the interest option is totally eliminated, and necessary changes in the fiscal and economic structure conducive to it are introduced. The practical experience of countries like Pakistan, Iran and Sudan, illustrates the nature of the institutional and structural changes required in the economy to make the PLS-based system a success.

Fundamental Objectives of Islamization of Economy

The discussion concludes with the issue of how to manage an Islamic economy. Two elements in particular distinguish an Islamic economy. Firstly, although considerable freedom of economic activity is allowed, the Islamic economy has a built-in mechanism to encourage the fruits of economic activity to be shared with the less privileged members of the society as well. This sharing is, in fact, instituted by Islamic teachings into the economic behaviour of individuals at micro level. This sharing behaviour is motivated by a kind of self-interest based on an absolutely secure promise of a certain return on anything shared with the needy (to be quantitative, the return is promised to be more than 70,000 per cent). Secondly, despite allowing, indeed promoting, competitive markets, there is an equally strong motivation (again with an institutional framework that supports individual upbringing and education) to ensure that dealings are just and fair, that no one systematically exploits others because of any special privilege that he might have obtained in the market while some other is in a less advantageous position to bargain.

The immediate issue is how to lead the economy to acquire the above-mentioned features? Chapter 13 briefly discusses this question in terms of the management of private and public sectors. Two fundamental principles for management of the private sector are highlighted:

(i) Ensuring 'economic peace' (eliminating all sources of economic disorder) in the society.
(ii) Fulfilling the minimum needs of all members of the society.

Two fundamental instruments to achieve implementation of these

principles are indicated for the managers of an Islamic economy, namely
al-'adl (which may be roughly rendered as justice), and *al-iḥsān* (which
may be roughly rendered as 'benevolence'). Some details are given in
Chapter 13. Regulation of the private sector to achieve the desired
objectives mentioned above will require institutional reforms in the
economy. The institutional reforms necessary to administer 'justice' and
'benevolence' are not difficult to identify in general terms; a detailed
description can only follow from an in-depth study of the society where
the reforms are required to be introduced. Only the broad principles of
the necessary reforms are indicated in Chapter 13. The management of
the public sector must complement the private sector for the same
objectives, besides (a) managing the collective interest and public good;
and (b) managing economic development and growth.

The discussion of Islamic management of an economy is deliberately
confined mostly to generalities to give a broad idea of the various
dimensions of the issue. Even so, the issue is too large to be discussed in
a single essay. The most important question, what exactly would or
should be the economic role of the state?, needs long research into the
problems of contemporary economics and into the role that the *Sharī'ah*
accords to government with respect to economic issues. It would appear
that the role of the state should be only to guide and regulate the private
sector and to ensure that the rules of *Sharī'ah* relating to exchange and
distribution are strictly adhered to, rather than take a substantial part in
production and distribution. In practice, the necessary in-depth work on
contemporary economic realities and *Sharī'ah* principles, requires joint
studies by economists and Islamic jurists working together.

Conclusion

The general conclusion of the papers in this collection is that, despite
elimination of interest, the economy remains viable. Further, the
elimination of interest, when coupled with other features of an Islamic
economy, can be expected to generate better results with regard to
efficiency, growth, stability, reduction in income disparity, elimination
of poverty, and fulfilment of needs of all members of the society.

For policy makers concerned with Islamizing their economies, it
should be satisfying and reassuring to note that:

(1)   There is no reason to believe that they may lose savings to plan
growth and development. On the contrary, there are reasons, after a

possible and in many cases very short-lived decline, to believe that savings may increase.

(2)   There is no reason to fear that the financial system may become less efficient. There are strong reasons to believe that the system may become more efficient and stable and conducive to growth and development.

(3)   No confusion will be created by the elimination of interest, in investment decision making, neither at micro level nor at macro level.

(4)   There is no reason to worry about the availability of policy variables to control and regulate the economy. The number of policy variables would rather increase offering greater flexibility and choice.

(5)   There will be enough potential in the economy to design a strategy to eliminate poverty and unemployment from the economy.

The analysis in the papers here presented is not comprehensive, particularly from the point of view of the system of property rights and the set of economic ethics that Islamic teachings instil in a society.

Ample evidence from the texts of original Islamic sources can be presented to argue that Islamic teachings in the economic domain aim at avoiding waste and promoting competitive markets. The literature of Islamic jurisprudence, very elaborate in the field of economic transactions, can readily be quoted to establish these two objectives. How Islamic jurisprudence has dealt with the issue of defining property rights to minimize market failures is an interesting question not so far studied. Such a study would not only be useful for the managers of Islamic economies but also offer helpful lessons to students of conventional economics as well.

Similarly, Islamic teachings provide a very elaborate system of ethics covering all aspects of human life, including those relating to economic transactions. How far Islamic ethics aims at minimizing the divergence between private costs/benefits and social costs/benefits, and how far they reinforce the system of property rights developed through Islamic jurisprudence, and hence how they contribute towards minimizing market failures, are again questions not yet investigated.

Research in these two areas falls within two distinct branches of Islamic studies, namely, Islamic law (*Sharī'ah*) and economics, and Islamic ethics and economics. Such research, appropriately focused, should aim to provide necessary guidance on how to manage Islamic economies in the contemporary world, and to establish the superiority of the Islamic system over all other human paradigms.

Notes

1. For example, Ahmad (1) and Metwally (7) worked out the effect of *zakāh* on savings, measured by the formula (d-b) (1+a-B) where

    d = marginal propensity to consume of *zakāh*-receivers.
    b = marginal propensity to consume of *zakāh*-payers.
    a = rate of transfer of income from *zakāh*-payers to *zakāh*-receivers.
    B = proportion of national income held by *zakāh*-payers.

    Let us consider a typical Muslim economy where we can assume the following values of the parameters:

    d = 0.95
    b = 0.80
    a = 0.025
    B = 0.90

    This means that the Ahmad and Metwally models imply that introduction of *zakāh* will increase the propensity to consume in the economy by 0.01, i.e. from 0.80 it will become 0.81. The increase is not very significant in terms of its macro-economic consequences in the Keynesian framework for an underdeveloped country. Similarly, Munawar Iqbal's calculations (2) show that even if we assume as ambitious a target as reducing *isrāf* to the extent of reducing consumption by 10% along with the imposition of *zakāh* of 2.5 per cent, the marginal propensity to consume will be lower in an Islamized economy, while the reduction in the propensity to consume will be very negligible. The same point was evident from Fahim Khan (3).

2. See M. Fahim Khan (6).

3. See M.P. Todaro (10), pp. 314–15.

4. See M. Fahim Khan (5).

5. See M.N. Siddiqui (9).

References

1. Ahmad, Ausaf, *Income Determination in an Islamic Economy,* Jeddah, Scientific Publishing Centre, King Abdul Aziz University, 1987.

2. Iqbal, M., 'Zakāh, Moderation and Aggregate Consumption in an Islamic Economy', in *Journal of Research in Islamic Economy,* Vol. 3, No. 1 (Summer 1985).

3. Khan, M. Fahim, 'Macroconsumption Function in an Islamic Framework', in *Journal of Research in Islamic Economics,* Vol. 1, No. 2 (Winter 1984).

4. ———, *Theory of Consumer Behaviour in Islamic Perspective.* Paper presented at the International Seminar for University Teachers in IDB Member Countries jointly organized in Islamabad by the International Institute of Islamic Economics, International Islamic University and the Islamic Research and Training Institute of Islamic Development Bank, Jeddah, August-September, 1987.

5. ———, *Distribution in Macroeconomic Framework: An Islamic Perspective,* Islamabad, International Institute of Islamic Economics, 1988.

6. ———, *Islamic Financial System and Human Resource Mobilization,* Jeddah, Islamic Research and Training Institute, Islamic Development Bank, 1991.

7. Metwally, M.M., *Macroeconomic Models of Islamic Doctrines,* London, J.K. Publishers, 1981.

8. ———, 'Rejoinder to Darwish and Zain', in *Journal of Research in Islamic Economics,* Vol. 2, No. 2 (Winter 1985).

9. Siddiqi, M.N., *Public Borrowing in Early Period of Islam.* Paper for the Third International Conference on Islamic Economics, Kuala Lumpur, 1993.

10. Todaro, M.P., *Development Economics,* New York, London, Longman, 1989, 4th edition.

PART I

CONSUMPTION

CHAPTER 2

Theory of Consumer Behaviour in the Islamic Perspective*

Allocation of available resources to the multitude of potential uses is the central problem of economics. The analysis of human behaviour that relates to this problem is called economic theory.

The mainstream analysis, which is called 'positive economics' has a theoretical aspect and an empirical aspect. In general, theoretical analysis precedes empirical analysis as its framework. Empirical analysis may, however, in some cases precede theoretical analysis. In that event, patterns and regularities in the data relating to economic decision-making are studied and theories then formulated and refined.

The theoretical analysis of this branch of knowledge that we call positive economics can be conceived in two perspectives: (a) in pure positive perspective, and (b) in some normal positive perspective.

In pure positive perspective, only those aspects of human behaviour are analyzed which are independent of norms or values; it is assumed that there is no normative or value-based restriction on the behaviour.

In normal positive perspective, those aspects of human behaviour are analyzed which are governed by some norms or values that a society imposes on its members, and which may be in the form of written legal injunctions or in the form of unwritten rules and traditions.

Positive economics in pure positive perspective has no real existence. Economics studies human behaviour in a society and every society has

---

*Adapted from a lecture delivered in the seminar on Islamic Economics for University Teachers, jointly organized by the Islamic Research and Training Institute of Islamic Development Bank, Jeddah, and International Institute of Islamic Economics, International Islamic University, Islamabad, 1987. Proceedings of the seminar have been published by the Islamic Research and Training Institute.

certain norms, values and rules for the behaviour of its members. The economics known to us as 'positive economics' is, in practice, the analysis of the economic behaviour of human beings in a normal positive perspective.

This paper attempts to present and compare the contours of the theory of consumer behaviour in two types of normal positive perspectives:

(a) The capitalist or *laissez-faire* type, i.e. a society governed by norms of what is called capitalist or *laissez-faire* society.

(b) The Islamic type, i.e. a society governed by the norms of Islam.

Let us take that part of consumer theory where we do not find any conflict between capitalist and Islamic norms. We assume the following:

1. A consumer is able to rank, according to his own preferences, commodities from which he has to make a choice.

2. The preferences of the consumer are consistent in the sense that they have the property of asymmetry and transitivity.

3. Positive prices of goods and income provide a certain choice space within which the consumer can make a choice.

Following these assumptions comes the behaviour part of the theory. And it is here that we must distinguish between capitalist and Islamic norms because, whatever the choice, it will have some value base. How to make the most preferred choice out of the choice space? Let us consider the two perspectives.

Capitalist Normal Choice

(i) It is assumed that preferences are capable of being represented by indifference curves. 'Indifference' here means that two goods, say x_1 and x_2, are perfectly interchangeable. The assumption is not a weak one. Rather, it is a strong assumption in that it implies that the underlying *needs* (as distinct from *desires*) which prompt consumption of x_1 or x_2 are also perfectly interchangeable.

(ii) Indifference curves are formed on the assumption of utility. The concept of utility, however, involves value judgement. In practice that comes to mean, by the capitalist norm, that desires are the best criterion for the formation of preferences. Desires and needs are not distinguished.

(iii) Non-satiation, i.e. more is always preferred to less.

(iv) Non-satiation implies that the most preferred consumption pattern must stretch the budget to the limit – all available income must be spent. (The implied value is that exhaustion of income is better than non-exhaustion.)

(v) The consumer selects the point which maximizes utility, i.e. where the highest indifference curve lies on the budget limit.

That, in a nutshell, is the essence of the theory in the capitalist normal framework. Elaborations of this analysis simply relate to logical and mathematical extensions of this theory.

The Islamic Normal Framework

We assume that the consumer is aware of Islamic norms and his behaviour is governed by them. Before we look at the process of his choice-making within the commodity space, we must consider one choice that has been excluded from the capitalist normal theory of consumer behaviour.

The choice is how much of the income is to be spent on worldly needs and how much in the way of Allah (*Infāq fī Sabīl Allāh*). Actions may be of the first or second type according to the intention of the person doing them. But, in this context, by 'spending in the way of Allah' we mean the spending that is not for one's own immediate worldly benefit. The consumer, in fact, faces two baskets. Let them be called X and Y. Basket X offers spending for fulfilment of worldly needs and basket Y offers spending in the way of Allah. The importance of the latter can hardly be over-stated. Several Qur'ānic verses and *Ahādīth* can be cited to explain the motivation that Islam provides for spending in the way of Allah. Even in present-day Muslim societies, we can observe that such spending is quite significant compared to non-Muslim societies. How does a consumer decide how much income to spend on Y and how much to keep for spending on X? This choice cannot be handled in the same way as the choice between commodities has been handled in the capitalist normal framework.

31

Let us assume a spending budget for the consumer which starts at point A. Now, his reward for every item of spending on the Y basket is higher than the worldly satisfaction he can obtain from any similar amount of spending on the X basket. However, he cannot start from A and go to the full limit of his budget on Y spending because there is some minimum amount of X that is essential for survival. Hence the most preferred point cannot be identified using the tools of conventional analysis which can locate the most preferred point for choice between two commodities. We must develop our own tools to determine the allocation of resources between X and Y. The *Sharī'ah* provides us the rule: 'Do not make your hand fastened to your neck nor stretch it out to its utmost reach, so that you become blameworthy and destitute' (17: 29). The balancing rule, in fact, is the fundamental rule of Islamic normal economics, corresponding to 'maximizing rule' in capitalist normal economics. This is a rule that keeps the individual in the best middle position. This is what one Islamic economist has called *Iqtiṣād,* and may be familiar to Western readers as the Aristotelian 'golden mean'.

As we have observed, for X or Y choices, the most preferred point cannot be located with conventional analytical tools. But conventional economic theory excludes such X or Y choices by making what is called the 'regularity assumption'. Conventional theory explains this assumption as the exclusion of 'bizarre' choice. In our case, the Y choice is not bizarre but perfectly normal, rational behaviour.

The tools which allow the application of the Islamic rule of balance should be different from the tools applied by conventional economists for their maximization rule. Once this choice has been made and a level of X (balanced amount to be spent on worldly needs) has been determined, then the question is how to allocate this amount to various uses.

Before going on to the commodity space, there is one more choice to be considered: how much to consume now and how much to save for future consumption. Conventional economic theory also addresses this question and answers it in terms of a positive time preference theory. According to conventional theory, the level of savings and present consumption will be determined by equating the rate of time preference and the rate of interest. This theory does nothing except explain (and try to justify) the existence of interest. The empirical evidence has failed to show that people save to earn interest. People save even if they do not get any interest and their saving habits remain more or less unaffected when the interest rate goes up and down. The motives for savings are varied and different. Earning income on the amount saved is only a small part of these motives.

The Islamic perspective on this issue is very clear. There are two aspects of this choice:

Firstly, it is perfectly permissible and desirable to save for future consumption. The Prophet's (peace be upon him) injunction that it is better to leave after death some resources for one's family than to leave them destitute, suggests that savings are desirable. But how much of the income to save and how much to consume now is again a question which does not require maximizing behaviour. The 'balancing' principle is again at work.

> Those who, when they spend, are not extravagant and not niggardly, but hold a just (balance) between those (extremes) (Qur'ān 25: 67).

Secondly, the expected rate of return on savings, and not interest rate, is the motivation for savings in the Islamic framework. The reason is obvious. A Muslim has to pay *zakāh* on savings. Savings will be depleted every year by *zakāh* and the purpose of savings will be defeated. In the presence of *zakāh,* savings make sense only if they also generate income so that *zakāh* may be paid out of the income from savings. Moreover, it is not merely *zakāh* that is to be paid out of savings. When a person has some savings, it becomes obligatory upon him to help the needy. The more he can earn the more savings he has, and the more he will be able to meet his obligations (arising out of savings), without adversely affecting his savings. Hence the expected rate of return on savings plays a positive role in motivating savings.

(It is worth noting here that a saver, in an Islamic framework, will have to be an investor at the same time. This implies the absence of a savings-investment gap and could go a long way towards determining the desired macro-economic equilibrium in the economy.)

After the allocation between present consumption and future consumption has been decided, there comes the choice of commodities for present consumption. Again the utility maximization principle is not entirely consistent with Islamic behaviour.

Islamic economics provides us an entirely different framework for analysis: desires or wants may not be the motivating force for consumer behaviour in Islam. An alternative which could be a base for consumer behaviour is needed.

Islam negates the assumption that all wants are equally important and that all should be satisfied. Instead, Islam recognizes that human beings have certain needs, some of which are more important and others less important. The more important needs should be fulfilled first, followed by fulfilment of less important needs. This fundamental element of the Islamic framework is not merely normative in content. It is a positive assumption. Civilized human beings do not treat all their wants as equally important. For them, some wants are more and some less important. More important wants are satisfied first. A man may want both bread and air-conditioners, but the two wants cannot be equally important. Even if the air-conditioner was offered at a price less than the price of the bread, bread would still have priority. Underlying needs determine priorities among wants.

The members of traditional societies in the contemporary world are not motivated to maximize satisfaction of their wants with the available resources; they find their needs adequately fulfilled and do not feel obliged to look for the satisfaction of wants beyond these needs which are defined either by themselves or by their environment. All development strategies thus fail to bring development in such societies because of the lack of motivation to earn more or to expand the disposable resources.

The question then arises about what need is and how it is different from want.

The Islamic Concept of Need

Need is as value-loaded a concept as want. Whereas want is determined by the concept of utility, need, in the Islamic perspective, is determined by the concept of *Maslahah*. The objective of *Sharī'ah* is the welfare of the human being (*maṣalaḥat al-'ibād*). Therefore, all goods and services which affect *maslaḥah* (welfare) will be said to be the needs of human beings.

Conventional economic theory describes utility as the property of a good/service to satisfy a human want. 'Satisfaction' is subjectively determined. Each individual must determine the presence of satisfaction according to his own criterion. Any economic activity to acquire or produce something is motivated by the utility in that thing. If something can satisfy a want, someone will be willing to make the effort to produce/acquire/consume that thing.

Maslahah, according to Shāṭibī, is the property or power of a good/service that affects the basic elements and objectives of the life of human beings in this world. Shāṭibī has described five fundamentals of existence in this world: life; property; faith; reason; posterity. All goods or services that have the power to promote these five elements are said to have *maṣlaḥah* for human beings, and are therefore needs.

But even so, all needs are not equally important. There are three levels of need:

(i)   The level where the five fundamental elements are barely protected.

(ii) The level where the protection of the five fundamental elements is complemented or reinforced.

(iii) The level where the five fundamentals are not merely assured but improved upon or adorned.

All goods and services that have the power or quality to promote (in any of the above-mentioned ways, i.e. to protect, reinforce or ameliorate) the five fundamentals are said to have *maṣlaḥah*. A Muslim is religiously motivated to acquire or produce all such goods and services according to the level at which the goods/services concerned promote these fundamentals. Goods/services that protect the fundamentals will have more *maṣlaḥah,* followed by goods/services that reinforce them, followed by goods/services that improve and adorn them.

Maṣlaḥah Versus Utility

For Islamic economists, therefore, *maṣlaḥah* is a more objective concept than utility for analysis of the behaviour of economic agents. Analytically, the concept of *maṣlaḥah* can more easily be manipulated than the concept of utility.

Though *maṣlaḥah,* like utility, remains a subjective concept, its subjectivity does not make it as vague as utility. Some of its peculiarities are:

1.   Though *maṣlaḥah* is subjective in the sense that the individual consumer himself is the best judge of whether a particular good/service has *maṣlaḥah* for him, the criterion of what constitutes *maṣlaḥah* is not itself subjective. The concept of *utility* is, by contrast, vague and subject to individual caprice.

Whether a Mercedes car has utility can be decided on the basis of different subjective criteria. For example, because it is comfortable; or because it is good to show off in; or because one likes its design; or because it is manufactured by one's own country or by a country that one likes; etc. There could be innumerable criteria on the basis of which one may decide whether something has a utility. This is not so in the case of *maslahah*. The criteria are fixed for everyone and the decision has to be made on the basis of this criteria. This property of *maslahah vis-à-vis* utility is capable of enhancing the predictability and validity of economic policies because the criteria available for decision-making are known.

2. The individual *maslahah* will be consistent with social *maslahah* unlike individual utility which will often be in conflict with social utility. This is again because of the absence of shared criteria for the determination of utility. The promotion of the five fundamentals is desirable not only for the individual but also for the society. By contrast, individual satisfaction of a particular want may not be desirable for the society. Alcohol may have some utility for those individuals who like to drink it, but it may not have social utility.

3. The concept of *maslahah* underlies all economic activities in a society, it is the underlying objective of consumption as well as of production and exchange; unlike the conventional theory, where utility is the objective of consumption and profit is the objective of production. Also *maslahah* remains the objective whether economic activities are being performed at an individual level or state level.

4. It is not possible to compare the utility person A gets from consuming a good (say an apple) with the utility person B gets from consuming the same good in the same quantity. In other words, how much satisfaction A or B enjoys or gets by consumption is not objectively describable. Comparison of *maslahah* in several instances, however, may be possible. It is at least possible to compare different levels of *maslahah*. For example, one can compare the situation where person A may be protecting his life by eating an apple while for person B the same act may only improve his health. In this case the *maslahah* for A is more than for B.

The Rule for Allocation of Resources to Needs

The basic principle is very simple. Resources should be first allocated to the essentials or *ḍarūriyyāt*. If the consumer has resources left over after meeting the essentials, he can go on to whatever complements the essentials, to *ḥājiyyāt,* and if there are still some resources left, these may be allocated to whatever improves or adorns, to *taḥsīniyyāt*. This classification provides the first level of preference ordering. This ordering is in the nature of lexicographic ordering and cannot be represented by convex indifference curves that neo-classical economics assumes for preference ordering.

The second level of preference ordering comes when choice is involved within the three categories of needs. In this event, the concept of indifference can be applied but in the case of *ḍarūriyyāt* and *ḥājiyyāt* we may not be able to construct a preference ordering that yields smooth convex indifference curves. The governing rule remains that of balancing. It is only with *taḥsīniyyāt* that we may be able to form preference ordering that can be represented by smooth convex indifference curves. The balancing rule again applies and there will be no room for prodigality or *isrāf*.

What is the Difference?

Let us recapitulate on the difference it makes if we use the concept of fulfilling needs instead of maximizing satisfaction of wants.

1. *The nature of the problem:*
In the conventional framework, the problem is assumed to arise because of the scarcity of resources. Suppose, the scarcity of resources is removed. Would the problem be solved? Most probably not. This is because of the inherent inability of material resources to satisfy all human wants. Can human wants be fully satisfied when 'wants' have no objective definition?

Their satisfaction thus remains vague and the economic problem defined in these terms also remains vague. Some Western economists too have expressed their dissatisfaction with describing the economic objective in terms of wants. Galbraith (*The Affluent Society,* 2nd ed., 1969) asks: How can production be defended as want-satisfying if that production itself creates wants?

The satisfaction of human wants is not merely a theoretical

assumption to define the economic problem. The capitalist ideology itself in practice leads individuals to pursue this objective irrespective of how vague or unattainable it is. The objectives of *Sharī'ah,* on the other hand, provide an entirely different dimension to the economic problem of an individual.

The reason for producing at all or for becoming involved in economic activities in the first place is that *Sharī'ah* requires individuals to look to and look after their welfare. Economic activities of production, consumption and exchange that involve *maṣlaḥah* (welfare) as defined by *Sharī'ah* must be undertaken as a religious duty to earn one's betterment not only in this world but in the world hereafter also. All such activities that have *maṣlaḥah* for human beings are called needs. These needs must be met.

'Fulfilling needs' rather than 'satisfying wants' is the objective of economic activities, and the pursuit of this objective is a religious duty. Man is obliged to solve his economic problem.

The definition of that problem in terms of unlimited wants relative to scarce resources may explain economic behaviour in a capitalist society, but it certainly fails to explain economic behaviour in an Islamic society.

2. *Concept of efficiency:*

The concept of efficiency in the conventional framework is to maximize satisfaction with the available resources. Efficiency in the Islamic framework is to maximize fulfilment of needs with the available resources. These two concepts are different.

The prime concern of conventional economics is efficiency. This concern emerges directly from its definition of the economic problem. If wants are unlimited and resources are scarce, then the only solution to the problem is to 'economize'. This is what is called efficiency, i.e. 'doing the best with what we have'. If our wants are virtually unlimited and resources are scarce, we cannot conceivably satisfy all of society's material wants. The next best thing is to achieve the greatest possible satisfaction of these wants.

By contrast, in the context of Islamic economics, this type of efficiency may not be a prime concern. As mentioned earlier, desirability is as important a concern as efficiency, the desirability being determined by *maṣlaḥah*.

Fulfilling needs is desirable. It is desirable that necessities be met as a first priority. Those who have more than their necessities are required to meet the necessities of those who do not have. All resources get devoted to the fulfilment of necessities. As necessities are limited, resources do not have to be unlimited to meet them. That resources should be unequal to necessities is against the promise of Allah and against reality. There is no question of economizing on necessities. Once necessities are met, whatever complements or improves can be sought after, and the seeking can be satisfied when and as resources become available. Efficiency and desirability are simultaneously required in fulfilling *hājiyyāt* and *taḥsīniyyāt*. Hence efficiency and desirability together are the prime concern of Islamic economics. Where there is conflict, desirability will get preference over efficiency. Desirability is determined by *maṣlaḥah* which was defined earlier.

3. *Tools of analysis:*

Conventional economics assumes maximization on the part of the consumer. Hence the mathematical tools of convex curves, differentiation, etc., can be applied. In the Islamic framework, we have the principle of balancing. The mathematical tools applicable for maximization will not be relevant in the case of the balancing principle. Also a large part of preference ordering, in our framework, is in the nature of lexicographic ordering rather than convex ordering. We will, therefore, have to formulate our own tools for our analysis.

4. *Scope of the theory:*

Some aspects of the consequences for the analysis of consumer behaviour in the Islamic framework can be represented in the following chart:

CHOICES FACED BY CONSUMER

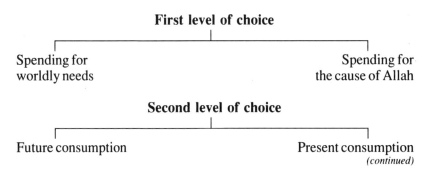

First level of choice

Spending for   Spending for
worldly needs   the cause of Allah

Second level of choice

Future consumption   Present consumption
(continued)

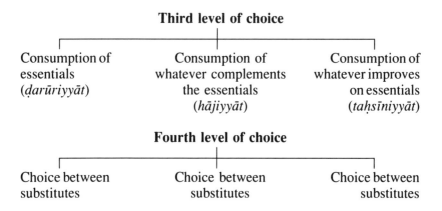

Third level of choice

| Consumption of essentials (*darūriyyāt*) | Consumption of whatever complements the essentials (*hājiyyāt*) | Consumption of whatever improves on essentials (*tahsīniyyāt*) |

Fourth level of choice

| Choice between substitutes | Choice between substitutes | Choice between substitutes |

The theory of consumer behaviour in the Islamic framework will, thus, have to analyze four levels of consumer choice, whereas conventional economics restricts itself to the second and fourth levels and chooses to ignore the first and third.

The tools of conventional economic analysis can be applied, though only partially, to the choices mentioned at the fourth level of choices. The scope of the theory of consumer behaviour in the Islamic framework is much larger than in the conventional framework.

Institutional Framework

What institutional framework will urge the Islamic consumer to behave in the manner outlined above? The conventional framework provides the market as the institution for consumers to pursue their objectives in a capitalist economy. The capitalist economies also have special institutions to meet the specific needs of those individuals who are unable to use the market to satisfy their wants. All these institutions are also required to guide consumer behaviour in an Islamic economy. There will, however, be some additional institutions to guide and monitor certain particular aspects of consumer behaviour, most importantly,

(i) to ensure abstinence from *isrāf* (prodigality);

(ii) to ensure consistency in the fulfilment of needs at the three levels (*darūriyyāt, hājiyyāt* and *tahsīniyyāt*);

(iii) to ensure abstinence from gross deviations from Islamic principles.

(iv) to motivate, organize and manage individual spending for the cause of Allah.

Consumers may not be inclined to pursue their own *maṣlaḥah* and instead indulge in *isrāf*. For example, consumers may like to eat their fill while their neighbours are starving, or to earn more by hoarding and hence cause harm to others, and so on. Moreover, a consumer may continue fulfilling *ḍarūriyyāt, ḥājiyyāt* and *taḥsīniyyāt* relating to his *nafs* (life) or *māl* (property) and may pay no attention to even the *ḍarūriyyāt* of *dīn* (Faith) or *'aql* (Reason) or *nasl* (Posterity). What institutional framework does the *Sharī'ah* provide in such cases so that individuals and society do not deviate from the objectives of *Sharī'ah*? The same question arises in relation to the fulfilment of social needs which individuals on their own may not be inclined or able to fulfil – education, health, research, defence, etc., are examples.

Also, individuals may not strictly be following Islamic principles of consumption and yet claim to be doing so. For example, an individual may indulge in conspicuous consumption on the pretext that he is pursuing *taḥsīniyyāt*.

The objectives of *Sharī'ah* described above may imply the following institutions:

(i) Voluntary institutions developed through the adequate education and training of the masses in *Sharī'ah*. *Sharī'ah* basically provides complete freedom and autonomy to the individual to take his own decision and be responsible to Allah on the Day of Judgement. For Islamic behaviour, what is therefore required is adequate education and training in *Sharī'ah*. Mass education in *Sharī'ah* will not only induce individuals to exercise self-restraint and adhere to Islamic principles, but also develop voluntary social institutions to monitor (and control, where necessary), individual behaviour. Besides this, *Sharī'ah* promotes social institutions to fulfil social obligations (i.e. *Farḍ al-kifāyah*).

(ii) Enforcement institutions oblige individuals to refrain from activities that create social or economic disorder in the society. Individual freedom ensured in an Islamic framework is not allowed to disturb the peace and order of the society. Such institutions will mainly be state institutions, and may intervene in the following activities of consumers in an Islamic society:

(a)   Consumption of prohibited goods which amounts to violating the law and order of the society.

(b)   Conspicuous consumption at a level that creates unrest, feelings of envy and depravity, in the society.

(c)   *Isrāf* (prodigality), excessive indulgence in the consumption of *ḥājiyyāt* and *taḥsīniyyāt* when the *ḍarūriyyāt* of a major portion of the society are not being met.

(d)   Grossly deviant or inconsistent behaviour from the point of view of Islamic principles, such as spending the bulk of the budget on *taḥsīniyyāt* and ignoring *ḍarūriyyāt*.

Non-market institutions, thus, will have to play an important role, along with market institutions, in an Islamic economy.

Conclusion

The first question must be whether our projected theory of consumer behaviour would be a positive or a normative theory. Our argument is that conventional consumer theory provides a positive theory in the framework of capitalist norms and Islamic consumer theory provides a positive theory in the framework of Islamic norms.

Satisfaction of wants may be positive consumer behaviour in some developed capitalist societies. Similarly, fulfilment of needs is positive consumer behaviour in several traditional societies in general, and in Muslim societies in particular. We observe, particularly in rural areas of Asian and African societies, that people aim at fulfilling their self-defined needs. Beyond that they do not strive much. People remain satisfied with the fulfilment of their needs and do not want to strive to maximize satisfaction of unlimited wants. Whether a consumer would pursue maximum satisfaction of unlimited wants, or whether he would aim at fulfilling his needs, and if the latter how he would define his needs, depends on the socio-ethical, religious and educational background of the consumer. Hence the needs-based approach will yield a positive theory for the consumers who have Islamic education and live in a Muslim society where Islamic ethics, norms and *Sharī'ah* are in practice. For any other society, this theory will be a normative theory, just as the capitalist theory will be a normative theory for any society aiming to adopt capitalist norms.

The second question is what role the Islamic theory of consumer behaviour will play. Our theory will achieve all those objectives that any positive theory aims at, i.e. understanding behaviour and enabling prediction of that behaviour. If we are able to develop a good theory explaining consumer behaviour for a Muslim economy, then, since this theory will be a positive theory in its own perspective, it will provide predictions that can be used by public and private agencies in their decision-making. These predictions will be useful in market demand analysis, analysis of taxation policies, analysis of import policies, etc.

The third question is what Islamic economists are required to do in relation to the theory of consumer behaviour. Their first task will be to firm up the foundations of the theory. This will require integrating into the theory the *Fiqh* principles relating to consumption. After the foundations have been firmed up, the tools will have to be developed that can help in the analysis of behaviour on Islamic foundations. We have explained in detail above why existing tools may prove to be insufficient to analyze consumer behaviour in an Islamic society.

Islamic economists must also analyze empirical data relating to consumer decision-making in Islamic societies, identifying the patterns and regularities, and compare them with the theories of conventional economics, so as to arrive at their own conclusions about the theory of consumer behaviour in the Islamic perspective. For example, in countries which have Muslim and non-Muslim communities, like Malaysia and Indonesia, we can take comparable groups from either community and do a comparative study of consumer behaviour to determine the extent to which the practice of Islam affects, e.g.

(a) propensity to consume/save.
(b) share income with others.
(c) composition of consumption basket.
(d) equality/inequality of distribution of consumption.

Such findings would go a long way towards developing and improving a theory of consumer behaviour in the Islamic perspective.

CHAPTER 3

The Macro Consumption Function in an Islamic Framework*

Introduction

Consumer behaviour, i.e. how consumers allocate their income between different heads and how they decide how much to consume now and how much to save for the future, was the subject of the previous chapter. The study of consumer behaviour has implications for macro economic policies. Many modern economic theories conclude that savings are essential for economic growth. The more people save in a country, the more rapidly it will grow. Against this background, modern economists conclude that the level of savings in an Islamic economy will be lower if people have to pay *zakāh* on their savings. In this argument *zakāh* is considered as a tax on savings that switches allocation of resources from savings (i.e. future consumption) to present consumption. Also, it is argued, if part of the savings of the rich are given to the poor, who will obviously consume it all, the aggregate savings level in the economy, other things being equal, will naturally decline. The conclusion therefore follows that as Islamization of an economy will result in lower savings, it will adversely affect its growth.

Are savings really essential for economic growth? Only those will answer yes to this question who believe that capital accumulation is the engine of growth. Some economists, particularly Islamic economists (Khurshid Ahmad (1)), may not believe so. We will, however, set this question to one side. Within the popular view that savings are essential for economic growth, we will raise only the following question: 'Is it really true that savings in an Islamic economy will be lower than if the same economy was operating on a non-Islamic basis?'

*This chapter is adapted from an article published in *Journal of Research in Islamic Economics*, King Abdul Aziz University, Jeddah, 1985.

45

Our answer to this is no. We have developed two arguments to support this answer. One argument describes the Islamic premises on which a Muslim will determine his consumption. It is argued that these premises are such that the aggregate consumption level will be lower than if the Muslim were consuming on un-Islamic premises. The second argument is built on the basis of a macro economic model that includes the dynamic effect of *zakāh* in an Islamic economy. Through this model, it is shown that even if there is any chance of a short run decline in the aggregate savings level due to the Islamization of the economy (i.e. imposition of such injunctions as *zakāh*), this adverse effect will soon be wiped out and the long term savings and growth path will be higher than in the non-Islamic economy. This results from the income distribution effects of *zakāh* which lead the poor to eventually enter the group of savers as their economic conditions improve.

Section I builds up the first argument, i.e. of the Islamic premises on which consumption of Muslims will be determined. Sections II and III give a macro model for an Islamic economy. Section IV derives mathematical comparison of savings propensities between Islamic and non-Islamic economies. The numerical results of simulation under various parametric assumptions and policy conclusions therefrom have been left for a later exercise.

Islamic Premises on which a Muslim's Consumer Behaviour is Determined

Before I explain the Islamic premises within which consumer behaviour is determined, I will briefly describe the premises on which modern economists believe that a consumer decides his consumption pattern.

Modern economic theory studies consumer behaviour with the following premises:

(i)   It is assumed that a consumer will decide what to consume and how to consume only to gain material benefits and satisfaction.

(ii)   It is generally assumed that all his consumption is geared to satisfying his own needs. He is not bothered about satisfying anyone else's needs.

(iii)   It is assumed that a consumer behaves rationally. This, among other things, means: (a) that the consumer will neither be miserly nor unnecessarily spendthrift; and (b) that he will not hoard his wealth.

Modern economists explain what and how much a consumer will consume and how much he will save to invest for future earnings/consumption on these premises which are taken as axioms, i.e. assumed to be given in human nature. In other words, no argument is given to explain why a consumer would act on these premises.

It will readily be understood that these premises can be valid only if a consumer has been brought up in a particular cultural environment and has been taught a particular philosophy of life. This may not be true for all societies in the world. In fact, very few societies have such a cultural environment or such a philosophy of life. Take, for example, the assumption of rationality. The type of 'rationality' assumed by modern economic theory may not exist in many societies with different ethical, social and cultural norms and customs. Besides, individuals do like to spend on other than worldly ends. (Even in Western materialistic societies, people like to spend on non-material ends.) Or, individuals do spend on not only their own but also others' material welfare (the social structure and culture of societies like India and Pakistan and many other developing countries necessitate such spending). Or individuals do become unnecessarily spendthrift (a problem in many Western societies) or hoard their wealth (a problem in many underdeveloped societies).

Islam, with its distinct ethical, social and cultural framework, provides completely different premises for the analysis of consumer behaviour which will consequently be very different from the theories that secular economists propound.

A Muslim consumer in an Islamic economy is supposed to engage in two types of spending:[1]

(a) To meet his (or his family's) material needs. Let us denote this type of spending by E_1.
(b) To meet the needs of others (for the sake of Allah). Let us denote this by E_2.

The total spending E, therefore, can be written as

$$E = E_1 + E_2$$

It is left to individual discretion to allocate income between these two types of spending. Human behaviour, however, is guided behaviour for a Muslim – a person who is advised to be God-conscious or God-fearing. Thus allocation between E_1 and E_2 will be determined by:

(i) some of the parameters that determine the consumption pattern of a 'rational' consumer (as outlined by conventional economics), and

(ii) degree of God-fearingness or God-consciousness (*taqwā*).

The role of God-fearingness in the spending of Muslims is clear from various verses of the Qur'ān:

> O you who believe; Fear Allah as He should be feared (3: 102).

> Verily the most honoured of you in the sight of Allah is (he who is) the most righteous of you (49: 13).

> God fearing are those who believe in the Unseen, are steadfast in prayer and spend out of what We have provided for them (2: 3).

Muslims are the more honoured as they are more God-conscious and God-fearing; and one definition or expression of this state is to spend in the way of Allah. The Qur'ān does not specify exactly how much a person should spend in the way of Allah. At two places in the Qur'ān the question, posed by the Companions of the Prophet (peace be upon him), what they as Muslims should spend is answered. In verse 2: 219, the answer is simply 'Say al-'afw', that is, to spend what is left over after meeting one's needs. It is reported that the other verse refers to the following question from the Companions of the Prophet (peace be upon him):

> What should we spend from our wealth and where should we spend it?

The verse (2: 215) says:

> They ask thee what they should spend (in charity). Say: Whatever you spend, that is good; (it) is for parents and kindred and orphans and those in want and for wayfarers. And whatever you do that is good – Allah knows it well.

The emphasis is on where money should be spent; on parents, relatives, the needy and wayfarers. The answer to how much should be spent has been left unspecified. The phrase, 'whatever you do that is good – Allah knows it well', indicates that there is no upper limit.

'Whatever you can afford you should spend' is the guidance. It was agreed among the Companions of the Prophet, and the generation succeeding the Companions, and among the *fuqahā'*, that one should spend from what is left after meeting one's needs and not that one should spend all of what is left over.

Without specifying how much should be spent for others in the way of Allah, great emphasis has been placed on such spending. The more one spends on others (for the sake of Allah) the better for him in this world and the Hereafter. This emphasis is apparent in many verses of the Qur'ān.

> And spend of your substance in the cause of Allah and make not your own hands contribute to your destruction. But do good. For Allah loves those who do good (2: 195).

Other verses with a similar emphasis are 2: 177, 3: 92, 9: 34, 2: 254, 2: 262, 2: 245, 8: 60.

Spending in the way of Allah (E_2) is entirely different from the first type of spending (E_1), which is for worldly needs. From the second type of spending, no worldly advantage is intended to be obtained. It has to be for the sake of Allah with no worldly motives at all, as is apparent from several verses. For example:

> O you who believe: do not annul your charity by reminders of your generosity or by injury – like those who spend their substance to be seen of men, but believe neither in Allah nor in the Last Day. There are in parable like a hard barren rock on which is a little soil; on it falls heavy rain, which leaves it (just) a bare stone. They will be able to do nothing with what they have earned. And Allah guides not those who reject faith (2: 264).

The same sense is reiterated in verse 4: 38.

Though no exact amount or any upper limit has been specified in the Qur'ān or the *Sunnah* for E_2 (or for E_1) we do find that there is a lower limit for the amount of E_2 to be spent by those who are eligible. This lower limit is the amount of *zakāh* which is mandatory. But this is only a minimum. To acquire a higher degree of Islamic worth, a Muslim has to do as much E_2 type spending as possible (see Qur'ān 2: 3 quoted above).

The stress on E_2 should not be taken to assume that E_1 is less important. We find specific guidance in the Qur'ān and the *Sunnah* emphasizing the importance of E_1 (e.g. the Qur'ān 7: 32).

All good things of this world have been created for man. Muslims are not asked to abstain from them. The Prophet (peace be upon him) says that when Allah bestows good things of the world upon one of His servants He likes to see them reflected in his appearance (of course without any intention of personal pride). The Prophet (peace be upon him) is also reported to have objected to abstinence from the lawful enjoyment of material things. He is also reported as saying: 'You don't really possess of your wealth but only what you eat and use up, what you dress and wear out or what you spend on charity and preserve (for the life hereafter).' At another place, in the Qur'ān, we find:

> Eat of their fruit in their season, but render the dues that are proper on the day that the harvest is gathered. But waste not by excess: for Allah loves not the wasters (6: 141).

> Of the cattle are some for burden and some for meat; eat what Allah has provided for you, and follow not the footsteps of Satan; for he is to you an avowed enemy (6: 142).

Here, Allah gives two commands: to spend for one's own needs and to spend for others in the way of Allah. The command 'waste not' refers to reasonableness in both types of consumption. Among other verses stressing E_1 type spending are 7: 31 and 2: 168.

Reasonableness in all spending is a vital aspect of Muslim consumer behaviour. This emphasis on reasonableness is unique to the Islamic economic system. The theory of consumer behaviour in secular economics assumes a 'rational' consumer who takes 'rational' decisions. But 'rationality' is in practice identical with selfish self-interest. In reality this quality is not discussed but assumed, and except as self-interest, there is no discussion on how rationality is to be achieved in an economy. Secular economics by-passes the question and that is why its theories lose practical relevance for most societies. Secular economists treat 'rationality' as an axiom relating to human behaviour, whereas, except as equated with self-interest, the type of rationality assumed by them is something that needs appropriate education. Developing or applying economic theories without imparting this appropriate education will be futile.

The maxim of reasonableness required for Islamic economic theories of consumer behaviour is not simply an axiomatic assumption which may or may not be true. It is something that a Muslim has to learn and acquire. Islam urges reasonableness with the same emphasis with which it urges how to spend and where to spend. The verse quoted above (6: 141) stresses reasonableness in spending. The same point is made in the verse

Do not make your hand tied (like the niggard's) to your neck, nor stretch it out to its utmost reach so that you become blameworthy and destitute (17: 29).

Reasonableness in spending is required not only for worldly spending (E_1) but also for spending in the way of Allah (E_2) as is clear from the following verses:

And render to the kindred their due rights, as (also) to those in want, and to the wayfarer; but squander not (your wealth) in the manner of spendthrifts (17: 26).

Those who, when they spend, are not extravagant and not niggardly, but hold a just (balance) between those (extremes) (25: 67).

In all the verses that allow E_1, the only limit that is commanded is not to consume prohibited goods and to consume only permitted goods. This reduces, other things being equal, the consumption basket of a Muslim consumer compared to a secular consumer.

Nothing has so far been said about saving for future consumption or investment to improve quality of life in the future. This is actually a part of E_1 type of spending, and it is legitimate in Islam. There is evidence from the Qur'ān and the *Sunnah* that justifies savings/investment.

To those weak of understanding, do not make over your property which Allah has made a means of support for you (4: 5).

In the explanation of this verse, commentators state that wealth is the capital of life and to preserve it by intelligent spending is obligatory on Muslims. The Prophet (peace be upon him) is reported to have said that poverty is likely to lead to disbelief. This implies that Muslims should try to improve their economic condition, which, in turn, justifies investment and hence savings. Another saying of the Prophet (peace be upon him), that to leave one's inheritors better off is desirable compared to leaving them poor, also emphasizes the importance of savings.

Unlike the secular economic system which does not penalize hoarding (savings that are not invested), the Islamic economic system

51

does place a specific penalty on hoarding in the form of *zakāh*. *Zakāh* will ultimately eat up all savings if they are not productively used to yield at least 2.5 per cent return per annum. Thus a Muslim has the following options with respect to his savings:

(a) Hoard it and pay at least 2.5 per cent of it every year in the way of Allah.
(b) Lend it as *Qarḍ Ḥasan* (free loan) and earn reward in the world hereafter.
(c) Invest it to earn at least 2.5 per cent return per year.

A rational consumer, obviously, has no alternative but not to hoard all his savings. If he decides to be irrational he will ultimately lose all that he has hoarded. Thus, savings have to be channelled towards investment. (This property of the Islamic economic system also reduces the chances of planned investment lagging behind or ahead of savings, to create deflationary or inflationary pressures, in the Keynesian framework. See also Kahf (3).) A Muslim will try to make investment with the following motives:

(a) to acquire permissible comforts of this world;
(b) to be able to have more to spend in the way of Allah and more reward in the Hereafter.

To recapitulate, the main elements of Muslim consumer behaviour are:

1. A Muslim consumer's total spending can be classified into the following major categories:

(a) Spending to achieve satisfaction in this world (E_1).
This includes:
(i) Present (immediate) consumption (let us denote it by (C_1).
(ii) Savings/investment for consumption in the future (let us denote it by (S_1).
(b) Spending for others with a view to earning reward in the Hereafter (E_2). This includes:
(i) what is immediately consumed by the recipients (let this be C_2).
(ii) What is invested for social purposes or community benefits or what is saved by the recipients for their own investment (S_2).

2. The consumption basket of a Muslim is likely to be smaller than that of a secular consumer as it includes only permissible things and excludes prohibited things.

3. The allocation between E_1 and E_2, and between C_1 and S_1 within E_1, or between C_2 and S_2 within E_2 has been left to rational consumer choices which should be guided by God-fearingness.

4. God-fearingness is an essential parameter in determining the consumer behaviour of a Muslim.

5. The only limit that has been specified is the minimum limit of E_2 for those who are under obligation to make these types of spendings.

6. A Muslim is allowed to save. A major part of his savings must be invested in order to earn at least a return that will prevent them from being depleted by *zakāh*.

From these premises, it is not very difficult to see that an Islamic economy will have a lower consumption propensity than a secular economy. The most important basis for this argument is that (a) the Muslim consumer is likely to face a smaller basket of consumptions to pick from than a secular consumer; and that (b) from within this basket he has to pick without crossing the limits of prodigality.

This is an immediate perspective. In a longer term perspective, we can visualize that the spending that is done for others will help them to improve their economic condition. Islam does not encourage people to keep receiving *zakāh*. They must improve their situation so as to enter the *zakāh*-payers category or at least to get out of the *zakāh*-receivers category.

Able-bodied poor people are allowed to receive *zakāh* only as a stop-gap to find an opportunity for them to improve their economic condition. In a dynamic economy, those people who are presently poor and cannot save anything are likely to be able to save as *zakāh* helps them to improve their economic status. Thus, even if in the short run, there is some reason to believe that savings propensity and hence economic growth in the economy are likely to be lower, there is no reason to believe that this will be true in the long run. This argument is further developed in the framework of a macro model discussed in the next section.

Deriving Consumption Function for an Islamic Economy

A. *Micro Consumption Function*

The consumer derives utility from both types of spending, E_1 and E_2. We may write the utility function as

$$U = F(E_1, E_2)$$

with the income constraint $Y = E_1 + E_2$

This utility function has the following properties.

$$F_1 = \frac{\delta U}{\delta E_1} > 0 \text{ i.e. marginal utility of } E_1 \text{ is positive.}$$

$$F_{11} = \frac{\delta F_1}{\delta E_2} < 0 \text{ i.e. marginal utility of } E_1 \text{ goes on declining as its volume is increased.}$$

$$F_2 = \frac{\delta U}{\delta E_2} = a > 0 \text{ and is a constant.}$$

This implies that the marginal utility of E_2 is a positive constant[2] for an individual with a specific level of God-consciousness. A declining marginal utility of E_2 is out of the question because the want for reward in the Hereafter is insatiable and unlimited. Increasing marginal utility of E_2 is also not possible as the reward of E_2 in the Hereafter is unknown. A person's evaluation of the reward will thus remain constant for each additional unit of E_2 spending. With this type of utility function, a consumer will go on consuming E_1 as long as its marginal utility is above 'a'. The more God-fearing a person is the more will be the 'a' value and more of the total spending will go to E_2. Thus:

$$E_2 = F(a, Y); \quad \frac{\delta E_2}{\delta a} > 0; \quad \frac{\delta E_2}{\delta Y} > 0$$

$$a = F(T) \quad \frac{\delta a}{\delta T} > 0$$

where T (the level of God-fearingness) is parametrically given.

E_2 type spending is done by that class of the population who can afford it. In Islamic terminology, E_2 will be spent only by the owner of *niṣāb*. Let us define owner of *niṣāb* as a person whose income exceeds a certain level, say Y^*

54

Thus: $\qquad E_2 = F(a, Y) > 0$ when $Y > Y^*$

$$= 0 \text{ otherwise}$$

For an owner of *niṣāb*, E_2 spending is not 'consumption' as understood in secular economics. In secular economic terminology E_2 is a transfer from the owner of *niṣāb* to the poor class of the population. E_2 may go entirely into consumption by the poor class or part of it may go to building up of their capital (physical or human). Let us use subscripts U and L to denote the values for owner of *niṣāb* (i.e. rich) and non-owner of *niṣāb* (i.e. poor) consumers respectively. We can write the following equation for the two types of consumers in the society:

$$E_L = Y_L + E_2 \text{ when } Y_L < Y^*$$

This means, the spending of the lower income consumer is equal to his total income plus the transfers from the upper income groups. (It has been assumed that all transfers are consumed by the lower income consumer. The possibility of the transfers being used to build up capital of the lower income consumer can be taken up later.)

$$\left. \begin{array}{l} E_2 = F\ (a,\ Y_u) \\ E_1 = Y_u - E_2 \\ a\ = F\ (T) \end{array} \right\} \quad \text{when } Y_u > Y^*$$

E_1 includes spending to build up durable consumer goods or to build up productive capital. This may also include hoardings in the form of jewellery, gold, silver, diamonds, etc. For the sake of simplicity let us classify the components of E_1 into the following:

(a)   All such spending as is termed consumption in secular economic terminology (C_u)

(b)   Savings (S).
   i.e. $E_1 = C_u + S$, where C_u = Consumption of the upper income group.
   and S = Savings of the upper income group.

How would the total amount of E_1, already determined by the parameter, T, be allocated between C_u and S? As already discussed, the allocation has been left to normal consumer behaviour except that Muslims have been categorically advised not to be extravagant.

This constraint on a Muslim will keep the level of C_u lower than the level of C_u of a secular consumer. How much lower the level will be will depend on how God-conscious a person is.[3] Thus we may define C_u in case of a Muslim as

$$\frac{1}{1-\beta} C_u = C_u^*, \text{ where } C_u = \text{level of consumption of a consumer.}$$

where $\beta = G(T)$ i.e. is a function of the level of God-fearingness with $\dfrac{d\beta}{dT} > 0$

C_u^* for a normal secular consumer is generally determined by the level of income, i.e. $C_u^* = F(Y_u)$ where $Y_u = $ income. Thus

$$C_u = (1 - \beta)\, F\,(Y_u)$$

For a Muslim consumer, it is not Y_u that is allocated between consumption and savings. It is E_1 left with the Muslim consumer (after spending E_2) to be allocated between consumption and savings. Hence,

$$C_u = (1 - \beta)\, F\,(E_1)$$

The above discussion is summarized as below:

Let us assume that there is no borrowing so that spending (including savings) is equal to income in the case of the upper income consumer, and equal to income plus transfers in the case of the lower income consumer.

Thus, the following equations describe the elements of consumption pattern in an Islamic economy.

$$
\begin{aligned}
C_L &= Y_L + E_2 \\
E_2 &= F\,(a, Y_u) & a &= F(T) \\
Y_u &= E_1 + E_2 \\
E_1 &= C_u + S \\
C_u &= (1 - \beta)\, F\,(E_1) & \beta &= G(T)
\end{aligned}
$$

B. *Aggregation for a Macro Framework*

(i) *Lower Income Group Consumption Function:*
Consumption of a lower income consumer depends on:

(a) his own income;
(b) the income of all the persons in the upper income group living in his neighbourhood;

(c) the level of God-fearingness of the individuals (particularly of the upper income group) in the community.

If we want to aggregate, the aggregation of the consumption of the lower income group will simply be the addition of the individual consumptions in the group. Aggregation is assumed to be a simple (unweighted) addition to the variables for all the individuals.

(ii)   Upper Income Group Consumption Function:
Consumption of a consumer in the upper income group depends on:

(a) his income;
(b) level of God-fearingness.

Ignoring the effect of income distribution and of variation in God-consciousness on consumption, the form of aggregate consumption function will require simple addition of the consumption and income of the individuals in the group. The level of God-fearingness is assumed to be the same at an average level for all individuals.

C.   *Dynamics of the Consumption Pattern*

Dynamism in the consumption pattern of an Islamic economy rises as people of the lower income group move into the upper income group over time (or vice versa). The possibility of movement from lower to upper group arises because of the improvement in the economic condition of the lower group. This will require:

(a) a desire to increase income, and
(b) an opportunity to attain this desire.

The desire to increase income is strong for a Muslim consumer because he will wish to spend in the way of Allah and earn a reward in the Hereafter. Also, it is a Muslim's religious obligation to improve his economic condition so that he becomes a *zakāh*-payer rather than a *zakāh*-receiver.

The opportunity to increase his income arises from the consumption relief that he gets from the transfer from the upper income group. This transfer, taking care of his and his family's consumption, gives him the opportunity to look for a better job or to build up his capital for the expansion of his work opportunities.

The growth in income at some point in time will shift the consumer from *zakāh*-receiver to *zakāh*-payer. In aggregate terms this means that the growth in income of the lower income group will shift some proportion of the population to the upper group. We can make this shift a function of per capita consumption in the lower income group. Thus, we can write:

$$\frac{N_L}{N} = F \left\{ \frac{C_L}{N_L} \right\}_{-1}; F` < 0$$

where $\dfrac{N_L}{N}$ = proportion of population in the lower income group

and $\left\{ \dfrac{C_L}{N_L} \right\}_{-1}$ = per capita consumption in the lower income group

i.e. the proportion of the population of the lower income group in the previous year will decline as per capita consumption in the group increases.

D. *Aggregate Consumption Function of an Islamic Economy*

With the above, we can now describe a consumption function in the economy as below:

$$
\begin{aligned}
C_u &= (1 - ß) F (E_1) \\
E_1 &= Y_u - E_2 \\
E_2 &= F (a, Y_u) \\
C_L &= Y_L + E_2 \\
\frac{N_L}{N} &= F (C_L/N_L)_{-1} \\
S &= E_1 - C_u = Y_u - C_u - E_2 \\
C &= C_L + C_u \\
Y &= Y_u + Y_L
\end{aligned}
$$

Macro Economic Model to Trace the Savings, Growth and Income Distribution Effects of the Consumption Function Described Above

A very simple macro model with the above consumption function is described below:

1. $C_u = (1 - \beta)\{a_0 + a_1 E_1\}$
2. $E_1 = Y_u - E_2$
3. $E_2 = d_0 - d_1 S_{-1}$
4. $C_L = Y_L + E_2$
5. $C = C_L + C_u$
6. $S = E_1 - C_u = Y - E_2 - C_u$
7. $Y_L = \{(Y_L)_{-1}\} \times (1 + g_L) + \gamma E_2$
8. $\Delta Y_u = I/K$
9. $Y_u = \{(Y_u)_{-1}\} + \Delta Y_u$
10. $Y = Y_L + Y_u$
11. $I = S$
12. $M = \dfrac{N_L}{N} = (M_{-1}) + \gamma_{-1}\left\{\dfrac{C_L}{N_L}\right\} + \gamma_2\left\{\dfrac{C_u}{N_u}\right\}$

$$\text{where } \gamma_1 < 0 \text{ if } \left\{\dfrac{C_L}{N_L}\right\} > \left\{\dfrac{C_L}{N_L}\right\}_{-1}$$

$$= 0 \text{ otherwise}$$

$$\text{and } \gamma_2 > 0 \text{ if } \left\{\dfrac{C_U}{N_u}\right\} < \left\{\dfrac{C_u}{N_u}\right\}_{-1}$$

$$= 0 \text{ otherwise}$$

13. $N = (N)_{-1}(1 + gn)$
14. $N_L = M.N.$
15. $N_u = (1 - M).N$

These equations are explained below:

1. $C_u = (1 - \beta)(a_0 + a_1 E_1)$

This equation determines the consumption level of the class that does not receive *zakāh*. We have already shown that the consumption function of this class can be written as

$$C_u = (1 - \beta) F(E_1)$$

We know that $F(E_1)$ is the consumption function that will prevail in a secular economy. A conventional form of this is

$$C = a_0 + a_1 Y$$

where C = consumption
Y = disposable income

We have E_1 instead of Y. E_1, in fact, is the disposable income of a Muslim consumer that he can spend to satisfy his material needs. Thus we can write

$$C_u = (1 - \text{ß}) (a_0 + a_1 E_1)$$

2. $E_1 = Y_u - E_2$

This is an identity which says that the amount at the disposal of the upper income group consumer for his spending is the difference between his income (Y_u) and what he decides to spend in the way of Allah (E_2).

3. $E_2 = Z + Z_1 (Y_u)$

   or $E_2 = d_0 + d_1 S_1$ $d_1 = 0.025$

This equation determines the amount to be spent in the way of Allah.

We have already shown that the function for E_2 can be written as $E_2 = F (a, Y_u)$. This specifically can be written as $E_2 = Z_1 (Y_u)$ where Z_1 is a parameter that will depend on God-consciousness. We know there is a minimum of spending (i.e. *zakāh*) that is obligatory upon the upper income group (though it may spend more out of its income). The level of God-consciousness will determine how much more will be spent out of its income Y_u. A more appropriate form, therefore, will be $E_2 = Z + Z_1 (Y_u)$ where both Z and Z_1 are the parameters. For the purpose of simulation, some simple manipulations are done as below:

The amount of *zakāh* $Z = 0.025 (A_{-1} + S)$
   where A_{-1} = *zakāt*able assets in the last year, and
   S   = savings

Also $Y_u = (Y_u)_{-1} + \Delta Y_u = (Y_u)_{-1} + \dfrac{1}{K} \cdot S$

Thus $E_2 = 0.025 A_1 + 0.025 S + Z_1 \{(Y_u)_{-1} + \dfrac{1}{K} S\}$

$= \{0.025 A_{-1} + Z_{-1} (Y_u)_{-1}\} + \{0.025 + \dfrac{Z_1}{K}\} S$

Since all values in the first part are pre-determined, we can denote this as d_0. Also the values $(0.025 + \dfrac{Z_1}{K}$ are all parametrically given.

Therefore, we denote them as d_1.

$$\text{Thus} \qquad E_2 = d_0 + d_1 \, S$$

It is not unreasonable to assume that the *zakāh* and other E_2 type spending are calculated by individuals on the basis of the past year's figures of assets, savings, income, etc. Therefore, we finally write the equation for E_2 as

$$E_2 = d_0 + d_1 \, S_{-1}$$

All these manipulations have been done to enable the simulations to be simple and easy. These manipulations will not be necessary and only the equation ($E_2 = Z + Z_1 \, Y_u$) can be used if a complex simulation programme can be afforded or if only mathematical analysis is done as is shown in part IV.

In the equation $E_2 = d_0 + d_1 \, S_{-1}$ it can be easily seen that d_1 cannot be less than zero. It will be equal to 0.025 if $Z_1 = 0$ and d_1 will be greater than 0.025 the higher the value of Z_{-1}, i.e. the level of God-consciousness, is.

4. $C_L = Y_L + E_2$

This determines the consumption level of those who are in the lower income group. Their consumption level has been assumed to be their own income (Y_L) plus transfers from the upper income group (E_2). It is assumed that all E_2 is consumed. An alternative variant of this equation could be to include only a part of E_2 as going to C_L and the rest of E_2 going to savings (building up the capital stock of those who are in the lower income group). To avoid complexities in the analysis here this variant is not being considered, but its effect will be considered later on.

5. $C = C_L + C_u$

This is an identity indicating that consumption in the economy is the sum of the consumption of two classes of population in the economy.

6. $S + E_1 - C_u = Y_u - E_2 - C_u$

This identity indicates that savings will be done by the upper income group and that savings will simply be that income minus what they consume or spend in the way of Allah.

7. $Y_L = \{(Y_L)_{-1} (1 + gL)\} + \gamma E_2$

This equation determines income for the population in the lower income group. The first part of their income, i.e. $(Y_L)_{-1} (1 + gL)$ has been assumed to be increasing at some exogenous growth rate (gL). This group obviously do not have capital stock. But they know that to be always in the receiving class of *zakāh* and charities is not encouraged in Islam and that they must improve their economic condition. Also, they will want to earn the reward of spending in the way of Allah as the upper income group are doing. So they will make efforts to increase their income.

Note that Y_L has been kept independent of Y_u. In fact, in an Islamic economy, Y_u may positively affect Y_L at least for those who are employed by the upper income group. In an Islamic economy, the wage pattern will be different from that in a capitalist society. The 'fair wage' theory or an employer's paternalistic considerations will be more relevant in an Islamic economy. This dependence in Y_L and Y_u is ignored here to keep the analysis simple.

Apart from this exogenous growth, some increase in the income of this group will be contributed by the transfers from the upper income group. The transfers, even if they do not contribute to the savings of the lower income group, will contribute to their efficiency. The use of *zakāh* on health and education will improve their human capital and hence will contribute to their income. The second part γE_2 represents this contribution.

8. $Y_u = I/K$

9. $Y_u = \{(Y_u)_{-1}\} + \Delta Y_u$

These two equations determine income for the upper income group. The change in the income of this group is determined by the investment that they make and the incremental capital output ratio – K (a parameter) of the economy. This assumes a fixed coefficient production function for simplicity. Any other form of the function could also be used.

The change in Y_u is thus $\Delta Y_u = I/K$. The current year's Y_u, therefore, is simply the sum of the past year's Y_u and current year's change in Y_u.

10. $Y = Y_u + Y_L$

This identity determines national income as a sum of the incomes of the two groups of population.

11. $I = S$

The assumption of absence of borrowing (external or internal) leads to this identity between savings and investments in the economy.

12. $M = \dfrac{N_L}{N} = (M)_{-1} + \gamma_1 \left\{ \dfrac{C_L}{N_L} \right\} + \gamma_2 \left\{ \dfrac{C_u}{N_u} \right\}$

This equation determines the percentage of population that will be in the lower income (*zakāh*-receiving) group.

In a dynamic economy where the income of both classes is increasing, where there is a mechanism for transfer of incomes, and where there are motivations and opportunities to move to higher groups, the percentage of population in the two groups cannot remain constant. The percentage will be a function of numbers in the lower group and will decline as consumption in this class increases and some of them move into a position to pay *zakāh*. γ_1 (a parameter) will determine how much decline in M will be brought about by a certain increase in the per capita consumption of this class. If $\left\{ \dfrac{C_L}{N_L} \right\}$ does not increase or rather declines, then γ_1 will be zero and M will remain the same as in the previous year.

Also it is possible that due to decline in the income of the upper income group some part of this population may enter into the *zakāh*-receiving group. γ_2 (a parameter) will determine how much increase in M will be brought about by a certain decline in the per capita consumption of this group. If $\left\{ \dfrac{C_u}{N_u} \right\}$ does not decline or increase then M will remain the same as in the previous year (i.e. will be zero).

$$M = (M_{-1}) + \gamma_1 \left\{ \dfrac{C_L}{N_L} \right\} + \gamma_2 \left\{ \dfrac{C_u}{N_u} \right\}$$

$$\text{where } \gamma_1 < 0 \text{ If } \left\{ \dfrac{C_L}{N_L} \right\} > \left\{ \dfrac{C_L}{N_L} \right\}_{-1}$$

$$= 0 \text{ otherwise}$$

$$\text{and } \gamma_2 > 0 \text{ If } \left\{ \frac{C_u}{N_u} \right\} < \left\{ \frac{C_u}{N_u} \right\}_{-1}$$

$$= 0 \text{ otherwise}$$

13. $N = N_{-1} (1 + gn)$

Population in the economy is assumed to grow at a constant rate (gn) per annum.

14. $N_L = M.N.$

15. $N_u = (1 - M) N$

These two equations determine the population in the two groups.

Implications of Islamic Consumption Function

1. *Savings – Short Term*

The savings function in an Islamic economy will be of the type

$$S = F_0 + F_1 \, WY$$

$$\text{where } F_1 = \frac{1 - z_1}{1.025 - 0.025a(1 - \beta)} \{ 1 - (1 - \beta) a_1 \}$$

The implication for savings under different situations is discussed below.

CASE I: *Zakāh treated as tax so that only zakāh is paid and there is no God-consciousness.*

This means no other spending is made in the way of Allah and no restraints on personal consumption are exercised and a Muslim behaves as a secular consumer. This means:

$$\beta = 0 \text{ and } Z_1 = 0$$

$$F_1 = \frac{1}{1.025 - 0.025a_1} (1 - a_1)$$

For a secular consumer in a secular economy, the savings function is:

$$S = a_0 + (1 - a_1) \, WY$$

Since the denominator in F_1 is greater than unity because a_1 is less than unity, hence

$$F_1 < 1 - a_1$$

Thus the propensity to save is reduced with *zakāh* in this case.

The difference, however, will be very low at high levels of propensities to consume and will be marginally higher at lower propensities to consume. In an economy that has a marginal propensity to consume equal to 0.80 (a too optimistic figure for a developing country) the introduction of *zakāh* as a tax will reduce marginal propensity to save by 0.5 per cent, i.e. instead of 0.20, it would be 0.199 (see Table below).

TABLE I

Effects of Introduction of *Zakāh* as a Tax on Short-Term Savings at Different Levels of Marginal Propensity to Consume

Marginal propensity to consume before introduction of *zakāh* (a_1)	Value of F_1 (marginal propensity to save after *zakāh*)	Value of $(1-a_1)$ marginal propensity to save without *zakāh*	F_1 as % of $(1-a_1)$	Percentage decline in marginal propensity to save as a result of *zakāh*
1.00	0.0000	0.00	0.00	0.0
0.90	0.1998	0.10	99.8	0.2
0.80	0.1990	0.20	99.5	0.5
0.70	0.2977	0.30	99.2	0.8
0.60	0.3960	0.40	99.0	1.0
0.50	0.4938	0.50	98.8	1.2
0.40	0.5910	0.60	98.5	1.5
0.30	0.6880	0.70	98.3	1.7
0.20	0.7840	0.80	98.0	2.0
0.10	0.8802	0.90	97.8	2.2
0.00	0.9756	0.00	97.0	2.5

The maximum effect will be a 2.5 per cent decline when the marginal propensity to consume is zero. This simply means that whatever they save from additional income will be reduced by the amount of *zakāh* at the rate of 2.5 per cent. If they save all of their additional income, then this saving will be reduced by 2.5 per cent and if they save only 20 per cent, this will be reduced by 0.5% of 20 per cent by *zakāh*. The marginal propensity to save will be 19.9 per cent instead of 20 per cent if *zakāh* is treated as tax.

CASE II: *Muslims understand the importance of spending in the way of Allah but their consumption patterns are the same as those of secular consumers.*

This means ß = 0 but Z_1 is positive.[4] In this case

$$F_1 = \frac{(1 - Z_1)}{1.025 - 0.025\,a_1} \{1 - a_1\}$$

F_1 in this case is less than in case I. That is savings in the short run are further reduced. The reduction will be more, the higher the value of Z_1.

CASE III: *Muslims are not inclined to spend in the way of Allah more than the minimum required. They, however, rationalize their consumption pattern as taught by the Qur'ān and the Sunnah.*

This means Z_1 is zero but ß is positive. In this case marginal propensity to save, MPS = F_1 W.

where $$F_1 = \frac{1 - (1 - ß)a_1}{1.025 - 0.025\,a_1\,(1 - ß)}$$

Let us compare this with the secular marginal propensity to save

$$MPS = (1 - a_1)\,W$$

W is common in both so we compare F_1 and $(1 - a_1)$.

The numerator of F_1 is greater than $(1 - a_1)$. The numerator of F_1 is, however, reduced by the denominator being larger than unity. Whether $\frac{1 - (1 - ß)a_1}{1.025 - 0.025\,a_1\,(1 - ß)}$ is greater than $(1 - a_1)$ will depend on the values of ß and a_1.

The restraint on personal consumption reduces the overall consumption by a certain factor. But reduced consumption means more *zakāh*. The net effect is shown in the following table. The table shows MPS* (i.e. MPS of an economy that has some positive values of ß). The values of MPS* have been shown for different values of ß at two alternative levels of MPS (which is the propensity to save in the absence of Islamic injunctions). The two alternative values have been assumed to be 0.20 and 0.10 which is a range generally observed in present-day Muslim countries.

TABLE II

Values of MPS* for Different Values of ß When $Z_1 = 0$

ß	When MPS = 0.20 i.e. when $a_1 = 0.80$	When MPS = 0.10 i.e. when $a_1 = 0.90$
0.01	0.209	0.100
0.02	0.217	0.118
0.05	0.241	0.150
0.10	0.282	0.191
0.20	0.363	0.282
0.30	0.445	0.373
0.40	0.527	0.465
0.50	0.609	0.558

The MPS* will be higher for higher values of ß.

Cases II and III are also unlikely in an Islamic economy. Both ß and Z_1 depend on the level of God-fearingness. It is very unlikely that one of them is zero and the other positive.

In comparing case III with case II, we find that one parameter of an Islamic economy (Z_1) will have a negative effect on saving propensity whereas the other parameter (ß) will have a positive effect. Their combined effect is considered in case IV.

CASE IV: *Muslims not only spend in the way of Allah but also rationalize their consumption as taught by the Qur'ān and the Sunnah – a likely reflection of an Islamic economy*

In this case marginal propensity to save is $MPS^* = F_1\ W$

$$F_1 = \frac{(1 - Z_1)}{1.025 - 0.025\ a_1\ (1 - \beta)}\ \{1 - (1 - \beta)\ a_1\}$$

Let us compare this with secular marginal propensity to save, $MPS = (1 - a_1)\ W$.

MPS^* (i.e. marginal propensity to save of an Islamic economy) will be greater than MPS if

$$\frac{(1 - Z_1)\ \{1 - (1 - \beta)\ a_1\}}{1.025 - 0.025\ a_1\ (1 - \beta)} > (1 - a_1)$$

MPS^* has two components

(i) $1 - (1 - \beta)\ a_1$

(ii) $\dfrac{1 - Z_1}{1.025 - 0.025\ a_1\ (1 - \beta)}$

It is obvious that the first component is greater than $(1 - a_1)$ as $0 < \beta < 1$. But the second part is clearly less than unity because $Z_1 > 0$ and

$$\{1.025 - 0.025\ a_1\ (1 - \beta)\} > 1 \text{ as } a_1, \beta > 0 \text{ and } < 1$$

The outcome, whether MPS^* is greater than MPS, will therefore, depend on the empirical values of Z_1 and β (which in turn will depend on the level of God-fearingness in the society).

Let us assume $Z_1 = 0.025$. It should be remembered that this is a proportion of his annual income that a God-fearing man will spend in the way of Allah, in addition to 2.5 per cent *zakāh* that he is obliged to pay on his savings. Also let us assume MPS in the economy before Islamization to be 0.20 (i.e. $a_1 = 0.80$). Now, assuming different hypothetical values for β that may be observed after Islamization, the impact on the marginal propensity to save is shown in the following table:

TABLE III

Values of MPS* for Different Values of ß When Z = 0.025

ß	MPS*	MPS* - MPS
0.000	0.194	-0.006
0.005	0.198	-0.002
0.008	0.200	0.000
0.010	0.202	+0.002
0.020	0.209	+0.009
0.050	0.233	+0.033

It can be seen that when ß = 0 (which is the same as case II discussed earlier), there will be an immediate negative effect on the marginal propensity to save. But a very small value of ß would make the marginal propensity to save higher even in the short run. This means that if people are willing to slightly change their life-style to reduce what Islam calls *isrāf* (prodigality), *zakāh* cannot have a negative effect on the (macro) marginal propensity to save in the economy. As is evident from the table, even as low a ß as 0.008 would not allow any negative effect on the propensity to save. A ß value equal to 0.008 would mean that if a person had a propensity to consume 0.80 when operating in an un-Islamic environment, the Islamic environment and Islamic values would cause him to reduce this to at least 0.794, a not unreasonable assumption. The injunction to avoid prodigality can be expected to have a much stronger effect on consumption, particularly in the modern environment of developing countries where consumption patterns are substantially dominated by conspicuous consumption. The higher the value of ß, the more the positive effect on the propensity to save.

If Z_1 value is greater than 0.025 (i.e. people like to spend more in the way of Allah), a higher value of ß will be required to avoid the negative effect on the propensity to save. Since both Z_1 and ß depend on the level of God-fearingness, ß is expected to move with Z_1, hence reducing the negative impact on the propensity to save.

Thus, in an Islamic society, the marginal propensity to save is likely to increase even in the short run.

Long Run Savings

This part has been left to be worked out by the interested reader by assigning different values to the parameter to see the growth path of savings. Since transfers from upper income groups contribute to the income growth of the lower class, savings will ultimately be higher in each of the four scenarios, compared to the scenario of a secular economy.

Growth and Income Distribution Effects

This part too is left to be worked out by the interested reader. Theoretically, it is easy to visualize how within the framework of the above model, growth and income distribution implications of an Islamic consumption pattern will be favourable, i.e. growth will be higher and income distribution more egalitarian.

Conclusions and Policy Recommendations

Comparison of savings, growth and income distribution effects by simulating the model under different scenarios can highlight various implications and trade-offs. The following general conclusions can be drawn on the basis of the above analysis even without running the simulations.

For developing Muslim countries striving for resource mobilization for development, Islamization provides a new hope for the economy. The motivation to consume less and save more to improve one's own economic conditions as well as the economic conditions of the less privileged in the community comes from one's conscience, i.e. from one's religion.

It cannot be denied that all policies of development and resource mobilization of developing countries fail because they lack motivation on the part of the individuals and because their policies are hardly in harmony with the social and religious norms of the individuals. Muslim countries, thus, have nothing to fear from the process of Islamization in the context of savings and capital formation.

The process of Islamization that would bring favourable results as indicated in the earlier sections assumes that Muslims practise Islamic values. The process of Islamization, therefore, should aim at inculcating Islamic values in the life of Muslims. Improving Islamic economic injunctions through legislation, though, may still be beneficial in the long run. It can be shown from the simulation model that if we impose *zakāh* through legislation without inculcating Islamic values (particularly economic values), there is likelihood of an immediate adverse effect on savings. The speed with which favourable effects on growth and income distribution in the long run are achieved will be extremely slow compared to the situation where people understand and practise Islamic economic values. Priorities in Islamization of the economy should be on bringing about Islamic values in the society through mass media as well as educational institutions.

Comparison of cases I to IV, as discussed earlier, suggests that if the government wants to implement the *zakāh* system by legislation, it should simultaneously launch an educational and moral suasion programme to reduce *isrāf* (prodigality) in consumption. Reforms in import policies and the tax structure can help in achieving this objective. In short, the starting point for any government should be the one suggested by case III, i.e. impose *zakāh* at the rate of 2.5 per cent along with policies to reduce *isrāf* in consumption both in the public and private sectors.

Notes

1. 'Spending' is used to include not only what is called 'consumption' in economics but also investment expenditures, transfers, lending and savings in the form of hoarding or otherwise.

2. It was argued by a commentator that the assumption $\dfrac{\delta U}{\delta E_2}$ = constant would not allow the indifference curve to be convex and would rather make it concave leading to a corner solution which is not a desirable Islamic solution. Without going into the implication of constant marginal utility of E_2 on convexity, I express my gratitude to Dr. Anas Zarqa for pointing out that the assumption of constant marginal utility of E_2 is not necessarily required. Instead, it is safe to assume a declining marginal utility of E_2. His argument, in brief, is as follows:

E_2 has a utility just as E_1 has. Even a secular consumer likes to spend E_2 to enjoy the satisfaction that he is not selfish and is nice to others. For a secular consumer this utility of E_2, however, will be too small leading to a too small level of E_2. For an Islamic consumer E_2 will be larger because he feels more satisfaction in E_2 due to his different objectives of life and belief in the reward of the Hereafter. E_2 will have a declining marginal utility as E_1 has. This is because a Muslim has been asked to be moderate in his spending even on E_2, as has already been discussed above. It can be safely argued that E_2 is in nature the same as E_1, thus having diminishing marginal utility. The analysis in this paper, however, continues on the assumption of constant marginal utility of E_2, the assumption of declining marginal utility of E_2 being supposed to have no effect on the conclusions.

3. The constraints requiring Muslims to be moderate may imply a higher level of C_u if the secular behaviour in the society is that of a niggard. This is, however, very unlikely, particularly in view of the consumption pattern of existing societies in Muslim countries.

4. Note that Z_1 is spending in the way of Allah beyond *zakāh*. This is the proportion of annual income that is spent by a God-fearing person in the way of Allah in addition to spending 2.5 per cent *zakāh* from his wealth.

References

1. Ahmad, Khurshid, 'Economic Development in an Islamic Framework', in *Studies in Islamic Economics,* ed. Khurshid Ahmad. Leicester, UK, Islamic Foundation, 1980.

2. Faridi, F.R., 'A Theory of Fiscal Policy in an Islamic State', in *Fiscal Policy and Resource Allocation in Islam,* ed. Ziauddin Ahmad, et al., Islamabad, IPS, 1983.

3. Kahf, Monzer, 'A Contribution to the Theory of Consumer Behaviour in an Islamic Society', in *Studies in Islamic Economics,* ed. Khurshid Ahmad, Leicester, UK, Islamic Foundation, 1980.

4. Robb, E.L. and S. Tahir, *Does Distribution Matter in Aggregate Consumption Function? A test in the context of permanent income hypothesis.* QESP Research Report No. 13, McMaster University, 1981.

5. Zarqa, Anas, 'An Approach to Human Welfare', in *Studies in Islamic Economics,* ed. Khurshid Ahmad, Leicester, UK, Islamic Foundation, 1980.

APPENDIX

$$C_u = (1 - \text{ß}) a_0 + (1 - \text{ß}) a_1 E_1$$
$$= (1 - \text{ß}) a_0 + (1 - \text{ß}) a_1 (Y_u - E_2)$$
$$C_u + E_2 = (1 - \text{ß}) a_0 + (1 - \text{ß}) a_1 Y_u - (1 - \text{ß}) a_1 E_2$$
$$= (1 - \text{ß}) a_0 + (1 - \text{ß}) a_1 Y_u + \{1 - (1 - \text{ß}) a_1\} E_2$$
$$= (1 - \text{ß}) a_0 + (1 - \text{ß}) a_1 Y_u + \{1 - (1 - \text{ß}) a_1\} \{Z + Z_1 Y_u\}$$
$$= (1 - \text{ß}) a_0 + (1 - \text{ß}) a_1 Y_u + Z + Z_1 Y_u - (1 - \text{ß}) a_1 Z$$
$$- \{(1 - \text{ß})a_1\} Z_1 Y_u$$

Let $(1 - \text{ß}) = A;\ (1 - \text{ß}) (1 - Z_1) = B$

$$C_u + E_2 = (Aa_0 + (Ba_1 + Z_1) Y_u + (1 - Aa_1) Z$$
$$= Aa_0 + (Ba_1 + Z_1) Y_u + 0.025 (1 - Aa_1) A_{-1}$$
$$+ 0.025 (1 - Aa_1) S$$

Since $Z = 0.025 (A_{-1} + S)$

$$S = Y_u - C_u - E_2 = - Aa_0 + \{1 - (Ba_1 + Z_1)\} Y_u$$
$$- 0.025 (1 - Aa_1)A_{-1} - 0.025 (1 - Aa_1) S$$
$$\{(1 + 0.025 (1 - a_1A)\} S = - \{Aa_0 + 0.025 (1 - Aa_1) A_{-1}\} +$$
$$\{1 - (Ba_1 + Z_1)\} Y_u$$

Let $1.025 - 0.025\, a_1 A = E$ and $- \{Aa_0 + 0.025 (1 - Aa_1) A_{-1}\} = F$

$$ES = F + \{1 - (B a_1 + Z_1)\} Y_u$$

or $\displaystyle S = \frac{F}{E} + \frac{\{1 - (B a_1 + Z_1)\} Y_u}{E}$

Let $\displaystyle \frac{F}{E} = F_0;\ F_1 = \{1 - (Ba_1 + Z_1)\} / E$

and let $\displaystyle \frac{Y_u}{Y} = W$, i.e. share of upper income group in the national income

$$S = F_0 + F_1 WY$$

This is the savings function for an Islamic economy. The savings function for a secular economy in similar conditions will be:

$$S^* = Y_u - C_u = Y_u - a_0 - a_1 Y_u$$
$$= - a_0 + (1 - a_1) Y_u$$
$$= - a_0 + (1 - a_1) WY$$

PART II

BANKING AND FINANCE

CHAPTER 4

An Overview of the Financial System of Islam

Prohibition of Interest

The contemporary practice of financing is based on the principle of interest, which Islam categorically prohibits. It should be made clear at the outset that the prohibition of interest does not mean suppressing the interest rate to zero; that is a misunderstanding of some economists while analyzing the economic consequences of this prohibition. The prohibition of interest means the elimination of the very concept of interest, and the introduction of an alternative concept. The alternatives given by Islam are very clear from the following verses of the Qur'ān:

> Allah *Subḥānahū wa Ta'ālā* permitted trade and prohibited interest (2: 275).

> He (Allah *Subḥānahū wa Ta'ālā*) eradicates interest and gives growth to charity (2: 276).

The verse (2: 276) uses the verb *maḥaq* which means destroying by the very roots without leaving any sign of it. Eliminating interest and providing alternatives is a concept totally different from suppressing the interest rate to zero.

Before discussing alternatives to it, let us briefly consider what interest is. The definition of interest (for which the Qur'ān uses the term *Ribā*) is that it is any increase (large or small, nominal or real) received on a loan. The loan includes all such advances in which the principal amount remains guaranteed. In Islamic jurisprudence, it is defined as *an increase in one of two homogeneous equivalents being exchanged without this increase being accompanied by a return.*

There is a consensus on this meaning of *ribā* among renowned Islamic jurists. Muḥammad ibn 'Abdullāh ibn al-'Arabī defined *ribā* as follows:

It stands for every increase not justified by the return.

Thus all what is known as interest in present days falls within the definition of *ribā*. This means that whenever financing is in the form of loan there cannot be any income or return on it.

Return on Financing

The prohibition of interest does not, however, mean that there is a prohibition on earning any return on financing. It is possible, within the Islamic framework, to earn income on financing. The principle on which it may be earned is: *al-ghunm bi'l-ghurm* or *al-kharāj bi'l-ḍamān*. This implies that for every real economic gain there has to be a real economic cost in return.

The application of this principle requires that financing should give something in return in order to earn an income. The only real thing that financing can earn is profit and any real thing that financing can provide in return to justify a profit is bearing the risk associated with the earning of profit that the financing is supposed to earn.

Thus, there are only two alternatives to interest-based financing. One is *qarḍ ḥasan* in which only a loan is made whose principal is guaranteed without any interest or profit or loss. The other is risk-bearing financing. It may perhaps appear that certain Islamic financing techniques do imply a fixed rate of return and hence the principle of risk-bearing may not seem to apply. As will be discussed in the subsequent chapter, none of the Islamic financing techniques really allow a fixed and predetermined rate of return for the finance-provider, though in some cases there may be fixed cost of capital for the capital-user. The fixity and/or predetermination of the rate of return is prohibited for the finance-provider because of the maxim *al-ghunm bi'l-ghurm* or *al-kharāj bi'l-ḍamān,* quoted earlier, which means in sum: no risk no income. Risk-bearing financing can take several forms, all of which are permissible as long as the maxim is adhered to.

Institution of *Zakāh*

The institution of *zakāh* may not seem to be directly a part of the financial system as such, but it does have several direct repercussions on the system. *Zakāh* includes all obligatory payment in the cause of Allah, and is imposed on various types of assets, some of which may fall into the category of capital. From the point of view of the financial system, it is important to note that all financial holdings and working capital are subject to such obligations. The main features of this institution are as below:

(i)   There is a minimum obligation specified for different forms of wealth. Financial assets, working capital (including stock-in-trade of any kind) are subject to 2.5 per cent payment per annum.

(ii)   These payments are made for no worldly reward or compensation in return, pecuniary or non-pecuniary.

(iii)   The heads or uses of these payments are fixed and include: the poor, the needy, those employed to administer (the fund), for those whose hearts have been (recently) reconciled (to truth), those in bondage, those in debt, travellers, and in the cause of Allah (Qur'ān 9: 60–2).

Three Unique Categories of Financing

Financing is encouraged in Islam. But the mode of finance depends on who and what is to be financed. There are three categories of financing:

(a)   Return-bearing financing for a potentially commercially profitable activity, where the finance-owner is also willing to bear the risk of possible loss. Neither the principal nor the return on it are guaranteed.

(b)   Return-free financing for commercially non-profitable activity or for the poor or needy. No return can be claimed. The principal is claimable subject to the borrower's ability to pay.

(c)   Charity financing for the poor and needy. No return and no principal is claimable.

Within the Islamic framework, no other form of financing is admissible. Category (c) is legally obligatory to a minimum limit depending on the wealth held by the finance-owner. Category (b) is morally obligatory, if a needy person approaches a finance-owner who has spare funds. Category (a) is voluntary and the market is allowed and expected to take care of supply and demand in this category of finance.

Islamic Financing Techniques

Several financing techniques are possible which conform to the categories mentioned above. Some of the techniques were prevalent in the time of the Prophet (peace be upon him) and the *Khulafā' al-Rāshidūn* and have been discussed in traditional *fiqh* literature. Other techniques have emerged recently to meet contemporary financing requirements within the light of the teachings of Islam. A very brief review of the various techniques currently used in theory and practice is given below:

Loan with Service Charges:

This is the same as *qarḍ ḥasan* except that the lender is allowed to charge any cost that may have to be incurred by the lender in making the loan available to the borrower. This technique is especially meant for financial institutions extending loans to their clients/members. Since such institutions necessarily incur certain costs in making this facility available, they are entitled to charge this cost to the borrowers. The service charges are not profit. These are actual costs in respect of rental of premises, workers' wages, stationary, etc., which arise in the process of supplying *qarḍ ḥasan*.

Muḍārabah:

This is a financing technique in which the capital-owner provides funds to the capital-user for use in some productive activity on the condition that the profits therefrom will be shared by the capital-owner and the capital-user. The loss, if any, incurred in the normal process of the business (and not due to wilful neglect or misconduct on the part of the capital-user) is borne by the capital-owner. The user does not invest anything in the business except his human capital and does not claim any wage/salary for conducting the business. The capital-provider simply provides the finances and is not authorized to interfere in the management of the business. The ratio in which profits are distributed is fixed and predetermined and known in advance to both parties. In the event of loss the capital-provider loses his capital to the extent of the loss, the user of the finance loses all his labour. The willingness to bear the risk of loss justifies a share in the profit for the finance-provider. The profit-sharing ratio is mutually agreed upon between finance-provider and finance-user and is influenced by market forces.

Mushārakah:

This is a financing technique in which a capital-owner invests in another party's business. Additional finance is provided to the party (individual or group) who already has some funds for investment. The finance-provider provides the additional funds on the condition that he shares in the profits from the business. The ratio in which the finance-provider shares the total profits of the business with the party receiving the additional funds is fixed and predetermined, and known in advance to all concerned. The loss, however, will be shared in the exact proportion of the capital invested by each party. The profit-sharing ratio is left to be mutually agreed upon and may be different from the ratio in which the two parties (finance-provider and user) have invested in the total capital of the project. This is because the two parties may share the work of managing the project in any amount mutually agreed upon. Market forces will influence the determination of the profit-sharing ratio. Both parties are allowed to charge a fee or wage for any management or other labour put into the project. If the two parties invest only financial capital and do not invest any part of their human capital, there is no reason why in a competitive market, the profit-sharing ratio should be determined otherwise than the ratio of the initial financial investment.

Mushārakah is different from *muḍārabah* in at least one respect. In the latter, the financier has no right in the management of the project in which his finance is being invested. *Mushārakah* arrangements, by contrast, do allow the financier to participate in the management. Otherwise, these two techniques are very similar in that the provider of finance directly shares the profits and is willing to bear the losses, if any, to the extent of his investment. That is why these two techniques are often lumped together in one category popularly known as Profit/Loss-Sharing or PLS techniques.

Muzāra'ah/Musāqāh:

These techniques, basically, are known to be agriculture financing techniques and in principle they are similar to *muḍārabah* as described above, with only the difference that, in this case, it is the output that is shared and not the profit as in the case of *muḍārabah*.

Leasing/Ijārah:

Financing can be done on the basis of leasing as well. An individual with scarcity of funds can approach another with surplus funds to fund the purchase of a productive asset or assets. The financier may purchase the asset and rent the asset to the person needing the asset. This is a financing technique because the investor's financial difficulties (with respect to purchasing the required asset) are overcome. He pays only the rent and does not have to incur the huge capital investment that may be involved in the purchase of the asset. Two things must be kept in view while considering leasing as a financial technique. Leasing, in the Islamic framework, requires certain conditions to be fulfilled, of which the principal are the following:

1.   The service or benefit that the asset is supposed to provide and for which it is being rented should be definitely and clearly known to both parties.
2.   The asset remains in the ownership of the lessor. He is responsible for its maintenance so that it continues to give the service for which it was rented.
3.   The leasing contract is terminated as soon as the asset ceases to give the service for which it was rented. If the asset becomes damaged during the period of the contract, the contract will not remain valid.
4.   The asset cannot be sold to the lessee at a predetermined price at the expiry of contract. If it is to be sold, its price will be determined at the time of the expiry of the contract.

These conditions directly imply that the financier or the owner of the asset is not entitled to earn a fixed, predetermined return on his finance/capital. The actual rate of return on his capital remains undetermined and will be known only on *ex post* basis.

The rent for an asset cannot be treated as rate of return on capital invested in the asset for the following reasons:

1.   The owner of the asset is uncertain about the total life of the asset.

It can bring him income only during its productive life. Also, he does not know what price the asset will fetch if he decides to dispose of it at any time during its productive life.

2. The owner of the asset is also uncertain about the extent to which the asset will remain on lease during its productive life. After the contract with the first lessee expires the owner is uncertain about how long it may take him to find the next lessee, nor can he be sure how much rent will be agreed upon with the next lessee. Even if the first lessee renews the contract, it is quite possible that at any point of time he may demand revision in the rent against a possible defect that may adversely affect the productivity or service for which it was rented.

Bay' al-Salam:

This technique has an application in agriculture. Under its terms, a producer can get finance against the sale of produce before the produce is actually available. The price and quantity of the produce in question is, of course, to be determined very specifically and precisely at the time of the contract. The rate of return remains unknown until the time the goods in question are delivered to the financier and he is able to dispose of them in the market. At the time of making the contract and while fixing the purchase price of the goods, the finance-provider makes a guess about the price at which he will be able to dispose of the goods in the market after the goods are delivered to him. He therefore agrees upon a price with the producer that is expected to bring him (the finance-provider) a certain rate of return on his capital. His actual rate of return, however, depends on how the actual prices when he takes delivery of the goods compare with the prices at which he purchased the goods when advancing finance to the producer.

A similar arrangement in industrial activities is called *Ju'ālah*.

Bay' Murābaḥah bi Thaman Ājil:

By this technique a party needing finance to purchase certain goods gets the necessary finance in the form of a sale contract on a deferred payment basis. The finance-provider purchases the required goods and sells them on the basis of a fixed mark-up profit, agreeing to defer the receipt of the value of the goods even though the goods can be delivered immediately.

The need for finance of the one in need is thus met. He needed funds to purchase certain commodities (e.g. raw material or capital goods or even consumer goods). His purchase is financed, and paid for at some later date though he may end up paying more than he would have paid if he had his own money to purchase these goods. The desire of the finance-owner to earn income on his capital is also met. He makes a profit in terms of the mutually agreed upon mark-up.

This financing technique too is sometimes considered to be the same as interest because a person who needed say $1,000 to purchase certain goods gets the funds but ends up paying an additional value which does look like paying interest. However, this mark-up is not in fact in the nature of a fixed compensation for time or deferred payment though the cost had to be incurred because the needy person did not have the means at hand to make the purchase he wanted. The mark-up includes reward for the services that the finance-owner provides, namely, seeking out and locating and purchasing required goods at the best price. This is a recognized service which can be paid for and whose value is predeterminable. Furthermore, the mark-up is not related to time since, if the financed person is unable to pay in time as agreed, the amount of mark-up remains as fixed in the contract – it does not increase due to the delay in payment.

Consider the position of the finance-provider. What justifies his earning the fixed mark-up? Firstly, he provides a definite service in the form of obtaining the goods for his client, for which service he can charge a fixed price. Secondly, in obtaining the goods, he is taking a risk. The client may not accept the quality or price at which he purchased and the financier is then stuck with the goods. This risk is over and above the risks normally involved in trading activity – such as storage costs, damage in storage or in transit, etc. All these risks justify his earning profit; they also mean that, though he has fixed mark-up, he may not necessarily end up making a profit or getting the rate of return on his capital equal to the amount of mark-up fixed at the time of contract.

Main Features of the System

With the above description of the principles and techniques, we now briefly describe some features of the whole system.

Elements of the System

1. There is no interest in the economy. Financial capital can earn income only by bearing and sharing the risk of loss. All banks,

commercial financial institutions and development financial institutions, will seek and provide finances which always have some element of risk bearing. Though there may be several different ways (to be discussed in more detail later in this chapter), all must entail some risk bearing in some form on the part of the finance-supplier.

2.   If financial capital is not willing to bear and share risk, it can then be advanced on *qarḍ ḥasan* basis. In this case financial capital neither earns any income nor bears or shares any risk of loss. Commercial financial institutions, of course, will not deal in such transactions on a large scale. The system will develop special institutions for this type of financing, either on a co-operative basis or through the public sector.

3.   There are both *zakāh* and charity in the system, the former, the minimum obligatory levy, being 2.5 per cent on financial assets, goods or capital. Besides serving as a deterrent to keeping financial capital idle, *zakāh* also serves as an obligation-free financial support to the lowest-income groups of the population.

4.   Public borrowing is constrained by the absence of interest in the economy. Public borrowing will either come in the form of risk-bearing capital for commercially productive projects or it will come in the form of *qarḍ ḥasan* to the government. Government securities bearing an uncertain return can be issued only for such borrowings as are linked to commercially productive activities.

5.   In general, there is nothing that prohibits the government from printing money. It is assumed to be permissible if the benefits of doing so outweigh the costs.

Forms of Financing

From Islamic teachings, we can identify two categories of financing permissible within a system which prohibits interest and replaces it with risk-carrying lending. These two categories are, respectively, *direct* and *indirect* financing.

Direct Financing. Within this category two modes of financing are permissible, namely, *qarḍ ḥasan* and profit/loss-sharing. Under *qarḍ ḥasan* the finance-provider can claim only the principal he advanced, and not any return, small or large, nominal or real, direct or indirect. Further, he is also obliged to reschedule or postpone repayment of the principal, if the borrower's circumstances are such that he cannot repay.

The postponement is required to be given until he becomes able to pay.

If a finance-owner intends to benefit commercially from his financing activity, he must enter into a PLS arrangement with the finance-user in the context of some particular productive/commercial enterprise. The PLS arrangement is not allowed if the finance is for consumption purposes or for general purposes (in either of which cases *qarḍ ḥasan* is the only option). There are no other avenues for direct financing.

Indirect Financing. There are or may be several Islamically permissible ways of indirectly providing finance. Some of these are or have been in practice, while others may be discovered or identified in future. Before explaining some major forms of indirect financing, let us first clarify the fundamental principle underlying them. Just as in direct financing, there can be no return earned on one's capital unless this capital has borne some part of the risk associated with the activity in which the capital is being used. Whereas, in direct financing intended to be profitable, the risk of loss is borne in exact proportion to the investment of the contracting parties and for the entire period of the use of the investment, the risk in indirect financing may differ from the proportion of the investment of the contracting parties. Sometimes it may be possible for the finance-provider to substantially reduce his part of the risk bearing (though it cannot be totally eliminated) and it may also be possible to substantially reduce the period of risk bearing (though it cannot be reduced totally).

Indirect financing, some major forms of which we shall briefly mention, falls into one of three major categories, namely:

  (i)   trading-based modes,
  (ii) leasing-based modes, and
  (iii) service-based modes.

Trading-based Modes: There are two principal forms under this category. One may be referred to as 'deferred delivery forms'. These were discussed briefly above under the heading *bay' al-salam* and *bay' murābaḥah bi Thaman Ājil*.

Leasing-based Modes: Leasing is an alternative to financing in that it relieves a business of making capital investment. However, leasing is not in itself a mode of financing and is only an alternative to financing. Leasing only meets the need for the use of some item of equipment or of

86

real estate. If ownership of the item of equipment or real estate is intended (and not use) then leasing is not a mode of fulfilling the financing needs. There are, however, ways in which leasing can be used for financing purposes. One of these is a form of hire-purchase in which the capital-user pays an instalment of the capital and an amount of rent for the capital. This rent diminishes as the instalments are paid, becoming zero when the total value of the capital has been paid and ownership is transferred.

Service-based Modes: A skilful individual may need capital to make use of his skills. He may for example, need finance to purchase raw material. The trade-based mode which allows for deferred payment may not be suitable if he is not a trader and does not know how to market his goods. Service-based financing can help to meet financing need in such a case. The individual can be offered all the materials he needs to produce a certain quantity of goods by a finance-provider whom he then repays on the basis of completed output. The financing needs of the skilled person are thus met, and he at the same time is relieved of the work of marketing. The finance-provider for his part expects to gain by selling the goods in the market at some margin of profit.

Institutional Framework

The system will generate its own institutions to meet the needs of the society. Commercial banks may continue to exist for the purpose of financing intermediation, but their modes of operation will change. On the liabilities side they can do *muḍārabah* with their clients. They will, thus share with their depositors the profit earned from their assets. On the asset side they have two avenues for earning income. They may either decide to work as mere financial institutions, in which case they will deal with their clients only on the basis of direct modes of financing, i.e. *mushārakah* or *muḍārabah*. Or they may choose not to remain free financial institutions and become instead trading banks or leasing banks to earn mark-up or earn income from the indirect modes of financing in trading-finance or leasing-finance activities.

Since the system provides for *qarḍ ḥasan* for the needy, and since this is a highly encouraged institution in Islam, both the public and the private voluntary sectors are expected to raise funds to meet *qarḍ ḥasan* needs.

The system of social insurance in the form of *zakāh* and charities is meant to meet the subsistence needs of those whose subsistence is threatened for any reason. State institutions as well as the private voluntary sector are expected to organize *zakāh* and charity funds and make arrangements to meet the survival needs of the less privileged.

CHAPTER 5

Comparative Features and Economics of Some Modes of Islamic Financing Techniques*

Introduction

The previous chapter explained several Islamic modes of financing as alternatives to interest-based financing. There is, however, a divergence between theory and practice on the order of preference of these modes of financing. The theory is, generally, that profit/loss-sharing should be the most widely prevailing mode of financing in the financial system of Islam.[1] Contemporary practice in Islamic banking, however, is, overwhelmingly, dependent on the use of mark-up based techniques. Profit-sharing is the least popular mode of financing in most of the Islamic banks in the modern world.[2] Some theoreticians have been quite critical of this practice.[3] This controversy can be understood and synthesized by analyzing the economics of the various types of Islamic financing techniques.

There are five basic modes of financing, namely *muḍārabah, mushārakah, ijārah* (leasing), *bay' al-salam, bay'-murābaḥah (bay' bi Thaman ājil)* or mark-up. All Islamic financing techniques in theory and practice are direct or indirect reflections of these five modes, or combine features of two or more of them. The present chapter concentrates on only these five basic modes.[4]

---

*This chapter is a part of the paper on *Comparative Economics of Islamic Financing Techniques* published by the Islamic Research and Training Institute, Islamic Development Bank, Jeddah, 1991.

Economic Features of Islamic Modes of Financing

A lot of literature is available, mostly in Arabic, that explains in detail the legal structure of the above-mentioned individual financing techniques. Comparison of these structures from an economic point of view has not so far been a subject of any rigorous study. The following distinctive features have been derived from a review of the relevant literature.

Nature of the Financing

Financing modes can be distinguished from the point of view of the nature of financing involved in different techniques. *Bay' al-salam* and mark-up based modes can be regarded as debt-creating modes of financing since financing in these two modes is in the nature of a debt. The finance-user stands obliged to pay back the entire financing (or its equivalent as agreed in *bay' al-salam*). The repayment by the finance-user is, in fact, predetermined in advance and hence becomes a sort of debt from his point of view. On the other hand, *mudārabah* and *mushārakah* are non-debt creating modes in the sense that the user is not obliged to pay back the total amount of finance. To some extent *ijārah* can also be regarded as a financing mode as it too is a non-debt creating mode of financing. In *mudārabah* and *mushārakah,* the finance-user pays according to the profit/loss that he makes out of the use of the finance, while in *ijārah,* only the rent is paid which, for any particular user, may be a small part of the total value of the asset. The debt-creating modes involve a debt burden on the user irrespective of how much he benefits from the funds. Non-debt creating modes do not carry a debt burden; the user pays according to the benefit he gets from the financing.

Role of the Finance-Provider in the Management/Use of Funds

In *bay' al-salam,* the finance-providers have no role in the management of the funds by the finance-user. Once the finances have been handed over, the finance-user is free to use them as he thinks best. In a sense, *mudārabah* can also fall into this category because the finance-provider is not allowed to interfere in the management of the enterprise in which his funds are being used. In *mushārakah,* on the other hand, the finance-provider does have a role in the management of the funds. In the case of mark-up based and lease-based financing, the finance-provider has full control over the use of the funds since these are deployed by himself.

Risk-Bearing by the Finance-Provider

Both in *mudārabah* and *mushārakah*, the whole of the capital invested by the finance-provider is at stake. The finance-provider in *mudārabah* is responsible for the whole financial loss of the enterprise in which the finances were used. His whole financial investment is thus at stake until the project is completed and the finances have been recovered. In the case of *mushārakah*, the finance-user bears the financial loss in proportion to his capital in the total investment of the enterprise. In this case too, the whole of the capital invested by the finance-provider remains at stake until the project is completed and the finances have been recovered. Almost similar is the case with leasing where the entire amount of capital remains at stake as the capital-owner is responsible for all the risks attached to it during the life of the asset. The capital will be at risk until the asset successfully completes its anticipated productive life. The risk-bearing in *bay' al-salam* arises due to the uncertainty of the future prices of the commodities involved in the contract. In each of these four cases, i.e. *mudārabah, mushārakah,* leasing and *bay' al-salam,* the finance-provider puts at stake the whole of his capital investment as well as the opportunity cost of capital for the whole period until the capital is received back.

In mark-up based financing, there is risk but less than that involved in the above-mentioned four techniques. The risk in mark-up is borne only until the goods are handed over to the capital-user, and not, as in the other techniques, until the capital is recovered. Once the goods are handed over to the finance-user, all risk lies with him and the finance-provider shares no risk during the rest of the period till the recovery of finance.

Other things being equal, mark-up based financing may involve the minimum risk for the finance-provider compared to the other techniques for the following reasons:

(i) The finance-provider does not bear risk for the entire period of the contract, the risk is only for that period in which a spot sale is to be made and the goods handed over to the client. For the remaining period of the contract, the amount of financing plus the agreed mark-up on it is

91

in the nature of debt and is risk-free. In all the other financing techniques the risk remains alive throughout the period of the contract.

(ii) Mark-up based financing requires only knowledge of the current prices of the goods to determine the financing and the return on it. In the other techniques, some anticipation or forecasting has to be made about values of the various variables involved in financing. This introduces an element of risk to the extent that the anticipations or forecasts may not prove correct. *Bay' al-salam* requires forecasting future market prices; leasing requires forecasting the productive life of the asset; and *muḍārabah* and *mushārakah* require forecasting the profitability of the enterprise/activity in which investment is made.

Uncertainty of Rate of Return on Capital for the Finance-Provider

It has been mentioned above that all Islamic financing techniques involve risk-bearing by the finance-provider. The finance-provider has, in some way, to bear the risk of loss of capital if he allows the use of money in any of these modes. This means that any return that he may expect, *ex ante,* on his finances has some element of uncertainty. It is a common misnomer to regard the trading-based and leasing-based financing techniques as fixed return techniques. The misunderstanding arises on the basis of the following argument:

Mark-up: Since the mark-up is fixed and predetermined as a percentage of the capital amount, this technique is considered to involve a fixed rate of return. The mark-up itself is considered the fixed rate of return.

Leasing: Since rent is fixed and predetermined, it is considered to imply a fixed rate of return because renting an item of equipment worth US $100,000 at an annual rent of US $10,000 means a 10% fixed rate of return on capital.

Bay' al-salam: Since the quantity and price of the goods to be purchased from the finance-user are known and fixed in advance, the finance-provider is assumed to have fixed the rate of return in advance.

In all these cases, the amount charged to the finance-user is usually assumed to be also the rate of return on capital. This is not actually the case. There are risks of losses involved for the finance-provider in all these techniques. In mark-up based financing, the financier faces all the costs and risks normally involved in a trading activity such as locating and buying goods, storage, damage in transit, etc. Furthermore, the finance-provider also runs the risk that the goods purchased for the finance-user may not be finally accepted by the finance-user on account of quality or other reasons. These risks thus keep the rate of return uncertain until the goods have been finally handed over to the finance-user.

In *bay' al-salam* financing, though the price, quality and quantity of the goods to be delivered to the finance-user are predetermined, the actual rate of return remains unknown until the time the goods in question have been delivered and he is able to dispose of them in the market. His actual rate of return will depend on how the actual prices at the time of disposing of the goods compares with the prices paid for the goods and on the cost incurred between the two transactions.

The rent on an asset cannot be treated as rate of return on capital invested in the asset because:

1. The owner of the asset is uncertain about the total life of the asset. The asset can yield income only during its productive life. Also the owner cannot know what price the asset will fetch if he decides to dispose of the asset at any time during its productive life.

2. The owner of the asset is also uncertain about the extent to which the asset will remain on lease during its productive life. On expiry of the contract with the first lessee, the owner cannot be certain how long it may take to find another lessee or how much rent will then be agreed. Even if the first lessee renews the contract, it is quite possible that he might demand a reduction in the rent against possible defect that may adversely affect the productivity or service for which the asset was rented.

Mudārabah and *mushārakah* generate risk primarily at the use end of the financing. The finance-provider has but a slight role in the case of *mudārabah,* and only a secondary one in the case of *mushārakah,* in attempting to control the risk of loss. On the other hand, leasing, mark-up and *bay' al-salam*-based financing involve a risk that is not generated at the use end of the financing. In leasing, the risk is associated with the anticipated life of the asset and its continuous employment on rent. In mark-up based financing, the risk is involved during the purchase of the required goods and hand-over to the client. In *bay' al-salam* the risk is during the receipt of goods from the client and their disposal in the market. In all three modes, the finance-user has nothing to do with the risk being faced by the finance-owner.

Cost of Capital for the Finance-User

The amount that the finance-user ends up paying to the finance-owner over and above the original finance obtained is referred to here as the cost of capital.

The cost of capital in the case of *muḍārabah, mushārakah* and *bay' al-salam* remains uncertain until completion of the contract. The cost of capital in the case of leasing and mark-up based financing is predetermined and fixed.

Thus, whereas rate of return on capital is always supposed to be variable and uncertain and cannot be predetermined, it is possible for the cost of capital to be fixed and predetermined, if leasing and mark-up modes are used.

Relationship Between Cost of Capital and Rate of Return on Capital

In the case of *muḍārabah* and *mushārakah,* the cost of capital and rate of return are explicitly the same. In the case of leasing, mark-up, and *bay' al-salam*-based financing, the cost of capital and rate of return on capital are explicitly divergent. The case of mark-up and leasing is straightforward. The finance-owner does not bear or share any risk at the use end of the financing. The finance-user, instead, is paying a fixed and predetermined cost. In the case of *bay' al-salam,* the rate of return for the finance-owner (being dependent on the price that he is able to get in the market minus the cost of marketing), may be not only different from but also unrelated to the cost that the finance-user is obliged to pay. (For a summary overview, see Table I.)

Table I

Comparative Features of Islamic Financing Techniques

Techniques:	*Muḍārabah*	*Mushārakah*	Leasing	Mark-up	*Bay' al-Salam*
Features:					
Nature of Financing	Investment Based	Investment Based	Leasing Based	Combination of Trading and Debt	Combination of Debt and Trading
Role of the Capital-Provider in the Management of Funds:	Nil	Full control	Full control on the use of the Finance	Full control on the use of the Finance	Nil
Risk-bearing by the Capital Provider:	i. To the full extent of the capital as well as of the opportunity cost of capital	Same as in *Muḍārabah*	i. To the full extent of the capital as well as of the opportunity cost of capital	i. To the full extent of the capital	i. To the full extent of the capital as well as of the opportunity cost of capital

(continued)

95

(continued from p.95)

	ii. For the entire period of the contract	Same as in *Mudārabah*	ii. Until the asset completes its life or is finally disposed of	ii. Only for a short period until the goods are purchased and taken over by the finance-user	ii. Even after the expiry of the contract until the goods are finally disposed of
Uncertainty of Rate of Return:	Complete uncertainty	Complete uncertainty	Complete uncertainty	Uncertainty only for a short period of the contract	Complete uncertainty
Cost of Capital:	Uncertain *ex ante*	Uncertain *ex ante*	Fixed and predetermined	Fixed and predetermined	Uncertain *ex ante*
Relationship of Cost of Capital and Rate of Return on Capital:	Perfect correlation	Perfect correlation	Weak correlation	Strong correlation but not perfect	No correlation

Economic Role of Islamic Financing Techniques

This section discusses the economic role of different modes of financing in the following dimensions:

(i)   Household consumption – savings choice.
(ii) Firms' investment decision making.
(iii) Financial intermediation.

In the existing literature, there is not much discussion on comparative aspects of various Islamic financing modes in the above-mentioned dimensions. All these, however, do appear in the joint discussion of the economics of *muḍārabah* and *mushārakah* which are jointly referred to in the literature as profit-sharing modes. An attempt has been made in this section to infer the comparative economics of various modes from the discussion so far on the economics of profit-sharing modes.

Household Consumption – Savings Choice

Two Ph.D. theses written in American universities have attempted to rigorously show that profit-sharing techniques make the lender,[5] i.e. the saver, worse off.[6]

For example, Rafi Khan (49, pp. 112) tried to prove that irrespective of the profit-sharing ratio, eliminating interest and introducing a pure profit-sharing system would inevitably make the lender worse off, compared to what he would have been in the interest-based system.[7]

Aside from the Shylockian flavour in this argument (which has emphasized the 'lender's' welfare without weighing it against the welfare of other members of the society),[8] there is a fundamental flaw in the methodology behind such arguments. They are always based on the assumption that the profit/loss-sharing system means suppressing the interest rate to zero for savers. In theory, as well as in practice, it has been made clear that the Islamic financial system does not mean a non-positive expected rate of return on savings.

If we intend to make the comparison with the interest-based system, we must ask: 'Will the banks working with Islamic financing techniques be able to provide a risk-return package, on the average, better than, the same as, or worse than, that in an interest-based system?' It will be argued later in the section on financial intermediation that the portfolio diversification and choice of various financing modes can enable an

Islamic bank to reduce its overall risk on investment to an almost negligible level, and still make at least as much profit as it would have made had it operated on the basis of interest.

If a saver wants to use leasing or mark-up or *bay' al-salam* modes to advance his money to the user, then obviously the bank's risk-return package will be the reference point when he makes any investment according to these techniques. Lenders, being small savers, are unlikely to have the know-how to take up a leasing or trade-business that will yield them a risk-return package, on the average, better or even equal to, the profit-sharing based, risk-return package offered by the banks.

In the case of leasing and mark-up based techniques, the welfare of the finance-user is expected to be lower than it is in profit-sharing techniques (and may be close to what it is in the interest-based system) because these techniques imply fixed cost of capital for the capital-user in almost the same way as in the case of interest.

The user may well be a little better off in the case of leasing-based financing compared to trading-based financing because of fewer repayment problems in the former than in the latter in the event of a loss in his project. In leasing-based financing, if there is a loss, the lessor will simply take his asset back and the lessee will have to worry only about the unpaid rent, if any. In the case of trading-based financing, if there is a loss, the finance-user will have to worry about the repayment of the entire capital plus the mark-up agreed upon.

In *bay' al-salam,* since the cost of capital is unrelated to the rate of return, the user may end up worse off compared to profit-sharing techniques. Also, in case of loss, the user faces the same problems of repayment as in the case of mark-up based techniques.

The leasing, mark-up and *bay' al-salam*-based techniques, however, have one additional use over *mudārabah* and *mushārakah* from the point of view of the welfare of the finance-user. The former techniques can be utilized for meeting household consumption needs, whereas profit-sharing techniques of *mudārabah* and *mushārakah* cannot be utilized for this purpose. In the profit-sharing based system those needing funds for consumption purposes will face difficulty in getting their needs financed. This problem can be overcome through leasing and mark-up based financing. The users of funds for consumption purposes thus may find themselves better off under mark-up, leasing and *bay' al-salam* modes than under *mudārabah* and *mushārakah.*

Firms' Investment Decision-Making

Profit-sharing techniques make the capital share profit according to its actually realized productivity. The actually realized return on profit is thus the price of capital which will determine its allocation.

Modigliani and Miller (60) have proved very convincingly in the context of corporate finance that it is not the interest rate which determines the cut-off point for the selection for investment in an enterprise. According to their analysis, irrespective of whether the source of financing is own savings or interest-based loan or issuance of common stocks in the share market, investment in an enterprise will be made only if the expected rate of return in the enterprise is greater than or equal to the actual rate of return in the comparable class of firms.[9] This is a clear argument against those who believe that interest plays an important role in the allocation of capital resources[10] and that its replacement by profit-sharing techniques may deprive the economy of the benefits of a useful instrument.

Within PLS techniques, *mushārakah* may have an edge over *muḍārabah* in the sense that in *mushārakah,* the capital-owner has a right to enter into the management and hence have some control over the problems created by informational asymmetry and moral hazards. *Muḍārabah* is void of any such control.

The role of leasing and mark-up based techniques for investment decision may be close to what it is in the case of interest, because as far as the capital-user is concerned he knows with certainty how much he will have to pay for the capital. But for the capital-owner, investment decision will depend on the rate of return on capital which will be different from the cost of capital to be paid by the capital-users, because the capital-owner has to make an allowance for uncertainties and other things, as mentioned earlier. Hence, there will be a divergence in the supply price and demand price of capital. This divergence is the result of the fact that the capital-user has not been made to bear the uncertainties that the capital-owner is bearing. It may also be noted that since an upper limit on their profit becomes fixed (by the rent or mark-up) which is unrelated to the profitability of the enterprise, these techniques, therefore, may not have as primary a role in the investment decision making as profit/loss-sharing techniques do.

It is argued that *muḍārabah* financing will imply an infinitely elastic demand for *muḍārabah* funds.[11] This is because the *muḍārib*'s stake in the enterprise remains constant at the level of the opportunity cost of his labour, irrespective of the total financial investment of the finance-pro-vider in the enterprise, whereas the expected rate of return is an increasing function of the financial investment. Every *muḍārib* would, therefore, wish to have as much investment as possible from the capital owner.

This argument, though correct, has no economic significance unless we also discuss the supply of *muḍārabah*-financing and the simultaneity in the determination of supply and demand. Supply of *muḍārabah*-fi-nancing will not be independent of profit-sharing ratio for the supplier. Suppliers' profit-sharing ratio in turn will depend on the expected income and the risks involved in the project for which finances are being demanded. The increased supply of funds may increase the income (depending on the nature of production function) but may also increase the risks (depending on the nature of human capital of the entrepreneur using the finance). An equilibrium level of profit-sharing will thus be simultaneously determined at which supply and demand will be equal. The argument of infinitely elastic demand under *muḍārabah* is the result of the misconception that cost of capital under *muḍārabah* is zero.

Cost of capital is the share in the profit that the *muḍārib* will be paying to *rabb al-māl*. A utility-maximizing *muḍārib* will, of course, be motivated by the higher expected profits. The increased supply of capital, however, will not come at a constant profit-sharing ratio. The profit-sharing ratio will be an increasing function of supply of capital because the risks of giving higher amounts to a single *muḍārib* may increase at an increasing rate. This may simply be reflective of the diminishing marginal enterprise of an entrepreneur (compared to the diminishing marginal productivity of labour). On the other hand, the productivity of the enterprise increases at a declining rate as more and more capital is invested. It is obvious that a *muḍārib* will demand capital at a level where his total profit is maximum.

It may be noted that the upper limit on the supply of the capital will depend on the asset that the *muḍārib* is putting at stake in the business. If the *muḍārib* is a skilled or professional labourer, the capital-owner may be willing to invest high amounts of capital with one particular *muḍārib*.

The same argument will apply to *mushārakah*. Since in *mushārakah* the capital-user has his own capital as well, and since the capital-owner has a right to enter into the management, the supply of capital may be relatively higher than it would be under *muḍārabah* for a given price of capital (i.e. for a given expected rate of return on capital).

Since leasing and mark-up based techniques imply a fixed cost of capital in the same fashion as in the case of interest rate, the nature and determinants of the demand for investible resources may not be very different from what it would be in the interest-based system. Leasing-based techniques may sometimes be advantageous for the capital-user, compared to mark-up based techniques, because the capital-user is responsible only for the payment of the cost of capital and is not responsible for the capital goods themselves. Under other circumstances, however, mark-up based financing may be preferred over leasing-based, as already discussed.

Nadeemul Haq and Abbas Mirakhor (27) argued that under profit-sharing techniques the level of investment will increase because elimination of interest will allow the firm to invest up to a level where the marginal productivity of investment becomes equal to one. A simple interpretation of this conclusion is that investment will continue until the return or profit on the last unit of invested money becomes zero. Waqar Khan (52) also shared this line of argument.

Note that investment decision-making requires that marginal unit of investment at least yields $1 + r$, where r is the opportunity cost of capital. In an interest-based system, this decision rule means that the last unit of investment brings a return at least equal to the rate of interest. The argument of Nadeemul Haq and Abbas Mirakhor, endorsed by Waqar Khan, implies that the profit-sharing techniques mean zero interest, therefore, investment can go on, until its marginal productivity becomes zero. This is not a correct line of argument.

Islam does not suppress the opportunity cost of capital to zero. In an Islamic framework a profit-maximizing firm[12] will continue investing until the marginal productivity of capital becomes equal to the opportunity cost of capital. Without getting into the debate about whether or not interest rate represents the opportunity cost of capital appropriately, it requires no argument that when the capital is scarce, the opportunity cost of capital can well be represented by the rate of return on comparable alternative opportunities for investment.

The presence of Islamic banks that can, through diversification of their portfolio, offer a positive rate of return on deposits with negligible risk, produces a lower limit to the opportunity cost of capital.[13]

It can easily be visualized that in the case of leasing-based financing, there may be, at least in the short run, a mis-match between the demand for assets needed by entrepreneurs and assets that capital-owners can possibly supply because of the divergence in the cost of capital and rate of return on capital. Hence, in the event of overwhelming use of leasing-based financing, it is possible that a substantial amount of capital may remain unemployed for a considerable time and there still be an excess demand for capital. The same may be true in the event of overwhelming use of all techniques where cost of capital and return on capital do not converge and are not interrelated.

Financial Intermediation

Financial intermediation is an important institution in a modern economy. Banks make the economy more efficient. Islam has nothing against efficiency. The emphasis in the Qur'ān and the *Sunnah* on avoiding waste and doing things in their best way is a reflection of the simple fact that efficiency with resources is a religious duty.

This section discusses the economic role of various Islamic financing techniques in the banking system.

On the liabilities side, while dealing with depositors, the banks as well as depositors, in principle have only one option and that is *muḍārabah* (albeit present practice shows some deviation from this principle). The bank promises to its depositors to share, in a certain ratio, whatever profits it makes by using their funds. The depositors' share will then be distributed amongst them on a *pro rata* basis. In the event of the bank undergoing a loss with the funds of the depositors, then all depositors will bear the loss on the same basis.

Since the bank, as an institution of financial intermediation, invests only depositors' funds and does not mix its own capital with the depositors' funds, the *mushārakah* techniques may not be applicable on the liabilities side. The same applies to leasing and trading-based (mark-up as well as *bay' mu'ajjal*) techniques because the depositors do not become involved in either leasing or trading when they deposit their savings with the bank. The bank will, however, have the option of offering packages to the depositors with varying degrees of return and risk. This makes banks working with Islamic financing techniques more flexible in taking care of the preferences of depositors and thus mobilizing their savings. All depositors will be exposed to some risk as they stand liable to share the losses of the bank in case of such an eventuality.

The banks, however, can minimize the total risk by spreading their investments to a large number of clients on the asset side. The larger the spread, other things being equal, the lower the risk. In this process, obviously, the bank may not be able to make high profits, yet there is no *a priori* reason why the banks should not be able to make as much profit as would be possible in an interest-based system, particularly in a capital-scarce economy, while keeping the risk at a negligible level.

On the asset side, the theorists of Islamic banking argue in favour of *muḍārabah* and *mushārakah* as quite suitable instruments for the banking system. *Muḍārabah* has the following advantages:

1.   It is consistent with the financial intermediary nature of the bank. The bank simply selects a suitable entrepreneur and invests its funds with him and awaits the result to share in profit/loss.

2.   It is capable of use for varying periods of investment and with a variety of entrepreneurs, small or large, allowing the bank a whole spectrum of varying degrees of risk and return.

The disadvantages of *muḍārabah* for the banking system are:

1.   The concept of the *muḍārib* being *amīn* (trustworthy) is the cornerstone of the application of the technique. The fact that the *rabb al-māl* (in this case the bank) bears all the loss in *muḍārabah* may result in moral hazards[14] (behaviour, on the part of the capital-user, not consistent with the interest of the capital-owner).

2.   The presence of moral hazards may not allow the bank to make large investments with an individual *muḍārib*. This may affect the profitability of the bank. Use of the bank's investment funds will depend, among other factors, on the stake that the *muḍārib* puts in. Unless a secondary market is functioning well for *muḍārabah* (through *muḍārabah/muqāraḍah* certificates/bonds), no individual *muḍārib* will be able to offer a business in which he could have a very large stake on his own. The *muḍārabah* investments of banks will therefore be low in the absence of secondary markets.

The advantages of *mushārakah* are the following:

1.   The possibility of moral hazards is reduced because the client would be making his own investment as well. The problem of informational asymmetry too would be reduced as the bank would have a right to enter into the management of the project in which it has invested.

2.   The bank is able to invest in large concerns because clients owning a large stake in the business would not put the bank in a

disadvantageous position in terms of risk. This may help improve the bank's profitability by enabling it to invest in larger and already established concerns with high profitability and low risk.

3.   It is possible to do *mushārakah* for long as well as short periods, and in the industrial as well as commercial, agricultural or service sectors.

Though *mushārakah* financing gives the banks the right to participate in the management of the funds, there remains the possibility that the bank simply waives its right to do so and just performs the role of financial intermediary. All economies are scarce in capital and particularly in risk-bearing capital.[15] Those in demand for bank capital will act in a fashion conducive to continued financial relations with the bank. It should, therefore, not be difficult for the bank to select from a large number of finance-seekers, those parties with which the bank may not feel the need to get involved in the management. Hence, the bank may, if it chooses, stick to its function of financial intermediation only.

Leasing and leasing-based financing would require a bank to deviate from its basic nature as financial intermediator. It will have to become involved in:

(i)   Purchasing an asset, which requires certain marketing expertise.

(ii)   Maintenance of the asset and bearing all costs associated therewith or with replacement if the asset is deficient or fails to perform the service for which it has been leased. This is likely to demand specialist knowledge and expertise about the assets being leased.

(iii)   Disposing of it, when the asset is no longer needed. This also requires, besides the risks resulting from price fluctuations, marketing expertise.

All these activities require the bank to go beyond financial intermediation. Any leasing contract that absolves the bank from all these activities will fall into the category of financial leasing which is not permitted according to *Sharī'ah* principles.

Since most of the deposits are short-term deposits and also the profit on the deposits is required to be declared periodically (say, annually or bi-annually) the banks will be compelled to depend on short-term leasing. Short-term leasing, however, will create an extra burden on the banks, because the frequency of purchasing, reselling and maintenance work will be higher as a result of shorter period leasing contracts. Banks which are interested only in doing financial intermediation may not wish to become involved in leasing-based financing.

Commercial banks thus may not use leasing-based modes overwhelmingly if they are interested in financial intermediation only. Leasing-based finance, however, can prove to be very useful in development financing. Leasing development finance corporations already exist in practice.

One advantage of leasing-based financing is that there is no informational asymmetry involved as is the case in *muḍārabah* and in *mushārakah*. If the bank is not satisfied that its clients have declared correct profits, it can provide them financing on the basis of leasing instruments/equipment/assets. The issue of moral hazards, however, remains as the clients may also use or misuse the assets in a way that imposes unnecessary costs on the bank (which is the owner of the assets).

Mark-up based financing is an instrument similar to leasing-based financing with the difference that in this case the bank is involved in trading instead of leasing to earn income. This financing technique has several advantages over leasing-based financing. The risk-bearing period in trade financing is shorter than in leasing-based financing. The bank knows its profit as soon as the purchase-sale transaction is completed, even though the bank's investment has not been fully recovered.

Such financing also makes the bank go beyond mere financial intermediation. It will have to take up the job of being a trade-house or a trade company as well as being a financial intermediary.[16]

Bay' al-salam also requires the bank to take up trading. But it is not as convenient to the bank as mark-up based financing in terms of the speed with which the bank's profit can be determined (which ultimately determines the level of return on deposits). Another disincentive of the technique is that it gives the bank no objective basis on which to anticipate its profits, obliging it to depend only on speculation about future prices.

It may be instructive to also note clients' preferences on the asset side of the banks.

In the initial stages of Islamization, when the whole economic structure has not fully adjusted to the Islamic financial system, and an appropriate commercial rapport has not been established between clients and bank, profit/loss-sharing financing will usually be preferred by only those entrepreneurs who expect low profitability or high risk in their projects. Clients with highly profitable or low risk projects will prefer fixed cost financing techniques (i.e. leasing and mark-up) so that they reap most of the benefits of their projects. For reasons already explained, mark-up based financing will be preferable to leasing-based financing.

Bay' al-salam may not be very attractive to clients because of the possibility of being exploited by the bank through speculation over future prices.

Liquidity is one of the main concerns of commercial banks. The profit/loss-sharing techniques may limit at least very short-term liquidity of the banks unless instruments are designed which have a secondary market as well.

Leasing-based techniques create liquidity problems more than profit/loss-sharing because leasing is generally more profitable the longer the period of lease. The money invested in leasing business cannot therefore be redeemed over short periods without adversely affecting the bank's profitability. However, if instruments are designed on the basis of leasing which have a secondary market also, then the technique may not pose such a liquidity problem.

Mark-up based financing is potentially better from the liquidity point of view, as compared to the PLS or leasing-based techniques.

Bay' al-salam may be better, in terms of short-term liquidity, compared to leasing-based financing, but inferior to the mark-up based techniques because of the time lag involved in the production of goods underlying the *bay' al-salam* contract.

Summary of Comparative Economics of the Islamic Modes of Financing

Bay' al-salam may have an extremely limited use in commercial banking. It could be most suitable for development financing. It may turn out to have some advantages over other financing techniques for certain commercial purposes as well, but the possibility of exploitation of the borrower on account of forecasting future prices may make it unattractive and inappropriate for commercial financing purposes.

Leasing, too, mainly finds its place in development activities in both the private and public sectors. It will not be so suitable for short-term commercial financing or for achieving short-term macro-economic objectives for the economy through the commercial sector.

Mark-up based techniques are, in general, superior to the leasing-based ones but inferior to the PLS techniques. Even in the commercial banking sector, mark-up based techniques may be suitable only in the initial stage of the formation of Islamic banks. After that period, commercial banks too may prefer the PLS over the mark-up based techniques.

For the economy as a whole, it will be desirable to promote the use of PLS modes of financing to benefit from the growth, equity, and efficiency aspect of these modes, which are discussed in more detail in the next chapter.

For commercial banking too, PLS modes are the only ones suitable for strictly financial intermediation purposes. Other modes require the banks to indulge in trading and leasing as well as financing, activities which take them beyond financial intermediation.

In sum, PLS-based modes seem to be the first best alternative to interest-based modes in general. Nevertheless, leasing, mark-up, and *bay' al-salam*-based techniques have a role to play, and give an added flexibility to the Islamic economy to run the financial system more efficiently and conveniently.

Notes

1. See M.N. Siddiqi (67), p. 9.

2. See Ausaf Ahmad (1), pp. 45–7.

3. See Ziauddin Ahmad (6).

4. *Qard hasan* (a pure loan without any return of interest) is also a mode of financing but is excluded from the discussion as it is not considered likely to have a substantial role in the financial market of the economy.

5. It may be noted that in the case of PLS and leasing and mark-up based techniques, the finance-provider cannot be termed a lender in the true sense of the word.

6. See Habibi (24) and Rafi Khan (50).

7. The argument of Rafi Khan (50) is the following, based on the framework borrowed from Branson (16):
A consumer who has surplus funds now has to decide how much to keep in money form and how much to keep in a risk-bearing asset like PLS. In a PLS-based system, a consumer will face a positive relationship between risk and rate of return. If he needs a higher return, he must face higher risk. This has been assumed to have a linear relationship as shown by the line OK in the diagram (a). The curve AA is the indifference curve showing the preferences of a saver between risk and expected rate of return. The

tangency of AA and OK lines at point E shows the situation where the saver (and hence the lender) would enjoy maximum welfare. He will invest OM* of his wealth and will earn a rate of return R*.

Rafi Khan then presents the interest-based situation and argues that the budget line will be at the position rK instead of OK, as shown in diagram (b). The line rK is shown to start at a point much higher than the starting point of OK. OK starts at origin implying no-risk-no-return. rK starts higher than origin because of the positive rate of interest without risk-bearing. Since the budget line in the interest-based system is higher than in the PLS system, the consumer will be at a higher indifference curve BB (enjoying increased welfare) in the interest-based system compared to that in the PLS-based system as shown by the indifference curve AA.

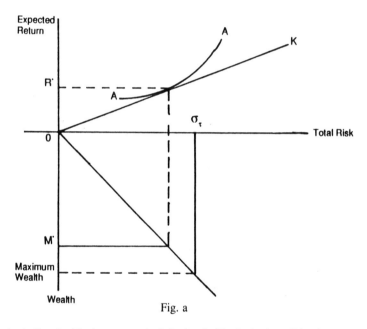

Fig. a

The basic flaw in this rigorous analysis is simple. No doubt, in an Islamic economy, there is 'no-risk-no-return' but this adage in no way implies that the starting point for the budget line in the above framework must be at zero, the point way below the starting point of interest-based budget line. It has been argued in the section on financial intermediation that the ability of banking institutions to diversify their investment/asset portfolios can help them minimize the risk on their profitability to an almost negligible level. This will obviously put a restraint on their profit-making capacity, but there is no *a priori* reason to believe that their profits (which in turn will determine the return on deposits) will force them to pay a return significantly less than interest rate. On the contrary, there are *a priori* reasons to believe that the rate of return on savings deposits in the PLS system may be higher than those in the interest-based system. Hence there is no *a priori* justification for the budget line in the PLS system in the above framework being so far below that of the interest-based system, as it will have a higher slope than that of the interest-based system. The banks, while anticipating higher profits, cannot give the depositors a very low rate of return. The budget line under the PLS-based system will depend primarily on opportunity cost of capital (productivity of capital in alternative opportunities). The PLS-based budget line will thus have the following features, compared to the interest-based budget line:

(i)   The budget line in the PLS-based system will not start on y-axis (as in the interest-based system), though the starting point may well approach y-axis very closely.

(ii)   The starting point in the PLS-based system will most likely be higher than that in the interest-based system because it will have to compensate for two elements – (a) productivity of capital and (b) risk-bearing. Thus a most realistic representation of the PLS-based system in the Branson framework will be as follows:

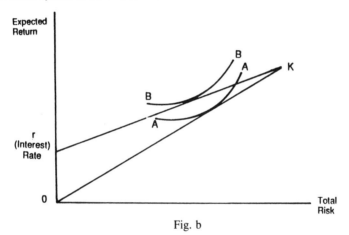

Fig. b

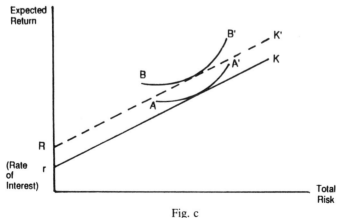

Fig. c

The lender's welfare will in consequence most likely be at a higher level in the PLS-based system as compared to that in the interest-based system.

8.   All attempts which have argued a worsening of lender's welfare have failed to identify what would happen to borrower's welfare. See Habibi (24) and Rafi Khan (50).

9.   See Modigliani and Miller (61), pp. 30 and 31.

10.   See also M. Anas Zarqa (79).

11.   See Habibi (24).

12.   A profit-maximizing firm, under competitive conditions, will simply minimize costs, which can be directly inferred from textual sources to be desirable in the Islamic economy. The prohibition of *isrāf* requires resources to be judiciously used which also means minimization of costs.

13.   See M. Fahim Khan (40).

14.   The term 'moral hazard' was initially used in the insurance business and basically refers to conduct where an agent acts against the interest of his principal, or where an agent behaves inefficiently as a result of the nature of his contract.

15.   See Albach (9).

16.   Though contemporary practice has designed some instruments based on mark-up financing which do not require the bank to become involved in actual trading, the validity under *Sharī'ah* of such instruments remains controversial in some circles.

References

1.   Ahmad, Ausaf, *Development and Problems of Islamic Banks.* Jeddah, Islamic Research and Training Institute, Islamic Development Bank, 1987.

2.   Ahmad, Khurshid, *Studies in Islamic Economics.* Leicester, UK, Islamic Foundation, 1979.

3.   Ahmad, Ziauddin, Munawar Iqbal and M. Fahim Khan, *Money and Banking in Islam.* Jeddah, International Centre for Research in Islamic Economics, King Abdul Aziz University, and Islamabad, Institute of Policy Studies, 1983.

4.   ———, *Fiscal Policy and Resource Allocation in Islam.* Jeddah, International Centre for Research in Islamic Economics, King Abdul Aziz University, and Islamabad, Institute of Policy Studies, 1983.

5.   Ahmad, Ziauddin, *Some Misgivings About Islamic Interest-Free Banking.* Annual Lecture in the Annual Lecture Series of Faisal Islamic Bank of Sudan, Khartoum, 1985.

6.   ———, *Concept and Models of Islamic Banking: An Assessment.* Islamabad, International Institute of Islamic Economics, 1985.

Comparative Features and Economics of Some Modes of Islamic Financing Techniques

7. ——, *The Present State of Islamic Finance Movement*. Islamabad, International Institute of Islamic Economics, 1985.

8. Akerlof, G.A., 'The Market for Lemons: Quality, Uncertainty and Market Mechanism', *The Quarterly Journal of Economics* (August 1970).

9. Albach, M., 'Risk Capital, Business Investment and Economic Co-operation'. Paper presented at the International Symposium on Islamic Banks and Strategies of Economic Co-operation, Baden-Baden, West Germany, 1983.

10. Ali, Syed Aftab, 'Risk Bearing and Profit-Sharing in an Islamic Framework: Some Allocational Considerations', in Ziauddin Ahmad, et al. (4).

11. Anwar, M., *Modelling Interest-Free Economy: A Study in Macroeconomics and Development*. Washington, DC, The International Institute of Islamic Thought, 1987.

12. Ariff, M. (ed.), *Monetary and Fiscal Economics of Islam*. Jeddah, International Centre for Research in Islamic Economics, 1982.

13. Attia, Gamal, 'Financial Instruments Used by Islamic Banks'. Paper presented at the Islamic Banking and Finance Conference, London, 1985.

14. Azhar, Rauf, 'Time Value of Money'. Paper presented in the seminar on Islamic Economics for University Teachers, organized by International Institute of Islamic Economics, Islamabad, and Islamic Research and Training Institute of Islamic Development Bank, Jeddah, 1987.

15. Bower, R.S., 'Issues in Lease Financing', *Financial Management*, 2 (Winter 1973).

16. Branson, W.H., *Macroeconomic Theory and Policy*. 2nd ed., New York, Harper & Row, 1979.

17. Chapra, M. Umer, *Towards a Just Monetary System*. Leicester, UK, Islamic Foundation, 1985.

18. Chaudhary, M.A., 'A Mathematical Formulation of Muḍāraba and Profit-Sharing in Islam', in *Proceedings of the Third Regional Conference of Muslim Social Scientists of the US and Canada*, Indiana, Muslim Trust, 1974.

19. Chaudhary, M.A. and A.N.M. Azizur Rahman, 'Macroeconomic Relations in the Islamic Economic Order', *Journal of Social Economics* (1983).

20. Council of Islamic Ideology, 'Report on the Elimination of Interest From the Economy', Islamabad, Pakistan, 1980, also reprinted in Ziauddin Ahmad, et al. (3).

21. Flath, David, 'The Economics of Short-Term Leasing', in *Economic Inquiry*, Vol. XVIII, April 1980.

22. Friedman, Milton, 'The Yo-Yo US Economy', *Newsweek* (16 August 1982), p. 4.

23. Green, T.L., *Corporate Finance*, New York, Putnam, 1987.

24. Habibi, Nadir, *The Economic Consequences of the Interest-Free Islamic Banking System*. Unpublished Ph.D. Dissertation, Michigan State University, 1987.

25. Hamoud, Sami, *Islamic Banking*, London, Arabian Information, 1985.

26. ———, 'Utilization of Funds Generated Through Islamic Financial Instruments'. *Proceedings of the Seminar Developing a System on Islamic Financial Instruments*, Kuala Lumpur, 1986.

27. Haq, Nadeemul and Abbas Mirakhor, 'Optimal Profit Sharing Contracts and Investments in Interest-Free Economy Banks'. Paper presented at the Islamic Banking and Finance Conference, London, 1985.

28. Heal, G., 'Do Bad Products Drive Out Good?' *The Quarterly Journal of Economics* (August 1976).

29. International Association of Islamic Banks, *al-Mausū'ah al-'Ilmiyyah wa'l 'Amaliyyah. Volume 5: al-Uṣūl al-Shar'iyyah wa'l-A'māl al-Maṣrafiyyah.*

30. Iqbal, Zubair and Abbas Mirakhor, *Islamic Banking*, Occasional Paper 49, Washington, DC, International Monetary Fund, March 1987.

31. Al-Jarhi, M. Ali, 'A Monetary and Financial Structure for an Interest-free Economy: Institutions, Mechanism and Policy', in Ziauddin Ahmad, et al. (3).

32. Kahf, Monzer, 'Fiscal and Monetary Policy in an Islamic Economy', in M. Ariff (12).

33. Khalifa, M. Uthman, 'Islamic Banking: Experience of Sudanese Islamic Bank'. *Proceedings of the Seminar on Islamic Banking*, Leicester, UK, Islamic Foundation, 1988.

34. Khan, M. Akram, *Islamic Economics: Annotated Sources in English and Urdu*, Leicester, UK, Islamic Foundation, 1983.

35. ———, 'Inflation and Islamic Economy, A Closed Economy Model', in M. Ariff (12).

36. Khan, M. Ali, 'Capital Pricing and General Equilibrium in Islamic Framework'. Paper presented in the International Seminar on Monetary and Fiscal Economics of Islam, held in Islamabad in 1981 under the auspices of Planning and Development Division, Government of Pakistan.

37. Khan, M. Fahim, 'Profitability of Islamic PLS Banks: Comment', *Journal of Research in Islamic Economics* (Jeddah), Vol. 1, No. 2 (1984), pp. 73–8.

38. ———, 'Macro Consumption in Islamic Framework', *Journal of Research in Islamic Economics* (Jeddah), Vol. 3, No. 1 (Summer 1984).

39. ———, 'Development Strategy in an Islamic Framework'. Paper presented in the International Seminar on Fiscal Policy and Development Planning, held under the auspices of International Institute of Islamic Economics, Islamabad, 1986.

40. ———, 'Discounting for Time Value of Money in Islamic Perspective'. Mimeograph. Islamabad, International Institute of Islamic Economics, International Islamic University, 1987.

41. ———, 'Economic Rationality of Islamic Banking'. *Proceedings of the Seminar on Islamic Banking*, Leicester, UK, Islamic Foundation, 1988.

42. ——— (ed.), *Distribution in Macroeconomic Framework: An Islamic Perspective*. Islamabad, International Institute of Islamic Economics, 1988.

43. Khan, M.A. Jabbar, 'Non-Interest Banking in Pakistan: A Case Study'. *Proceedings of the Seminar on Developing a System of Islamic Financial Instruments,* Kuala Lumpur, 1986.

44. Khan, Mohsin S., 'Islamic Interest-Free Banking: A Theoretical Analysis'. *IMF Staff Papers* (Washington), Vol. 33, No. 1 (1986), pp. 1–27.

45. ———, 'Principles of Monetary Theory and Policy in Islamic Framework'. Paper presented in the International Seminar on Islamic Economics jointly organized by International Institute of Islamic Economics, Islamabad, and Islamic Research and Training Institute of Islamic Development Bank, Jeddah, 1987.

46. ——— 'Islamic Interest-Free Banking: A Theoretical Analysis', in Mohsin Khan and Abbas Mirakhor (48).

47. Khan, Mohsin S. and Abbas Mirakhor, 'The Framework and Practice of Islamic Banking', in Khan and Mirakhor (48).

48. ———, *Theoretical Studies in Islamic Banking and Finance.* Houston, Texas, USA, The Institute for Research and Islamic Studies, 1987.

49. Khan, Shah Rukh Rafi, 'Profit-Loss Sharing, An Economic Analysis of an Islamic Financial System', Ph.D. dissertation, The University of Michigan, 1983.

50. ———, 'An Economic Analysis of a PLS Model for the Financial Sector', *Pakistan Journal of Applied Economics,* Vol. 3 (1984), pp. 89–105.

51. Khan, Tariqullah, *Islamic Economics: A Bibliography.* Jeddah, Islamic Research and Training Institute, Islamic Development Bank, 1984.

52. Khan, Waqar M., *Towards an Interest Free Economic System.* Leicester, UK, Islamic Foundation and International Association for Islamic Economics, 1985.

53. ———, 'Investment Functions in Islamic Framework'. Paper presented in the International Seminar for Teachers of Economics in Muslim Countries, IIIE/IRTI, Islamabad, 1987.

54. Latif, Bijan, 'Inflation Caused by Monetary Functions in Both Islamic (Interest-Free) and Non-Islamic (Interest-Based) Banking System'. Paper presented at special seminar on Islamic Finance and Banking. Tokyo, The International University of Japan, November 1987.

55. Mannan, M.A., 'Mobilizing Muḍārabah's Other Half', *Arabia* (July 1984).

56. ———, 'An Appraisal of Existing Financial Instruments and Market Operations from an Islamic Perspective'. Paper presented in Seminar on *Developing a System of Islamic Financial Instruments* jointly organized by Islamic Research Training Institute of Islamic Development Bank and Ministry of Finance, Malaysia, in Kuala Lumpur, 1986.

57. ———, *Islamic Economics: Theory and Practice,* revised edition. Hodder & Stoughton, The Islamic Academy, Cambridge, 1986.

58.   Masri, Rafiq, *Riba and Discounting in Islamic Economics* (in Arabic), Jeddah, Centre for Research in Islamic Economics, King Abdul Aziz University, 1985.

59.   Mirakhor, Abbas and Iqbal Zaidi, 'Stabilization and Growth in an Open Economy', IMF Working Paper, Washington, IMF, 1988. Also in the Proceedings of the International Institute of Islamic Economics, Islamabad and Islamic Research and Training Institute of Islamic Development Bank, Jeddah, 1987.

60.   Modigliani, F. and M.H. Miller, 'Corporate Income Taxes and the Cost of Capital: A Correction', *American Economic Review* 53 (June 1963), pp. 433–43.

61.   ———, 'The Cost of Capital, Corporate Finance and the Theory of Investment', in A. Abdel (ed.), *The Theory of Finance and Other Essays*, Vol. 3, Cambridge, USA, The MIT Press, 1980.

62.   Najjar, Ahmad, *Banking Without Interest as a Strategy for Economic and Social Development of Muslim Countries*, Jeddah, King Abdul Aziz University, 1972.

63.   Naqvi, S.N.H., *Ethics and Economics*, Leicester, UK, Islamic Foundation, 1981.

64.   Neinhaus, V., 'Profitability of Islamic PLS Banks Competing with Interest Banks: Problems and Prospects', *Journal of Research in Islamic Economics* (Jeddah), Vol. 1, No. 1 (1983), pp. 37–47.

65.   ———, 'Principles, Problems and Prospects of Islamic Banking', *Intereconomics*, Vol. 20, No. 25 (September/October 1985).

66.   Sabbagh, Hasham, 'The Mechanics and Operations of Islamic Financial Markets'. *Proceedings of the Seminar on Developing a System of Islamic Financial Instruments*, Kuala Lumpur, 1986.

67.   Siddiqi, M.N., *Banking Without Interest*, Lahore, Islamic Publications, 1973.

68.   ———, *Muslim Economic Thinking: Survey of Contemporary Literature*. Leicester, UK, Islamic Foundation, 1981.

69.   ———, *Issues in Islamic Banking*. Leicester, UK, Islamic Foundation, 1983.

70.   ———, *Partnership and Profit Sharing in Islamic Law*, Leicester, UK, Islamic Foundation, 1985.

71.   ———, 'Islamic Banking: Theory and Practice', in M. Ariff (ed.), *The Muslims of Southeast Asia*, Singapore, Institute of Southeast Asian Studies, 1988.

72.   ———, 'Economics of Profit Sharing' in Ziauddin Ahmad, et al. (4).

73.   Stigler, G., 'The Economics of Information', *The Journal of Political Economy* (June 1961).

74.   Trolle-Schultz, E., 'Savings and Investments Through Islamic Banking and Finance'. Paper presented at a seminar on 'Islamic Economics – Theory and Practice' organized by the Pakistan-German Society for Friendship and Co-operation, in Bonn, 22 September, 1986.

75. Uzair, M., *Interest Free Banking,* Islamabad, Pakistan Publications, 1953.

76. ———, 'Some Conceptual and Practical Aspects of Interest Free Banking', in Khurshid Ahmad (ed.), *Studies in Islamic Economics* (2).

77. Wilson, Rodney, *Islamic Business: Theory and Practice.* London, The Economist Intelligence Unit, 1984.

78. Zarqa, M. Anas, 'Stability in an Interest-Free Economy', *Pakistan Journal of Applied Economics,* Vol. 2 (Winter 1983), pp. 181–8.

79. ———, 'Project Evaluation in Islamic Perspective', in Ziauddin Ahmad, et al. (4).

CHAPTER 6

The Viability and Economics of Islamic Banking*

Islamic banking is banking without *ribā* (interest). The economic rationale of Islamic banking cannot be understood without understanding the economic rationale of the prohibition of *ribā*. Prohibition of *ribā*, in turn, implies the following:

(a)   an alternative approach to pricing the factors of production and time value of resources; and
(b)   an alternative approach to the institution of 'lending'.

Approach to Pricing Factors of Production and Time Value of Resources

The prohibition of *ribā* is not merely the prohibition of an institution. It is in fact also the introduction of an alternative system. Failure to understand the alternative system often leads to the confusion that Islam might have prohibited usury and not the modern-day bank interest which plays such an important economic role and seems just like earning profit on investment. This confusion particularly arises because modern economic theory confuses the concept of interest by attaching different shades of meaning to it. The Islamic approach is first briefly explained below to elaborate what it is in the factor pricing and time value of money that Islam prohibits, and what it is that Islam permits, and what the difference is between profit and interest, and how factor pricing and time value of money in the Islamic framework are different from in the interest-based system.

*Adapted from a paper presented in the Seminar on Islamic Banking, at Loughborough University in July 1988, organized jointly by the Banking Centre of Loughborough University (UK), International Association for Islamic Economics, and the Islamic Foundation, Leicester.

Capital Pricing

The neo-classical production function $Y = F(K, L)$ is subjected to a price of capital called r and price of labour called w. The price of capital r is usually referred to as rate of interest, though it is the rent of the capital.

Islamic law does not mix up the two concepts, rent and interest. If K is in the form of physical assets, then it can claim a price which can be fixed and known in advance, i.e. rent. If K is malleable capital, then it cannot claim a rent. It can claim profit which cannot be determined *ex ante* and can be determined only *ex post*. The principle is simple. Rent is for the service or benefit provided by an asset. If the services of an asset are definite and known in advance, only then can rent be fixed and known in advance. This subject has been discussed in detail in the next chapter. Briefly, there are the following principal conditions that entitle an asset to receive rent:

(a)   It is capable of providing a service. In other words, the asset does not have to be altered into something else in the process of its use. Thus, textile machinery is rentable but cotton is not rentable. A coat is rentable but a cake is not.

(b)   The service to be provided by the asset should be identifiable definitely in advance.

(c)   If the asset goes out of order or gets destroyed (through no fault of the lessee), the lease contract expires irrespective of the period for which the contract was made.

Now if the capital is in the form of a fixed asset, it can claim a price which can be called rent. The rent can be fixed and predetermined. But if the capital is malleable then such capital cannot be rented, though it can be invested. Such capital cannot claim any predetermined reward. Its reward depends on the actual outcome of the activity in which the capital is used.

This means, in the Islamic framework, that capital may have two types of price:

(a)   A fixed, predetermined price which only fixed assets are entitled to receive.

(b)   An uncertain price (to be certainly determined only *ex post*) which malleable capital is entitled to claim. A fixed predetermined price for such capital will be *ribā*.

118

For neo-classical economic analysis which assumes uncertainty away and makes no distinction between malleable and non-malleable capital, the distinction between rent and interest can make no difference, even for Islamic economists. Interest as a price of capital in such a case can be acceptable to them, though they would still prefer to use the term 'rent' rather than 'interest' because of the abominable connotations attached to it by Islam. But when uncertainties have to be taken into account or when malleable and non-malleable capital have to be distinguished, interest and rent have to be distinguished as price of capital. The former (as price of malleable capital) is prohibited, whereas the latter (as price of non-malleable capital only) is permitted. The price of malleable capital will be determined on the basis of actual profit/loss on the total investment.

If therefore, in the economic analysis of neo-classical production, 'interest' means the price of non-malleable capital then that economic analysis is acceptable to Islamic economists because 'interest' is nothing but legitimate rent. If, however, 'interest' means the price of the use of malleable capital then Islamic economists part from the neo-classical economists.

In connection with the application of interest for malleable capital, it may be worth recalling the anonymous adage: 'How to have your cake and eat it: lend it out on interest.'

Time Value of Resources*

Time might have its own price, if it were capable of being bought and sold in the market on its own. But as time can be bought and sold only in association with some other resources, the value of time depends on the value of the use to which the resources are put over time. That is the economic concept of time value in Islam.

Islam does recognize the time value of resources and does allow that value to be realized, irrespective of whether the resources are physical assets or monetary. But time value is not allowed to be realized on the basis of any predetermined rate. Time is like malleable capital. The realization of time value requires awaiting the outcome of the use of resources over time. If the outcome is visible and tangible, it may justify time value of money. (If the money has been used for mere consumption purposes the money-owner is not entitled to claim a time value for his

---

*The issue is discussed at some length in Chapter 8.

119

money.) The time value of money within an Islamic framework can only be *ex post*.

For neo-classical economic analysis, this does create some problems because it does not fit with the time preference theory of neo-classical economics. Notwithstanding the controversy over it, let us leave the theoretical discussion of time preference to one side. The bare fact is that Islam does not allow time value of money to be realized on the basis of a rate determined *ex ante*; any realization on such a basis will be *ribā* which is prohibited.

There should be no confusion with the concept of rent. For example, it might be said that rent includes time value of money and, since rent is predetermined, a predetermined time value of money must be permitted in Islam also. This is wrong. It is true that the rent of an asset is calculated in a way that will realize not only the value of the asset but a certain time value of money as well. But this calculation is made over the life of the asset, which life is uncertain. Moreover, it is not necessarily the case that an asset will remain on rent throughout its life. Hence, how much time value of money is actually realized remains uncertain until the asset has completed its economic life.

Any attempt to guarantee the realization of an asset along with a certain predetermined profit is disallowed in Islam. For example, that type of finance leasing is not permitted in which the user of the asset undertakes to buy the asset at a predetermined price at the expiry of the contract.

Profit

Profit is, by definition, the reward for risk-bearing only.[1] It cannot be predetermined. Any reward that is predetermined can be rent (which includes wages) or interest but cannot be profit by definition. The principle is: profit is by risk-bearing only.[2] Interest is prohibited but profit is permitted in Islam.

In summary: sources of income in Islam are two:

(i)   renting one's assets.
(ii) making profit through entrepreneurial/risk-bearing economic activities.

All assets cannot be rented because certain conditions have to be fulfilled for rentability. Monetary resources are assets which cannot be rented. Monetary resources, however, are allowed to earn profit if they are invested in economic activities and if they are subjected to bearing the risk of loss in case such an eventuality should arise.

There can be no profit from loans as such, that is, loans in which the principal is guaranteed. Any profit on guaranteed principal means a predetermined positive time-value of resources, which is not permitted in Islam.

Basis of Operation for Islamic Banks

With this clarification of the nature of *ribā,* interest, rent and profit, let us now review the nature of Islamic banks before we turn to the economic rationale of Islamic banking.

The main function of commercial banks is to collect small and mostly idle savings and pass them on to investors. Banks are also supposed to make a profit out of this activity. They are able to provide capital to investors at a lower cost than the investors would incur if they had to individually find and negotiate with individual lenders. Banks are also able to provide savers with a return which, in most cases, will be higher than they would otherwise have obtained.

Commercial banks achieve this through the instrument of interest. They collect savings by promising depositors a predetermined positive rate of return while guaranteeing their deposits as well. They pass on these savings to investors requiring them to pay a predetermined positive rate of return (higher than they promised to the depositors) while also obliging them to guarantee the principal. Banks, in this way, indulge in *ribā* on the liability side as well as the asset side. Depositors and borrowers with such banks also indulge in *ribā.*

Banking is a useful service but how can banks operate without indulging in *ribā*? The answer given by Islamic scholars is that the banks should operate on the basis of profit. They can earn profit from the investors to whom they advance the money and whatever profit they earn can be shared with the banks' depositors. In both cases the condition for profit-earning will have to be fulfilled, namely, bearing the risk of loss.

Banks can earn profit in three ways – trading, leasing or by direct financing in profit/loss-sharing contracts (for details see Chapter 4). They are free to devise instruments to earn profit in any of these ways. But any instrument that ensures profit without carrying risk of loss will not be an Islamic instrument, irrespective of whether it is a trading or leasing instrument or a profit/loss-sharing one. This constraint implies the following:

1.   Commercial banks cannot extend loans because they cannot earn any profit on loans. They will have to invest with the associated risks of investment if they want to earn income.

2.   Commercial banks cannot advance money for consumption purposes because in this case there is no concept of sharing profit and hence banks will not be able to earn any income on such advances. Commercial banks will advance money only for commercially productive activities.

3.   Banks can, by diversifying their investment portfolios, minimize risk, but they cannot eliminate the risks associated with investment. There is a possibility therefore – and this possibility exists also for interest-based banks – that such banks may go into loss at some time. And if the banks lose, the depositors must share the loss.

Contemporary Practice of Islamic Banks

The contemporary practice of some Islamic banks is somewhat different from the theory of Islamic banks. This situation leads to the confusion that the Islamic concept of pricing capital and time value of resources is not so very different from what is implied in the concept of interest. The fact is that the contemporary practice of Islamic banks, to a very large extent, has not been able to meet the true spirit of Islamic banking. Leaving aside the social and philanthropic aspects, let us concentrate on the economic spirit of Islamic banking. The true spirit of Islamic banking, as already explained, is that banks may neither receive nor pay any return obtained without bearing economic[3] risks, associated with the return. If we examine the practice of Islamic banking, one peculiarity is very conspicuous. Of the three types of investment modes discussed earlier (i.e. trading, leasing and PLS), the banks have been found excessively inclined towards the trading mode to deploy their funds for earning income. There is certainly nothing wrong with earning income through trade (which is the noblest profession being in the tradition of the Prophet (peace be upon him)). What is disturbing is that while using the trading mode the banks rely upon the second option which is reselling the goods needed by their clients on a cost-plus basis, rather than sharing the profits and losses of their clients. Though, according to Islamic law, selling goods on a cost-plus or mark-up basis is admissible, when it is linked with financing as well, this type of trading becomes less desirable. Since the client is in need and is unable to pay cash for the goods needed by him he is obliged to accept the goods purchased by the bank. The mark-up that the bank charges while reselling the goods, thus, becomes in the nature of interest if the bank is implicitly facing no risk in this trade.

Some banks even went a step further and explicitly removed all trading risks by requiring the clients to repurchase the goods in advance of the purchase made by the banks. This happened in a country where the whole banking system had been converted and there was no fear of competition from the interest-based banks.

Those institutions which chose to use leasing mode to earn income also tried to by-pass the legal provisions that require them to bear the risk of loss associated with the income they want to earn. For example, the banks would require the lessee to keep the asset insured against all risks at his own expense whereas legally the lessor is required to bear all risks associated with the maintenance of the asset.

In the case of the profit/loss-sharing mode too, certain institutions introduced innovations which would reduce for them the possibility of getting a return below a certain predetermined rate. For example, the bank would ask the client to form a 'reserve account'. The bank would fix a predetermined rate (say 15 per cent) which would normally be lower than the rate of return that the client would expect to get from his project. The bank would then ask the client to pay a return every year according to this rate, with any excess profit accruing to the bank (due to higher profits in the project) to be deposited in the 'reserve account'. If, during any year, the client earned a profit less than the predetermined rate (15 per cent in the above example) or suffered a loss, the client would make up the bank's 15 per cent return out of the 'reserve account'. If the 'reserve account' failed to meet the bank's required 15 per cent rate of return the client would sell his equity shares to the bank in lieu.

In some cases banks reached an agreement with their clients in which if the client declares a profit that ensures the bank at least a certain predetermined rate (say 15 per cent), the bank asks no questions and does not bother to check the client's accounts to determine the correctness of the declared profit. But if the client declares a profit less than the rate (15 per cent in this case) or declares a loss, the bank goes through all the client's accounts and its assessment is final. In such agreements, clients prefer to declare a bare 15 per cent return whether they make more or less profit and hence banks end up getting a fixed, predetermined rate of return irrespective of the outcome of the activity in which their funds have been used.

There are four types of environment in which Islamic banks are currently operating:

1. The whole banking system in the country has been converted, and activities are overseen in some way by religious bodies.
2. The whole banking system in the country has been converted. The religious supervision of banking activities, however, is poor.
3. The interest-based system exists side by side and has a strong base in the system. The country, however, is a Muslim country and the government is sympathetic to Islamic banking and provides some assistance and a legal framework for the operations of Islamic banks.
4. In a non-Muslim country where the Islamic banks have to find their own way within the existing legal framework of the country.

A tendency on the part of the banks, to look for such instruments for dealing with clients on the asset side that would absolve them of the obligation to bear the risk of loss, has been found in each of the four types of environment, though in varying degrees.

Among the factors, described by the banks themselves, which force them to deviate from the true spirit of the Islamic system are:

(a)   The apprehension that the banks may lose the confidence of depositors if risky investment results in volatile changes in the banks' profits and hence in the rate of return to the depositors. Loss of confidence may mean reduced deposits and hence reduced business for the banks. This apprehension forces the banks to look for such financial instruments, particularly on the asset side, as can minimize the risk of loss as far as possible. Theoretically speaking, such an apprehension cannot be justified in environments where the whole banking system is required to operate on an Islamic basis, and particularly when there is no empirical evidence on the elasticity of bank deposits with respect to the rate of return on deposits. Further, even the apprehension that dealing with their clients on the asset side on a profit/loss-sharing basis would make banks' profits volatile does not so much reflect a drawback of the profit/loss-sharing (PLS) system, as inefficiency on the banks' part and failure to properly diversify their investment/assets portfolio to minimize risk.

(b)   The second factor is the asymmetry of information between the

124

bank and its clients. Banks fear that their clients may not declare the true profits/losses to be shared with the banks. Though this apprehension may be true for a small part of their clientele in some regions, it cannot be true for all of their clients everywhere. Moreover, most clients will not be dealing with the banks on a one-off basis. Clients needing a continuing relationship with the banking system will need to be competitive which in turn requires them to be honest in their dealings with their banks.

The general phenomenon is, however, curious. Why has a commitment to Islamic banking so far failed to get properly translated into practice?

Is it something inherent in the system or is it that Islamic banks are not yet mature enough to handle all the practical problems, or is it that some institutional reforms are required in the society before Islamic banking is put into practice? Possible answers to these questions will be discussed in later chapters. For the present, we shall not allow the contemporary practice of some Islamic banks to divert us from an exposition of the economic rationale of Islamic banking. We return therefore to the theoretical discussion.

The Islamic principle of financing whether by an individual or by an institution such as a commercial bank is the following:

(i)   No return on a loan may be expected or realized. A return can be expected only on investments.

(ii)   There can be no risk-free investment. Risk must be carried in proportion to the share in total investment.

The argument that an uncertain rate of inflation makes the real rate of return on an interest-based loan a risk-bearing investment is not acceptable in Islam. Once we call it a loan, *nothing* can be charged on it irrespective of whether inflation or any other consideration makes the charge positive or negative in 'real' terms. All financing is termed a loan when the principal remains guaranteed whether in nominal or real terms. This brings us to the next aspect of the prohibition of *ribā*.

Approach Towards Lending

Lending, in the Islamic framework, is allowed only for charity. No reward whatever is allowed to be sought in return for giving a loan. This means anyone who has money and wants to earn more money with it cannot do so simply by lending it.

Lending/borrowing can be done for commercial purposes as well as for consumption purposes. The position remains the same in either case – no return on a loan.

Basically, there are two classes of financial need which may compel one to rely on borrowing:

1. Urgent needs, postponement of which may inflict serious harm/loss.
2. Non-urgent needs which can be postponed.

Islam discourages borrowing for the second type of needs. Though individuals may, on a personal basis, engage in lending/borrowing for such needs, no institutions will develop to cater for these needs. By contrast, the Islamic economy not only encourages lending for urgent needs but also requires institutions to be developed to cater for them. Lending for the purpose of meeting urgent needs is encouraged by promising a seven-hundredfold or more reward in the Hereafter.

Since all lending has been forbidden to earn or generate any income, the lending institutions for urgent needs cannot be commercial institutions.

Urgent needs may include commercial as well as consumption needs. A commercial enterprise, for example, may be in such distress that the entrepreneur has no choice but to rely on borrowing. Self-evidently no-one is likely to come forward to *invest* in such a business, but someone may come forward to help the persons involved to get out of their distress. A poor individual unable to earn subsistence from his business may require a loan to help expand his business or to help his family survive while it becomes established. The motivation behind any lending in such situations has to be the spirit of brotherhood.

The commercial financial system in an Islamic economy, therefore, will have a very minimal role in lending/borrowing of this kind. Any lending/borrowing that takes place in an Islamic economy will be in the non-commercial sector for non-economic motives.

Economics of Islamic Banking

We are now in a better position to see the economic rationale of Islamic banking. What Islamic banking means is the following:

1. There will be no lending/borrowing.
2. The price/cost of capital will be determined by the actual rate of return on capital.

The economic rationality of an institution can be understood in terms of the economic functions that it is required to undertake in an economy. We can start with the most primary concern of modern-day economics, i.e. efficiency. Will the Islamic banking system be more or at least as efficient as the interest-based banking system is supposed to be?

Efficiency Argument

Capital should go where it is most productive. The profit rate, therefore is the only price of capital that will allocate capital most efficiently.

It is also recognized in modern economic theory that it is profit rate and not interest rate that allocates capital. Hence paying capital the profit instead of interest cannot be assumed to disturb allocative efficiency.

The distinction between profit and interest in modern text-book economic analysis is illusory. The text-book analysis assumes perfect information and certainty. Under such assumptions interest and profit are exactly the same, and efficiency cannot be identified as due to capital pricing on the basis of interest or on the basis of profit.

The efficiency of Islamic banking *vis-à-vis* interest-based banking follows from our observations earlier that Islamic banking favours the economic feasibility of the project whereas interest-based banking favours the creditworthiness of the user of capital. The interest-based system basically allocates loans against the creditworthiness of borrowers. Because the principal as well as return on it are guaranteed irrespective of whether the capital earns a profit or a loss, creditworthiness becomes important so that the principal and return are recoverable even in the event of the project's failure. Economic feasibility of the project may be only one factor in the determination of the creditworthiness of the user. Under the Islamic system, the owner of capital will get back the principal along with the return only if capital earns a profit. The capital and return cannot be recovered if the project goes into a loss even if the entrepreneur otherwise had the ability to pay. Economic feasibility and profitability, therefore, are the primary considerations. Theoretically, this argument is irrefutable. Various practical considerations are, however, supposed to give the interest-based system an edge over the Islamic system. Let us discuss a couple of such considerations.

It has been argued that when making investment decisions, an entrepreneur must know what he is going to pay for the inputs that he needs. If capital is to be paid according to the actual rate of return which cannot be known *ex ante*, then the entrepreneur cannot know the cost of the capital he will be using. Interest, thus, serves as a useful unit of accounting.

But it is well-established in the economic literature that interest does not reflect the cost of capital. It is the profitability of capital that measures the cost of capital. All entrepreneurs know what the expected rate of return on capital is in their project and in alternatives to it. This expected rate of return can serve, in the Islamic framework, as a cost of capital for accounting and decision making purposes. The owner of the capital will, however, not be actually paid according to the expected rate of return. The payment will be made according to the actual rate of return. Interest is not, therefore, so much of a convenience as to outweigh the efficiency argument.

Another argument relates to the asymmetry of information between user of capital and provider of capital about profitability and rate of return. It is possible that a capital-user may not correctly declare the profit he has earned by using the capital and hence may not pay the correct price to the capital-provider. The argument may turn out to be true in some cases. But does this possibility, if realized, affect the efficiency argument? It does not. If today an economy decides that every entrepreneur will get capital only on the basis of profit/loss-sharing, the scarcity of capital will force all entrepreneurs not only to offer the best projects but also the best declared ones. Capital-providers will rank all projects according to their economic feasibility and profitability as they judge it, and will allocate capital accordingly. Once this is done the allocative efficiency requirement is satisfied. The interest-based system will not rank projects according to profitability, but according to the creditworthiness of the capital-users, which defeats the allocative efficiency requirement. The asymmetry of information may create a problem only at the time of payment of return to the capital. The question is: Will the Islamic system always work to the disadvantage of capital-providers? This is basically an empirical question. There are *a priori* reasons for believing that this is only an apprehension. If the market is competitive, competition will force capital-users to be honest in their dealings with capital-providers. This is what happens in all economic activities.

Even if asymmetry of information affects allocation of capital, the argument that eliminating the need for information on either side makes the system more efficient is hardly persuasive. The interest-based system simply does away with the need for disclosing information about the project, which obviously implies that efficiency is not the criterion in capital allocation.

Stability Argument

A second criterion that modern economists would consider while evaluating the economic rationality of an institution is the stability of the equilibrium that the institution will achieve. There is no reason to believe that replacement of interest by profit as the payment for capital will make the equilibrium in the capital market unstable. The capital market will function like this. The users and providers of capital will negotiate a profit-sharing ratio (s). Given a certain productivity of capital, a reduction in s will increase demand but reduce supply. Similarly a rise in s will decrease demand but increase supply. There will be an equilibrium in the market at a certain s. The negatively sloped demand and positively sloped supply curve imply that the equilibrium will be stable. Exogenous shifts in supply and/or demand curve will instantly create disequilibrium but soon the supply and demand forces will bring the system back to equilibrium – which may be a new equilibrium.

What is more important, however, is the stability in the macro-economic general equilibrium framework. The macro-economic stability is more of an empirical question than a theoretical question. Theoretically, under the assumption of perfect foresight and certainty, there is hardly much need to prove the stability of an economy where price of capital is determined by its actual rate of return. There are several empirical studies which clearly hint that it is the fixity of return on capital (i.e. interest) in relation to uncertainty of entrepreneurial profit that has been the cause of business cycles. The Islamic system eliminates fluctuations in the entrepreneurial profits relative to return on capital and hence may help entrepreneurs to avoid volatile investment decisions leading to instability and business cycles.

Since we are talking of macro-economic stability in relation to the replacement by the Islamic banking system of interest-based banking, it makes sense to first consider the stability of the latter. It has been argued in the conventional literature that the interest-based banking system is inherently unstable. The liability side of the bank (deposits and interest) is fixed and guaranteed by the bank. On the other hand, its assets are subject to the solvency of clients. Insolvency of even a few clients could unbalance the bank's assets and liabilities making it vulnerable to bankruptcy. Substantial empirical evidence is available to show that the failures of several interest-based banks is significantly attributable to this factor. The liabilities of Islamic banks rise and fall with their assets because depositors must share in the profits as well as losses of the bank. Making banks operate on an Islamic basis would make them more stable, implying, other things being equal, greater macro-economic stability than in the interest-based system.

As regards instruments of control available to the monetary authority, the Islamic banking system has its own. The ratio in which banks share profit with the clients to whom they advance money can be controlled by the central bank. If bank capital needs to be made more expensive for investors, the central bank could ask commercial banks to raise the profit-sharing ratio. This would reduce demand for the banks' capital.

Thus far our discussion has referred to functions that conventional modern economists would wish or expect an institution like Islamic banking to perform in the economy. However, there are certain functions that an Islamic economy would wish and expect to see performed by banking. The foremost of these is equity.

Equity

There are several aspects of equity. We consider here only one aspect, namely, that equals should get equal treatment. (In the present context, we mean 'equal' only in terms of economic performance.) In the Islamic banking system, of two projects with the same expected rate of return, neither will be discriminated against on any grounds as capital gets its return from what the projects earn. If the return on capital is guaranteed and not linked to the returns from the project, several avenues of discrimination open up, the most important of which is creditworthiness. As an individual's creditworthiness is greater the richer he or she is, the bulk of bank advances go to the rich. This is what is seen in the distribution of bank advances in most modern-day economies. A point worth noting here (as in other contexts) is that Islamic banking ensures equity without sacrificing efficiency. The argument for equity can be made within the argument for efficiency. Efficiency and equity are not conflicting issues as modern economic theory believes.

Another aspect of equity is that capital should earn rent or profit according to the same rules as apply to other factors of production. If it intends to earn rent then it should fulfil the conditions of rentability as other assets do; if it wants to earn profit then it should fulfil the conditions for the same. Why should equity capital and bank capital expect or get different treatment if they are exactly the same in nature and perform the same function?

Reduction in Poverty and Economic Inequalities

Reduction in poverty and economic inequalities is one of the primary objectives of the Islamic economic system and Islamic banking can play an important role in achieving this objective. Consider a developing economy with a lot of surplus labour either unemployed or disguised unemployed. These people may have the option of indulging in a small trade which could generate some income to support their family but they lack the necessary capital to start the business, even though the actual amount they require is extremely low. They do not seek capital from a bank and prefer to wait for a job opportunity where they could get a fixed wage. The bulk of the stock of human resources in such developing economies is in wage-paid jobs or is waiting idly for such wage-paid jobs. They have no incentive to go into entrepreneurial activity even if they have the ability: the main constraint is need of capital.

It is not merely that the banking system cannot provide them capital because they are not creditworthy. It is also that these people do not raise a demand for bank capital. As will be discussed in more detail in a later chapter, interest-bearing capital cannot induce this stock of human resources to undertake entrepreneurial activity. They prefer to wait for a wage-paid job, because if they take up an entrepreneurial activity then in the event of a possible loss or low profit, they may find themselves unable to return the capital with interest to the capital owner. Islamic banks provide risk-bearing capital. With Islamic banking, the entrepreneurial risks are shared and the human resources encouraged to engage in entrepreneurial activities. Entrepreneurial activities have a higher potential for economic growth through growth in income and wealth. A person with a business of his own is likely to increase his income and wealth at a much higher rate than a wage-paid employee can possibly do. A businessman has more incentive to save because these savings will help him increase his business and his income.

The world is in search of an alternative financial system which can help transfer the needed resources from developed world to developing world without creating a debt crisis.[4] Islamic banking provides a viable and practical alternative. In fact suggestions coming forward in this respect are, by and large, suggesting nothing but an Islamic banking system.

Notes

1. Even where profit is defined as a reward for innovation or enterprise, it implicitly means reward or risk bearing, implying that profit cannot be predetermined.

2. This does not include gambling risk.

3. The adjective 'economic' has been attached to risk only to exclude gambling and speculation.

4. See D.R. Lessard and J. Williamson (5).

References

1. Ahmad, Ausaf, *Development and Problems of Islamic Banks,* Islamic Research and Training Institute, Islamic Development Bank, Jeddah, 1987.

2. Ahmad, Ziauddin, *Concept and Models of Islamic Banking: An Assessment,* International Institute of Islamic Economics, Islamabad, 1985.

3. Iqbal, Zubair and Abbas Mirakhor, *Islamic Banking,* Occasional Paper 49, International Monetary Fund, Washington, DC, March 1987.

4. Khan, Mohsin S., 'Islamic Interest-Free Banking: A Theoretical Analysis', IMF Staff Papers, Washington, DC, Vol. 33, No. 1, 1986, pp. 1–27.

5. Lessard, D.R. and J. Williamson, *Financial Intermediation Beyond the Debt Crisis,* Institute for International Economics, Washington, DC, September 1985.

PART III

PRODUCTION AND INVESTMENT

CHAPTER 7

Factors of Production and Factor Markets in Islamic Framework*

Introduction

Conventional economic theory uses a particular classification of factors of production which is recognized as arbitrary, and which has no scientific authority except that it is conventionally accepted. This chapter attempts to initiate a new classification derived from Islamic concepts, which may be considered more rational even within the conventional theoretical framework. A brief analysis of factor markets within an Islamic framework, along with the supporting Islamic institutional arrangements, has also been included. Detailed analysis of the supply, demand and equilibrium conditions in factor markets has been left for a later essay. The approach put forward in this chapter has implications not only for the theories of production and distribution but also for the theories of economic development since these are based on the supply and demand for the factors of production.

Factors of Production

Factors of Production in Conventional Economic Theory

Factors of production are inputs that provide a productive service in a productive process. Conventional economic theory distinguishes four such factors, simplified standard definitions of which are reproduced below. The objective here is to discuss the core of the classification rather than to discuss the technical details of the respective definitions.

---

*Adapted from a paper published in *Journal of Research in Islamic Economics*, Vol. 2, No. 1, pp. 25–45.

(i)   Land (which includes minerals, water and other natural resources).

(ii)   Labour.

(iii) Capital: this does not mean capital in the sense of money. It refers to man-made units like buildings, factories, machines, and tools, that produce goods and services. Capital without labour cannot possibly generate output.

(iv)   Enterprise: this is a special kind of human resources which co-ordinates the use of the capital, land and labour to produce output. Enterprise perhaps has the hardest task of all – decision making.

This division plays a role in explaining the theories of production and of distribution of output. All current theories of economic development try to explain the process of development within the framework of these four factors of production.

Some Observations on the Conventional Classification of Factors of Production

Some of the problems with this classification are as follows:

(i)   No economic rationale is given to justify adoption of this classification. Economists themselves have commented on its arbitrariness (Samuelson (b), p. 557), which, perhaps without serious implications for the theory of production, does have serious implications for the theory of distribution.

(ii)   The conventional theory does not recognize money capital as an explicit factor of production but recognizes interest as a reward for capital. The interest rate is the price of money capital but is treated as representing also the price of physical capital.

(iii) While determining the distribution of output, economists have advanced explicit theories about how the share of land, labour and capital is determined in the market, but there is no theory about how the entrepreneurial profit is determined. The fact that conventional theory is practically devoid of a coherent theory of the supply and demand for enterprise is recognized in the works of Leibenstein (5), Baumol (1) and Leff (4). This may be tolerable in static analysis with the assumption of perfect certainty and knowledge of input and output prices and a determinate and predictable production function. But it is of little help in understanding the development process of an economy.

(iv)   The reward for factors of production goes to those who own them. Thus rent goes to the landlord, interest goes to the capitalist, wages go to labour, and profit goes to the entrepreneur.

It is at best confusing to define, say, land and enterprise as two distinct factors of production when the landlord is himself the entrepreneur using his own land for production. It is irrelevant to speak of the landlord getting rent and the entrepreneur getting profit. In fact the landlord is getting rent plus profit/loss.

The distinction between profit and rent in this case serves no meaningful purpose. It is simpler and easier to comprehend if, in this case, we treat the landlord as the entrepreneur.

Rent is usefully distinguished as such only when the land is rented and the landowner does not assume the role of the entrepreneur to use his own land.

A direct consequence of this theoretical approach is its failure to take account of an important choice. Should owners of land, labour and capital decide to work for others for, respectively, rent, wages and interest, or should they take entrepreneurial risk to earn profit? This is a choice often made in reality but one that has never been explicitly treated in conventional economic theory. The theory discusses the choice between different non-entrepreneurial resources. The question why these resources should choose to be so and not become entrepreneurial is not raised.

(v)   The basis of distribution of the share of output is the same for the first three factors of production, land, labour and capital, namely, marginal productivity. A classification that requires the same basis for determining the rewards of all factors of production cannot be considered very meaningful if distributive justice is to be studied.

(vi)   Economic literature has generated a lot of confusion between rent of physical capital and interest rate. It is often said that interest rate is the rent of capital equipment (Scott and Nigro (7), p. 314; Samuelson (b), p. 557). Why is it quoted as a rate per monetary unit or 'per dollar value of capital goods'? Why is it not referred to as per machine, per building, per tool, etc., as is the case with wage for labour and rent for land. A conventional economist would argue that since it is not possible to account for all types of capital goods and their separate rentals, it is analytically convenient to consider all capital goods in money value and consider their rental as a rate per dollar value of capital goods. But in this way a real issue is obscured.

137

Land generates a service. The same is true of capital goods. Capital equipment is like land which is used without being fully consumed during use. The same is true of labour. There is no substantial difference between the rent for the services of capital equipment and the wages for the services of a human being. Both result from a contract for delivering a service in exchange for a compensation (rent or wages).

An analytical confusion is generated when interest rate is regarded as a rent for capital goods. Interest rate should enter into the rewards of factors of production only if money or finance is treated as an explicit and distinct factor of production capable of providing a service. No economist likes to do so.

The General Concept of Factors of Production in the Islamic Framework

All productive inputs can be grouped into two categories. The first category comprises those inputs that do not get 'consumed' in use in the production process. They retain their original nature and shape (except normal wear and tear). Let us call this category 'factor inputs'.

The other category includes those inputs which get 'consumed' during the production process and lose their original nature and shape. For example, raw cotton is an input in textile production. After the textile is produced, raw cotton is no longer there as raw cotton. This category can broadly be called 'consumed inputs'.

It may be mentioned that money can easily be recognized as a 'consumed input'. According to the above classification, money is useless unless it is 'consumed' to convert it either into factor inputs or into other consumed inputs. Money has to be 'consumed' to be useful in a productive process.

In an Islamic framework, factors of production can be identified according to either of the following functions:

(i)   They provide a definite productive service for which they are entitled to receive a definite reward (i.e. wages or rent). We will call these factors 'hired factors of production' or HFP.

(ii)   Or they choose to bear the entrepreneurial risks of a project rather than have a fixed wage or rent. We will refer to these factors of production as 'entrepreneurial factors of production' or EFP.

Although the conventional economic theory recognizes both the functions described above, most of its analytical framework centres around the first type of factors of production, i.e. the inputs that generate productive service for a fixed reward and do not get consumed. The second type of factors of production are generally kept out of the analysis by assuming perfect information which eliminates risk.

Factor inputs are allowed to serve as HFP as well as EFP. (As EFP they will not claim fixed rent or interest and instead will claim profit by bearing entrepreneurial risk.) Money is not allowed to serve as HFP, but can serve as EFP if it decides to bear risk. Besides assigning the EFP role to factor inputs, it is also a peculiarity of the Islamic economic system that it implicitly recognizes money as a separate independent factor of production to the extent that it is capable of bearing risk (and hence becomes entitled to the same reward as all EFP get, namely, profits).

In an Islamic framework, it is convenient to define and classify factors of production according to the method of determining their reward or price. The Islamic framework recognizes two categories of factor prices. One category is called *ujrah*. This is a broad name for rents which include the 'rent' for human services normally called wages in conventional economic theory. Thus, all factor inputs are paid *ujrah* for their use. Islam allows *ujrah* only for those inputs which are not directly 'consumed' in the production process. Thus money in an Islamic framework cannot be rented and cannot claim any *ujrah* or rent (interest). On the same grounds, raw materials cannot be rented or placed on *ujrah*. All *ujrahs* are fixed and known in advance with certainty. *Ujrahs* are always positive because the services or benefits for which they are hired have to be, by Islamic law, positive.

The other category of factor prices is called profit (which can be positive or negative). Profit is a reward for visualizing a profitable productive venture and bearing the risks (if any) associated with initiating and establishing it. Profit can be regarded as a reward for bearing risk as is sometimes recognized in conventional economic theory too. Islam categorically entitles factor inputs as well as money to earn this reward. Money, disallowed *ujrah, is* allowed profits provided it performs the function that justifies profit. Raw materials are generally priced in the commodity market and therefore are not allowed to share profits or to be placed on rent. The only way for the raw materials to earn profit is to treat their money equivalent as a financial capital invested in a productive project. In some special cases (mostly in agriculture), some inputs are sometimes allowed to share profits. These instances are, however, exceptional. All profits, by definition, are uncertain and are not known in advance or fixed in advance. Any so-called profits that are claimed to be fixed and known in advance come into the category of *ujrahs* by definition.

According to these two distinct factor prices, the Islamic framework can allow identification of only two categories of factors of production, namely:

(i) entrepreneurial factors of production (EFP) which claim only profits by bearing risk.

(ii) hired factors of production (HFP) which claim only *ujrahs* (rents or wages) and do not bear risk.

Before discussing the nature and function of these two factors in the following section, it may be instructive to summarize the main points of difference between our classification of factors of production and the classification used in the conventional economic theory.

First, our classification categorically separates and distinguishes financial capital from physical capital, according to each different type of factor prices. The confusion and overlapping of these two types of capitals in conventional economic theory, as already discussed, is absent in our framework. Second, financial capital is forbidden to earn a fixed, predetermined rent (i.e. interest) which is a cornerstone of the conventional economic theory. The rationale of depriving financial resources of a fixed rent has already been discussed. Since Islam does not allow *ujrah* on an economic resource that is consumed during the production process, the financial resources are not, therefore, entitled to any rent (or interest). The paradox in renting such a commodity becomes very clear from a quotation given by Samuelson himself in his chapter on interest: 'How to have your cake and eat it too. Lend it out on interest' (Samuelson (b), p. 557). Islam does not allow this irrationality.

Any resource which is consumed during the production process can be sold in an Islamic framework in a commodity market only. But Islam forbids money to be treated as a saleable commodity.[1] The conventional economic theory in fact does not consider it as a factor of production but treats it as a commodity. The theory determines its price not in the factor market but in the money market – a prohibited institution in Islam. This leads to the third major difference – institutional, in nature – arising out of our classification. The financial market which is, in our framework, a factor market for monetary resources, is a real sector and not merely a money-market.

We now discuss the nature and functions of the two types of factors of production recognized in Islam. It should be noted that the two types of factors of production are:

(a)   mutually exclusive (i.e. the same resource cannot be entrepreneurial and *ujrah*-receiving at the same time); and
(b)   perform entirely different functions.

Entrepreneurial Factors of Production (EFP)

Enterprise, in our framework, is to perform the following functions:

(a)   Making a decision about whether or not to participate in or initiate a particular productive activity.
(b)   Being willing to bear the risks associated with it.

Thus, in our framework, an entrepreneur does not need to be a specially gifted individual. If he is able to visualize a profitable productive venture, he can take the decision to initiate it if willing to subject the resources at his disposal to the risks, if any, associated with it. In doing this, he becomes an entrepreneur. He may not have the special organizational capabilities as highlighted in economic literature. It is assumed that organizational capabilities can be hired by offering appropriate *ujrah* to competent managers or executives. Organizers are thus *ujrah*-able resources rather than entrepreneurs.

The two functions, decision-making and risk-bearing are capable of being distinguished. Whereas decision-making rests solely upon human resources, the risk can be borne by the human resources, and/or physical resources and/or monetary resources. Suppose a person sees a productive opportunity. He can take the decision to initiate the project as well as bear the risk by investing his own human resources in the project. Alternatively, he may take the decision to initiate the project but may make his non-human resources bear the risk by investing only his physical capital or monetary resources. No human resource can become entrepreneurial simply on the basis of the decision-making function. Some resources have to be offered to bear risk.[2] The share in the profits of the project will be dependent upon the resources that are invested to bear risk. That is why we find it expedient to use the term 'entrepreneurial factors of production (EFP)' rather than simply entrepreneurs, to reflect the combination of human and non-human resources that are willing to bear the risks involved in initiating or participating in a productive economic venture.

This definition of enterprise obviously does not require the EFPs to be 'innovative' or 'social deviants'. We are assuming the EFPs are simply economic resources who, when confronted with a choice to work for a wage or to have their own work, i.e. whether to rent their resources or earn profit on them, decide in favour of the latter. In several situations, the economic resources may have no choice but to become EFP. This may occur, for example, in the following cases:

(a)   A man wants to pursue an economic activity but finds that it is religiously forbidden to rent the resources at his disposal (for example, if he has only money as a utilizable resource).

(b)   A man wants to pursue an economic activity but finds it uneconomic to rent the resources needed for it (for example, too low a wage level as rent for his labour, or too low a rent to lease buildings, assets, etc.).

It will be explained in the section on institutional framework that economic resources may not be allowed to sit idle nor may an individual decide to keep his resources idle. Certain penalties in the system will leave him no choice but to become an entrepreneur. This indicates a peculiar feature of the system, namely that it generates entrepreneurs in the economy. This feature will be discussed in detail in later sections.

The supply and demand of EFPs and their determinants will also be discussed later. It may, however, be useful to explain here what we mean by supply and demand in relation to EFPs.

By supply of EFPs we mean, briefly, the willingness or availability of the economic resources to initiate a productive venture and to bear the risk associated with it.

By demand for EFPs we mean the actual involvement of entrepreneurial resources in entrepreneurial jobs. In other words, demand for EFPs reflects the availability of entrepreneurial opportunities to engage the EFPs.

Hired Factors of Production (HFP)

All resources that offer definite productive services for a definite reward known in advance are called hired factors of production. All physical capital and human resources can fall into this category as long as they do not get 'consumed' in the process of production while offering their production services. 'Organization' and 'managers' as factors of production too are treated as HFPs as long as they are not willing to bear the entrepreneurial risks.

HFPs get employed only by the EFPs. Their employment, i.e. demand for them, will increase as the EFPs avail themselves of more and more entrepreneurial opportunities. The determinants of the supply of the HFPs are more or less as discussed in conventional economic theory. It will be worthwhile, however, to discuss the main features of the Islamic legal system relating to the renting of HFP resources since these features help to clarify the working of the factors market of HFPs in an Islamic framework. (See the discussion of institutional framework below.)

HFPs include land, labour, physical capital goods and human capital, but exclude monetary resources. HFPs are derived from resources which could also offer themselves as entrepreneurial resources. The supply and demand for HFPs thus competes with the supply and demand of EFPs. All resources have to opt for HFP and *ujrah* or for EFP and profit.

Some Features of the Institutional Framework in Islamic Economic System

It is not the intention here to describe the entire institutional framework of the Islamic economic system. Only some broad features, that are very basic to explaining the nature of factors of production and factor markets being developed here, are presented in this section.

Commodity Markets

Islam allows commodity markets as an institution of exchange. In fact, trade has been described as one of the most liked professions for human beings. Several verses of the Qur'ān and numerous sayings of the Prophet (peace be upon him) might be quoted to indicate the high value accorded to trade in Islam. The literature on the Islamic legal system gives a very elaborate code of rules and regulations for operation of the institution of trade. These rules more or less ensure a perfectly free commodity market except in circumstances where a free market may lead to misallocation of resources from the point of view of the objectives of Islamic law. Since the commodity markets in Islam have more or less the same features as are assumed by conventional economic

143

theory under ideal conditions, description of these features is therefore omitted.

Factor Markets for HFP

Ujrah, the price of the HFP, is determined in the market by the supply of and demand for them. The EFP resources share the residual output which is called profit. Profit determines the demand for EFP resources in the economy. The supply and demand of the factors of production, particularly of EFP resources, will be discussed later. In this section we discuss the provisions of the Islamic legal system that have a bearing on the market of HFP inputs.

Only those goods/resources may be rented or hired which are not 'consumed' as they are used. Renting or hire is the sale or purchase of the benefits/services of physical assets or resources including human resources. The assets or resources that generate benefits in the form of real produce (like a tree giving fruit or cattle giving milk) cannot be rented for such benefits. Financial resources cannot be rented because they cannot generate any service without being 'consumed'.

There is some difference of opinion about renting land for agricultural purposes. A minority of Islamic scholars disallow renting of land for agricultural purposes. The majority of Islamic scholars allow renting of land for agricultural purposes within the general principle of renting, which is, that any physical resource that is capable of generating a productive service is capable of being rented or hired. Land should not be confused with trees whose renting is disallowed because their benefits are in the form of real produce. Land rented for agricultural purposes is rented to benefit from its productive capacity which is a service and not a real produce. This service can be utilized to generate real produce only after providing adequate inputs (seeds, water, etc.). This is comparable to machinery which also provides a service in the form of productive capacity which can be utilized to produce real goods.

Rented goods may generate permitted economic benefits which must be definitely known. Where any doubt obtains about the nature or amount of the benefits or if the benefits are uncertain, the goods cannot be rented. Again, reference is to the service which the resources are rented to provide, and not to the output produced by using this service. For example, if a machine is being hired for producing a certain good then its capacity to produce such goods must be definitely known. Goods that are prohibited or which generate prohibited services, or which are by design capable only of prohibited goods, cannot be rented. Maintenance of the rented resource to sustain the flow of benefits/services for which it is rented is the responsibility of the owner. Any loss or damage (excepting that wilfully caused by the user) must be borne by the owner. The resource ceases to be on *ujrah* as soon as it becomes or is found to be incapable of providing the service for which it was rented.

The level of *ujrah* is determined by supply and demand. That the total rent over the entire life of the rented resource may exceed its cost is permitted in respect of the owner's entitlement to profit against the responsibility he bears for loss and damage. *Ujrah* should be fixed and known in advance – that is the defining condition of it. No uncertain element is permitted. If *ujrah* is uncertain it must be regarded as profit and the resources used against such an *ujrah* must be called entrepreneurial resources.

Ujrah can be paid in kind but not in the same kind as the benefits/services that the rented asset itself is providing. For example, *ujrah* for a machine cannot be paid in the form of allowing the use of a similar machine. It is, however, allowed to pay *ujrah* for a machine by allowing the use of a building, or the use of a different kind of machine.

Resources allowed to be rented or hired include:

(i)   Land (for cultivation, or construction, or plantation, etc.)

(ii)   Animals (for transportation or for help in cultivation).

(iii)   Human resources: this includes equally skilled or unskilled manual labour, as well as 'professional' services, such as those of doctors, lawyers, teachers, administrators, managers, etc.

(iv)   Buildings (such as houses, shops, factories, stores, etc.).

(v)   All such other goods as are capable of providing services without being consumed in the process of use (such as machinery, tools, clothes, tents, jewellery, etc.).

Though the factor market for HFPs is similar to the conventional factor market for land, labour and capital, there are still a couple of distinguishing features:

(i)   Monetary resources are out of the HFP category which is not the case in the conventional framework. There are two implications of this. First, the rental of goods is no longer regarded as 'interest rate' as is the case in the conventional economic theory. It is now a real rental, i.e. the price of a real service. Second, the supply of capital cannot be treated as a supply of savings which are generated in the process of a choice between present consumption and future consumption. The supply of capital is now generated by the output of the capital goods and has no links with the interest rate as is the case with the supply of other commodities.

(ii)   The supply of HFP factors, particularly of labour, results in the process of a choice whether to be a hired factor or an entrepreneurial factor. In the conventional theory, their supply results in the process of a choice between taking or not taking up employment. (This will be discussed in more detail in the section on supply and demand of factors of production, after discussing the institutional framework.)

Institution of Partnership

Islam encourages taking part in the production process. All economic resources are allowed to join to initiate a joint project. Thus it is possible that an individual with only his human resources and another with only financial resources should together initiate a productive venture. Their partnership will be entirely on a profit/loss-sharing basis; no other form is permitted. In other words, only entrepreneurial resources can join in a partnership. A combination where one person invests his resources to bear the risk of a project and the other simply rents his resources, will not be a partnership.

Partnership between non-human resources only is also possible. For example, it is possible that two or more persons initiate a project by investing financial resources only – they hire managers to organize and run the project.

Islam has laid down rules for sharing profit in any economic partnership. The principle is that profits of a joint project can be shared on any basis agreed in advance. For example, two partners may agree to share profits in proportion to their respective initial investment or on a 50:50 basis or any other pre-agreed ratio. Whether there is person A participating with no financial resources with person B participating with financial resources, or whether A and B are both investing only financial resources in a certain ratio, the partners are allowed to fix profit-sharing ratios irrespective of volume of investment through mutual bargaining. Since the participating resources are likely to be different in nature, as well as in such economic characteristics as productivity, scarcity, etc., it is wise to leave profit-sharing ratios to market forces which will function according to the relative supply and demand of the participating resources. It is important to remember that whereas the profit-sharing ratio can be agreed upon by mutual negotiation, the losses can only be shared in the ratio in which financial resources were invested.

The main economic function of partnership is to distribute entrepreneurial risk so that more and more potential entrepreneurial resources come forward to avail themselves of the entrepreneurial opportunities in the economy. Partnership also increases output. A and B's joint output will be larger than the sum of their individual outputs because of division of labour and specialization.

All capitalist economies permit partnership. What is peculiar about this institution within the Islamic system is the support given to it by various elements within the system. By contrast, the capitalist system, in which all productive resources are rentable, discourages partnership. In an economy with high business risks, all productive resources will prefer to be on *ujrah* rather than be entrepreneurial. Scarce factors will naturally command a high *ujrah*. They will have no compelling incentive to opt for partnership when entrepreneurial risks are very high; they will be willing to participate only in projects that ensure very high profitability, and will typically be looking for big ventures. Abundant factors will be able to command only low *ujrah*; most will be looking for entrepreneurial opportunities (discussed further below), but will not be able to find a partnership with the scarce resources. This is because being abundant (implying marginal utility or productivity close to zero) they have very little at stake, as compared to any scarce factor, when sharing in an entrepreneurial activity.

That is why we see, in labour-abundant developing countries operating under a capitalist system, that the bulk of the population of working age is idle.[3] This is because the wage level is too low to induce them to forego the leisure and family privileges they enjoy, or the social benefits that the family gets even from non-working members.[4] This so-called surplus labour will obviously fail to secure partnership with either physical or financial capital because the risk is great and the labour being surplus does not have much at stake in the event of a loss. There is nothing in a capitalist economy to motivate entrepreneurial partnership particularly between scarce and abundant resources.

The Islamic economic system has several elements to promote the institution of partnership. Leaving aside the ethical norms which urge a co-operative spirit among economic agents, let us look at only a few of the institutional provisions. Islam obliges one scarce factor to be fully available for entrepreneurial partnership, namely monetary resources. These resources while forbidden to earn rent, are encouraged to participate in entrepreneurial activities.

Disallowing the earning of rent is, obviously, not enough by itself to motivate a resource to take a risk rather than be idle. Aside from the ethical imperatives, the Islamic system provides an institutional penalty on idle resources in the form of *zakāh* at the rate of 2.5 per cent on financial assets. The revenue from *zakāh* is distributed among the poor. Any person who decides to keep his monetary resources idle will have to pay *zakāh* of 2.5 per cent every year, ultimately losing all his financial resources. The only way to save his financial resources is either to purchase capital equipment for renting or to become an entrepreneur, initiate a productive venture of his own, or to participate on a profit/loss-sharing basis in someone else's project. In this way, the income or means is earned to pay *zakāh* which is morally (as well as economically) worthy. Thus, there is incentive in the system for finances to opt for initiating own investment or partnering another's.

The capitalist system does not encourage partnership of big entrepreneurs with small entrepreneurs, even if small entrepreneurs can prove themselves to be more productive. In the interest-based system there is always a demand from entrepreneurs for financial resources on fixed rent (interest). These entrepreneurs must be entrepreneurs with the certainty of earning profits considerably higher than the interest rate. The system encourages existing entrepreneurs to get bigger and bigger because the bigger entrepreneurs can offer guarantees to the banking system for the payment of interest. This discourages small entrepreneurs from entering into projects, particularly those who cannot be sure of profits higher than the interest rate. The big corporations thus become bigger and bigger relying all the while on (mostly) interest-based finance. The constraint of making finance available only on a profit/loss-sharing basis reduces the attraction to big entrepreneurs. This induces new entrepreneurs to enter the market who were previously excluded because they were not big enough.

Also, an institution that compels a scarce factor to participate rather than claim *ujrah* creates demand for enterprise by sharing and hence reducing risk of the enterprise. Partnership is more fruitful the more it occurs between abundant and scarce factors. Such partnership promotes the interests of the abundant factor as the bulk of the risk-burden is carried by the scarce factor due to its opportunity cost.

Before closing this discussion, it will be instructive to comment, in the context of partnership, on the implications of insisting that the loss-sharing ratio corresponds strictly to the ratio of financial resources, whereas profit-sharing ratios may be bargained.

No project is initiated to make a loss. That is against common sense as well as against Islamic injunctions. The participating resources contributing to a partnership do so for profit, which is the reward for the investment made (human as well as financial) and the risk taken. This reward is in the nature of the price for entrepreneurial resources, in the same way that *ujrah* is the price for the services of hired factors of production. As *ujrah* is determined in the market by mutual negotiation, so too is the profit-sharing ratio. If two entrepreneurs decide to invest only financial resources, there is no reason why market forces of supply and demand will lead to a profit-sharing ratio different from the ratio of their respective financial investment. A pound will be valued as a pound in the market whether it is invested by person A or person B.

But if person A invests only financial resources while person B invests only human resources, the market will determine a profit ratio without regard for the ratio of financial investment by the two parties. Since expected profits are assessed in advance, the negotiated profit-sharing ratio would reflect the relative productive worth of the resources invested by A and B. As soon as one of the parties to a project enters human entrepreneurial resources into it, the ratio of financial investments loses its relevance to determine the basis for sharing the profit.

Now consider the sharing of losses. It is totally wrong from the economic point of view to consider losses merely as negative profits (though in simple accounting terms that is correct). Profit is a result of deliberate efforts geared towards achieving that result. Loss is not the result of deliberate efforts geared towards achieving that result. It is a result rather of the unforeseen factors which make up what is called 'entrepreneurial risk'.

The terms of partnership in the Islamic system insist on the contract being profit and loss sharing. The risk is shared as well as the hope or expectation of success. For the sharing out of profit, the market is competent to determine the value of the individual efforts that went into a project. But loss results from unforeseen, uncontrolled factors which are not offered in the market – they are by definition unknown. The market cannot be the mechanism for determining sharing of loss fairly.

When a loss arises, it is accounted a loss in financial terms (it is not an economic loss). This does not take into consideration the opportunity cost of the lost human resources that were invested in the project. The human resource has already lost what he invested, namely his labour. The remaining loss (that is financial loss) is to be borne by the remaining resource, namely the financial resource. The rule is that financial loss must be borne by the financial resources just as the human resource loss has already been borne by the human resources.

A basic requirement for the promotion of entrepreneurial partnership is that the risks of the project be distributed fairly among the participants. It will discourage partnership if human resources are asked to share the financial loss too (over and above the loss of labour and energy invested).

A further provision in the Islamic framework conducive to promoting the institution of partnership, namely social security, is discussed in the next section.

Thus there is not only a mechanism to promote the Islamic institution of partnership but also this institution creates a demand for entrepreneurial resources by:

(a)　encouraging new entrepreneurs to come into the market to avail themselves of entrepreneurial opportunities;

(b)　promoting partnership between scarce and abundant resources, thereby encouraging abundant entrepreneurial resources to come into the market as entrepreneurial rather than hired factors of production.

(c)　promoting partnership between large and small entrepreneurs, thereby creating a demand for small entrepreneurs;

(d)　reducing risk in the economy by distributing it fairly among entrepreneurs, thereby making potential entrepreneurs more willing to come forward.

Institution of Social Insurance

Islam requires a share for the have-nots in the resources of the haves. Muslims are required to assist the deprived section of the population who for whatever reason are unable to earn their living. This is largely a voluntary institution, whose strength and effectiveness depends on the practise by Muslims of Islamic ethical norms. However, besides charitableness and *sadaqah,* there is the institution of *zakāh* which authorizes collective authorities to take part of what is due from the resources of the haves and distribute it to the have-nots.

The presence of this institution in the Islamic economy is conducive to promoting participation and hence the demand for EFP resources. An individual with nothing else to live on would hesitate before becoming involved in entrepreneurial opportunities because in the event of loss, the risk is too great – starvation for himself and his family. He would, therefore, prefer to get a job at a low wage rather than initiate a higher profit venture which carries a chance, albeit slight, of ending up in loss. However, if the system ensures the minimum welfare of his family,[5] he is encouraged to take an entrepreneurial risk. He will have no compelling incentive to prefer a low wage.

Factor Markets

Supply and Demand of Hired Factors of Production

We do not disagree significantly with the theories of supply and demand of labour and capital in conventional economics, and can easily adopt them to explain the supply and demand of human resources and physical capital in an Islamic economy, except that rental of capital goods will really be a rental and not an interest rate. Marginal productivity will determine the demand for the human resources and physical capital to be employed on *ujrah* basis. The supply of labour will be determined by the marginal utility of leisure to the labourer. The supply of capital goods will be determined by the opportunity cost of producing capital goods.

Supply and Demand of Entrepreneurial Factors
of Production

The supply of such EFP resources as can be hired will be determined as a residual out of the total stock of such resources left over after employment on *ujrah*. Suppose S_R is the given supply of such resources. After S_U of these have been able to get placement on *ujrah*, the remainder, $S_R - S_U$, constitutes the supply of entrepreneurial resources. This is shown in the following diagram:

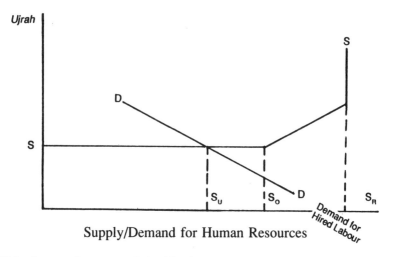

Supply/Demand for Human Resources

SS is the supply curve of the hired resources. Up to a certain level S_0, these resources are available at a constant opportunity cost. Between S_0 and S_R they can be supplied only at an increasing opportunity cost and beyond S_R, their supply cannot be increased at any cost in the short run. S_R is the total available stock. Out of these S_U get employed on *ujrah* u which is where the supply curve intersects the demand curve DD. The resources S_U - S_R will not find it economic to get employed on *ujrah* because opportunity cost is higher than what the employer is willing to pay. The resources beyond S_U, therefore, will prefer the entrepreneurial option and remain idle until they actually find an entrepreneurial activity to get involved in.

Two points need further elaboration before we turn to the demand for entrepreneurial resources:

(a)   How the S_R is determined, and
(b)   how the remainder S_R - S_U becomes EFP

S_R for human resources will be determined by the size and growth of population. Migration and other factors discussed in the literature are other sources of determining the stock of human resources in the economy. S for capital goods in the country will be total output of capital goods in the country minus exports plus imports. The total stock of capital goods may exceed demand at any one point in time. If this situation persists the holders of physical capital will have no choice but to look for an entrepreneurial activity utilizing their physical capital which, otherwise, will be depleted by *zakāh* deductions.

With regard to the second question: why a resource not finding an adequate *ujrah*-paid job would be willing to bear entrepreneurial risk, the answer is clear in case of physical capital. *Zakāh* deductions force the owner to deploy the physical capital in any project that would at least yield some positive expected profits, i.e. anything greater than zero, so that a part or the whole of the *zakāh* could be paid out of the profit, instead of from the asset itself. Thus all such capital goods that fail to get employed on *ujrah* are available for entrepreneurial employment. For human resources, though there is no such formal institutional compulsion as *zakāh* to dissuade an individual from sitting idle if he cannot get employed on *ujrah,* yet actual instincts do urge individuals to achieve something for themselves and their family. Social norms too encourage human beings to do some productive work. A man involved in productive work always has a social status higher than a person sitting idle. There do exist some societies where a sweeper or a domestic servant or a cobbler, etc. may have a social status less than an idle person. Such a social environment does not exist in Islam. There are specific Islamic injunctions that urge or oblige individuals to earn their own living. Sitting idle can be assumed to be a strongly discouraged option.[6] A person unable to get employment on the basis of *ujrah* can be assumed to be available for an entrepreneurial activity. Besides, 'profit' is a recognized motive even in conventional economic theory. Human beings want to make, even to maximize, profit. Those who are unable to get employment to earn 'profit' from their services will seek an opportunity where they can earn 'profit' by utilizing their ability to bear entrepreneurial risk.

Factors determining the demand for entrepreneurial resources may be listed as:

(a)   ability to visualize a productive activity that would yield him an expected profit greater than the prevailing level of *ujrah* for his resources;

(b)   risks involved in initiating the project;

(c)   supply of other productive resources;

(d)   institutional arrangements conducive to easy entry into the market.

The ability to visualize a profitable venture in turn depends on several factors like education, means of communicaton, level of income, consumption, spending patterns, etc. The risks in an economy are determined by the socio-political climate on the one hand and the moral fibre of the society on the other. The resources required to initiate the project can either be the entrepreneur's own resources or he can work with resources owned by others. Rent (reflecting the relative supply) of other productive resources will be a key factor in the demand for entrepreneurial resources. The higher the rents in the economy, the lower will be the demand for the EFP. The factors relating to free entry are promoted by the institutions of partnership and social security described earlier.

The supply of different kinds of EFPs raises the demand for itself. Thus availability of entrepreneurial, i.e. risk-bearing, capital will raise the demand for the entrepreneurial human resources and vice versa. Hence there is an indirect application of Say's Law to the EFPs in the sense that the aggregate supply of EFPs generates their own demand.

Factor Market Equilibrium

As discussed earlier, the supply of the two factors of production is determined as below:

Supply of Factors of Production = S_R determined by the choice between leisure income and *'ibādah* (worship) in the case of human resources, and by a choice between present consumption and future consumption in the case of capital goods and financial resources.

Supply of *ujrah*-based jobs = S_U = D_U i.e. determined by the entrepreneur's demand for HFP resources.

Supply of entrepreneurial jobs = S_N determined by S_R - S_U or S_R - D_U

Demand for entrepreneurs = D_N exogenously given.

Demand for hiring the resources is determined by the productivity of HFPs in entrepreneurial activities. Whereas productivity determines the slope of the demand curve, the level of entrepreneurial activities determines the shifts in the demand for hired resources. Any excess demand in the HFP market will result in raising the *ujrah* level hence clearing the HFP market. Any excess supply in the HFP market is available to become an EFP rather than waiting at the door of the entrepreneur as HFP. Thus the HFP market can be said to be always in equilibrium.

Not all available EFPs, however, may be able to get involved in entrepreneurial activities. In other words, there may not be enough demand for EFPs in the economy, there may be an excess supply or a disequilibrium in the EFP market. There cannot be excess demand in the HFP market because that would shift resources from the HFP market to the EFP market. The only reason for disequilibrium in the factor market is, therefore, the excess supply in the EFP market. Otherwise the factor markets are in equilibrium in the economy: the growth in the economy will simply raise *ujrahs* as well as profits; depression will result in lowering the *ujrahs* and profits till the *ujrahs* become downward rigid which will result in creating excess supply in the EFP market.

Physical capital has a choice to become HFP or EFP. The rent at which physical capital will be supplied in the HFP market will depend on the cost of production of these goods (which is to be recovered from the rent by the time it completely depreciates) plus the expected profits on the investment of resources used in the production of these capital goods. The demand for capital goods as HFP will depend upon the productivity of these goods as HFP. If there is an excess supply of capital goods, i.e. their marginal productivity as HFP falls, they will be offered a rent lower than they are willing to accept. This will cause the capital goods to shift from the HFP to the EFP market. An increase in the supply of capital goods in the EFP market may reduce the expected profits of capital goods. A new equilibrium level of rent and expected profits of capital goods will, therefore, be achieved clearing both markets for these goods.

It can easily be visualized that there cannot remain substantial excess supply of capital goods even in the EFP market. Suppose the stock of capital goods reached a level that brought the *ujrah* in its HFP market and profits in its EFP market to a level where a further decline would compel the owners to keep their assets idle till more profitable opportunities arose in the EFP market. The lack of demand will obviously lead to a decline in further production of capital goods. The excess supply will either be soon wiped out or not remain quite so substantial.

Similarly, human resources too have a choice to become HFP or EFP. The wage at which human resources will be supplied in the HFP market will depend on the marginal utility of time.[7] The demand for the human resources as HFP will depend upon the productivity of these resources as HFP. If there happens to be an excess supply of human resources, they will be offered a wage lower than they are willing to accept. This will cause the human resources to shift from the HFP to the EFP market. An increase in supply of human resources in the EFP market may reduce the expected profits of human resources in this market. A new equilibrium level of wages and expected profits (of human resources) will, therefore, be achieved, clearing the market for these resources.

There is, however, always the possibility that the excess supply of human resources, not employed in the HFP market, will also fail to get absorbed into the EFP market. This means that there are not enough entrepreneurial opportunities that these resources can visualize or initiate or participate in to yield them a profit equal to or more than the wage. In other words, there is not enough demand in the EFP market.

We treat this situation as a disequilibrium (excess supply) in the human resource EFP market. The HFP market will remain in equilibrium as the wage will be determined where markets clear supply and demand. The wage level determines the expected profit level in the EFP market. The demand for EFP resources at this expected profit is exogenously given and fixed in the EFP market. The EFP market will clear as the demand for EFP shifts upwards. Wage and expected profit levels remain the same. The EFP market may also clear if expected profits in the economy rise. But in this case, wages and profit levels increase too as the EFP market clears.

Money does not have a choice to become HFP. It can only become EFP. Savings that are not converted into assets or capital goods become money available for investment. The supply of monetary savings for investment will depend on the income as well as the profits on the investment that these savings can bring.[8] Some part of savings will always be in the form of monetary savings. As physical capital/assets are usually quite expensive, smaller savers have no choice but to hold their savings in monetary forms. Even all those who can afford to buy a physical asset may not do so as they have to take a double risk – first, at the time of buying the asset which requires adequate knowledge of the market and of the assets along with the ability to anticipate future prices for the assets, and, second, at the time of renting the assets which involves the risk of keeping the asset idle during the search for a tenant at the desired rent as well as the risk of loss or of damage to the asset during the period of tenancy.

An excess supply of monetary resources is hardly conceivable in any capital-scarce economy in general and in an Islamic economy in particular. An excess demand for EFP in monetary resources may arise. This will mean more profits on the monetary resources. The higher profits will lead to more savings in monetary resources till the market is cleared. The supply of monetary resources to meet the demand may become constrained by the capacity to save in the economy. This may allow excess demand in the economy to persist if adequate monetary and fiscal measures do not intervene in the EFP market in monetary resources or if monetary resources from abroad are not allowed to fill the gap.

Notes

1. The logic behind not treating money as a saleable commodity is very clear. A commodity is sold in the market at a price which is composed of the following:

(a) cost of materials which went into its production;
(b) *ujrahs* of HFP used to add value to it;
(c) opportunity cost of EFP used to bring this commodity to the market.

Commodities can be exchanged in the market only if they differ in terms of any of the above 3 features.

2. In fact, risk-bearing is the necessary and sufficient condition to define an entrepreneur. Any resources willing to bear the risks of a project implicitly are making a decision to initiate or participate in a project. The distinction between decision-making and risk-bearing has been made to highlight the nature of human resources which may make a decision without subjecting themselves to risk-bearing.

3. This is what Arthur Lewis calls unlimited supply of labour in his well-known work, 'Economic Development with Unlimited Supplies of Labour', The Manchester School of Economics and Social Studies (May, 1954), reprinted in B. Okun and R.W. Richardson, *Studies in Economic Development* (New York, Holt, Rinehart and Winston, 1961).

4. Empirical evidence of such a phenomenon has been discussed in M. Fahim Khan, *A Study into the Causes of Fluctuations in Real Wages in the Labour Surplus Economy of Pakistan,* Ph.D. Dissertation (unpublished). (Boston, Boston University, August, 1978).

5. For further information on the institutions guaranteeing minimum living needs in an Islamic system, see M.N. Siddiqi, 'Guarantee of a Minimum Level of Living in an

Islamic State', in Munawar Iqbal (ed.), *Distributive Justice and Need Fulfilment in an Islamic Economy* (Islamabad, International Institute of Islamic Economics, 1986), pp. 249–84.

6. Several sayings from the Prophet (peace be upon him) can be quoted to indicate that Islam discourages resources to sit idle and encourages human beings to earn resources:

(i) for their own living;
(ii) for the deprived and the have-nots in the society;
(iii) for the promotion and development of the society;
(iv) for the propagation of Islam.

Thus an Islamic setting has no place for idle people or unutilized resources.

7. We prefer to use the phrase 'marginal utility of time' rather than 'marginal utility of leisure'. This is because 'leisure' is not the only opportunity cost of getting involved in an economic activity. Time required to be devoted to Allah (such as prayers, social obligations, propagation of the words of Allah and *jihād (fī sabīl Allāh)* is a more important opportunity cost than leisure. We, therefore, like to refer to the utility of time rather than the utility of leisure.

8. The institution of moderation not discussed in this paper is a peculiarity of the Islamic system which enables the economy to generate more savings than in a comparable non-Islamic economy. Some discussion of this institution can be seen in M. Fahim Khan (3).

References

1. Boumal, W.J., 'Entrepreneurship in Economic Theory', *American Economic Review*, Volume LVIII (May 1968), pp. 64–71.

2. Khan, M. Fahim, *A Study into the Causes of Fluctuation in Real Wages in the Labour Surplus Economy of Pakistan.* Ph.D. dissertation (unpublished), Boston, Boston University, August 1978.

3. ———, 'Macro Consumption Function in an Islamic Framework', *Journal of Research in Islamic Economics*, Vol. 1, No. 2 (Winter 1984), pp. 1–24.

4. Leff, N.H., 'Entrepreneurship and Economic Development: The Problem Revisited', *Journal of Economic Literature* (March 1979).

5. Leibenstein, H., 'Entrepreneurship and Economic Development', *American Economic Review*, Vol. LVIII (May 1968), pp. 72–83.

6. Samuelson, P., *Economics*, 11th edition, New York, McGraw Hill, 1980.

7. Scott, R.H. and N. Nigro, *Principles of Economics*, New York, Macmillan, 1982.

8. Siddiqi, M.N., 'Guarantee of a Minimum Level of Living in an Islamic State', in Munawar Iqbal (ed.), *Distributive Justice and Need Fulfilment in an Islamic Economy*, (Islamabad, International Institute of Islamic Economics, 1986), pp. 249–84.

CHAPTER 8

Time Value of Money and Discounting in Islamic Perspective

Introduction

Several issues arising in the conventional techniques of project evaluation need to be reconsidered from an Islamic perspective, especially as many of them have not been resolved even in the conventional framework. Discounting for time value is one such issue. It assumes particular importance in the Islamic perspective in view of the prohibition of interest, which can be considered as a sort of denial of the time value of money. On the other hand, Islam does not prohibit contracts of sale (for example, *bay' mu'ajjal*[1] and *bay' al-salam*[2]) in which the price of a commodity can be different from its spot price if a time element is involved in the process of exchange. This (with important reservations as we shall see) can be considered a sort of recognition of the time value of money. Further, rents and wages also appear to recognize some reward for the time element. The rent of a house, for example, includes an element beyond depreciation, which (again with important reservations) can be considered as time value of money. Thus, while *bay' mu'ajjal,* rent and wages include a fixed and predetermined element as compensation for time, the prohibition of interest specifically denies recognition to the time value of money. The question then arises about what the correct position of Islam is on this issue? The answer is of primary importance in the context of project evaluation where cost of capital must be defined clearly, with some awareness of its time value. If Islam does not recognize the time value of money, then there would be no need for discounting or compounding for the time value of money in project evaluation and feasibility studies. If, on the other hand, Islam does recognize the time value of money, we need to know the principles

159

under which such a value is to be determined, the rationale of discounting, and the discount rate to be used in project evaluation. Several worthwhile attempts have been made to tackle this issue. The first was by Anas Zarqa (5) who concluded that discounting is permissible in Islam and that the rate of return in projects of comparable riskiness already in operation should be used as the rate of discount. However, he did not discuss the Islamic position on the time value of money and also questioned the relevance of time preference in determining the discount rate. Rafiq al-Masri (4) discussed the question of the time value of money in detail, arguing that Islam does allow time value of money. However, he did not discuss a number of important issues, such as why the time value of money is denied in the case of interest and what would be the appropriate determinant of the time value of money (and hence of the discount rate) in an Islamic economy. Rauf Azhar (2) discussed the consumer's time preference as well as productivity of investment and concluded that the rate of profit, and not the rate of interest, should be the appropriate rate of discount in an Islamic economy. But since he made the conventional assumption of perfect foresight and lack of uncertainty, his conclusion loses Islamic perspective. Also, he did not discuss issues like the concept and nature of time value of money and the principles under which it is to be distinguished in a loan contract from in an investment contract. Furthermore, his conclusion that money has no time value or is not entitled to a rate of return if it is in malleable form, whereas it is entitled to a profit if it is moulded into a productive asset, does not, in my view, reflect the correct Islamic position about return on money capital. A sum of money invested in a business enterprise is entitled to a share in profit irrespective of the form in which it is held by the entrepreneur. On the other hand, a definite sum of money loaned to a business enterprise with the principal guaranteed is not entitled to any return, however the money is converted by the borrower into productive assets.

In short, the issue of the time value of money and hence of discounting in an Islamic framework remains unsettled. The discussion that follows is a new effort to resolve some of the relevant questions.

Islamic Perspective on Time Value of Money

The conventional concept of discounting regards two similar goods at two different points of time as having two different values because of the time element involved. Since, in the conventional framework, present consumption is always assumed to be preferred over future consumption, future values need to be discounted to make them comparable with present values. The rate of interest serves as the rate of discount. Leaving aside for the moment the question of the suitability of interest rate as a measure of time preference, let us first consider whether time value is justified in Islam when a time element is involved in comparing the values.

Some Islamic economists have answered this question in the affirmative.[3] They start by arguing that *bay' mu'ajjal* and *bay' al-salam* are permissible modes of trade in Islam. In these types of sale, the price of a commodity sold on, respectively, credit or advance payment basis, can be different from its spot price. This, in their view, suffices to prove that Islam does recognize difference in value due to a time element, that Islam does have a concept of time preference.

It is true that Islamic jurists have allowed a difference between the price of a commodity if delivered immediately and the price if delivered some time in the future, or between the cash and credit price of a commodity. But this does not necessarily mean that they have recognized a predetermined time value for money. The difference in present and future values of the same commodity cannot be said to have been allowed by the jurists on account of the time element involved. They might have allowed this difference because they recognized that supply and demand forces are different at different points of time. That reasoning would explain their allowing the future price in a *bay' mu'ajjal* contract to be either higher or lower than or equal to the present price. As far as I know, they never say that the future price in *bay' mu'ajjal* must be higher than the present price. Similarly, in the case of *bay' al-salam,* permission for the difference in the price of a commodity to be delivered in future is likely to be simply a recognition of the forces of supply and demand that cause prices to fluctuate with time. It is conceivable that the actual market price of a good when delivered may turn out to be *less* than what the buyer paid at the time of contract. Indeed, it is precisely this risk that justifies the profit earned if the actual market price at the time of delivery turns out to be higher than at the time of contract. Hence, it is not correct to argue that the permission for *bay' mu'ajjal* and *bay' al-salam* is an unqualified recognition of the concept of pure time value. There may be recognition of some time value but its nature needs to be clearly understood.

It has also been argued that rents on physical assets are permitted in

Islam and the aggregate rental value allowed to be higher than the present value of an asset. The inference has then followed that Islam recognizes the time value of money and allows it to be cashed in the market. This argument has some weight. Rent can be interpreted as a time value of money. Suppose a person buys a machine for £10,000 and rents it out at £1,000 per year. He would be earning a gross return at the rate of 10 per cent per annum on his money. As the owner of the machine, he is responsible for its depreciation, and for maintaining it in full working order throughout the contract: if the machine through no fault of the user, fails to function properly the owner is liable for its repair or replacement. The net return to the capital would be calculated as follows:

$$r = \frac{(R \times t + C) - M}{M} \qquad [1]$$

where r = net time value of money;
R = rent of the asset per annum;
t = number of years the asset has actually been used under the rent contract;
C = nominal value of the asset at the time of termination of the rent contract;
M = money being invested.

It can be seen that both t and C are uncertain and can be determined only after the rent period terminates. Hence if rent is considered to involve time value, it is a value that cannot be predetermined.

In order to further clarify the point that Islam does not permit a *predetermined* time value of money, the example of a conventional financial lease contract can be presented. In such a lease, a physical asset is rented out on the following conditions:

(a)   The user of the asset is responsible for maintenance of the asset in working order.

(b)   The user undertakes to purchase the asset on expiry of the contract, and to do so at a predetermined price, irrespective of the condition of the asset and even if the asset does not actually exist at the time of expiry of the contract.

(c)   The contract is irrevocable before the date of its expiry.

In this case, all values for R, t, C and M in the equation are predetermined and hence r is also predetermined and fixed. There is no element of uncertainty in r. Financial lease, in this form, is not permitted in Islam, from which it can be inferred that Islam does not permit a fixed, predetermined time value of money.

That prohibition is also evident from another *fiqh* principle which states, 'no compensation for time (alone)'. For example, if an individual takes from another a loan of say £1,000 to be repaid after one year, and then either he or the other party wants to arrange (say after six months) that £500 be paid immediately and £500 be exempted in lieu of early payment, it would be disallowed. Such negotiation is not permitted in the Islamic framework.

From the above discussion, we have tried to establish that if there is a concept of time value of money in Islam, it can only be an *ex post* one. But in *bay' mu'ajjal* a predetermined higher price is permitted if deferred payment is agreed. An individual is authorized to, for example, sell goods at, say, £100 if the payment is made now, and to sell at £120 if the payment is to be made after a year. Does this not imply a fixed and predetermined time value of money?

To understand the Islamic position in this case, we need to identify correctly the possible reasons for the difference in the prices quoted for two different points of time. The possible sources can be:

(i) Time preference. One is not necessarily indifferent about the same value of two different points of view, i.e. £100 now may not be the same as £100 after a year because of the time element involved.

(ii) Supply-demand conditions. One may not assume that present supply-demand conditions and hence price will hold constant at some point in the future.

Thus the higher price in case of deferred payment in *bay' mu'ajjal* contract cannot be attributed only to time preference. It has been allowed in view of *both* factors, namely time preference and supply-demand conditions. Therefore, we can say that there may be time value involved in *bay' mu'ajjal* contract but this time value is certainly not predetermined.

From the above discussion, we can infer that Islam does not have anything against realizing time value of money but it cannot be claimed as a predetermined value.

Rate of Return on Capital as a Measure of Time Preference

Having outlined the Islamic position about the time value of money, we now turn to the question of how it can be integrated with investment decision making. To do so we must review, from the Islamic viewpoint, the concepts of time preference and of rate of return on capital as a measure of time preference.

Concept of Time Preference

Once we admit the existence of interest in the society, it is easy to develop a theory of time preference. People can be assumed to have a certain rate of time preference which is predetermined. Taking interest rate as a parameter, a utility-maximizing consumer will make a choice between present and future consumption such that his rate of time preference is equal to the interest rate at the margin. Similarly, in investment decision making, an individual will discount future cash flows (or compound present values) at the given interest rate in order to make the present and future values comparable. But if we deny the existence of interest rate in the society, the above treatment of time preference in the context of investment decisions loses its validity. It has already been argued that the time value of money in an Islamic perspective cannot be predetermined. In the presence of an uncertain time value of money, how can we justify use of a predetermined rate of time preference?

One approach could be to use the average rate of return on capital in the economy as a proxy for the expected time value of money. We may use, as suggested by Zarqa (5), the rate of return in alternative uses of comparable risk, assuming that this rate of return represents the expected time value of money. One problem in this approach is that the expected rate of return on capital in the economy may over-estimate the expected time value of money because the rate of return on capital may include several elements other than time value of money, e.g. reward for bearing the risk not associated with time. Furthermore, it has been observed that long-term projects have expected profits higher than short-term ones. Thus, the expected rate of profit on capital may change with respect to time. In other words, the expected rate of profit may be a function of time. If the expected rate of return on capital is to represent the time value of money, then we will have to think of the rate of time preference as a function of time as well. Therefore, the whole concept of time preference needs to be reviewed, a task to which we now turn.

The rate of time preference can be determined by confronting a consumer with the choice between present and future consumption and locating the point of indifference. If a consumer is indifferent between £100 now and £110 a year from now, then his rate of time preference is 10 per cent. This is how the rate of time preference is defined. In the conventional framework, this rate is assumed to be fixed. However, if this rate is to reflect uncertainties associated with time, then this rate cannot be assumed to be fixed over time. It should vary as uncertainties associated with time vary. In other words, the rate of time preference for an individual will depend on the time-frame for which he is taking the decision. In a three-year framework, the rate can be expected to be different from that relevant for a two- or four-year framework. The reason is that time preference depends on time-related uncertainties which are compounded by the length of time involved.

In the light of the above discussion, the present value of a future cash flow would be worked out as follows:

$$PVF_t = F_t (1 + d_t)^{-t} = F_t e^{-d} t^t$$

where F_t = flow accruing in period t

PVF_t = present value of F_t

d_t = rate of time preference relevant for the period t, and

$d_{t+i} > d_t > d_{t-i}$ for any positive value of i.

As an example, suppose a person is indifferent between £1,000 now and £1,210 two years from now. The rate of time preference in this case will be

$$d_2 = 10\% \text{ because}$$
$$£1,000 = 1,210 (1 + \frac{10^{-2}}{100})$$

In the above framework this rate cannot be taken to imply that this individual will also be indifferent between £1,000 now and £1,331 three years from now, since

$$£1331 \frac{(1 + 10)^{-3}}{100} = 1000$$

The rate in a three-year framework should be higher than in the two-year framework. Therefore, the individual is expected to be indifferent between £1,000 now and a figure higher than £1,331 after three years. In this framework, it would be justifiable to equate the rate of time preference with the expected rate of return, both being functions of time.

Rate of Return and Investment Decision Making in Islamic Perspective

In making investment decisions, it is mostly money capital that is under consideration. In the conventional framework, the rent on this capital is called the rate of interest, which rate serves as a measure of time preference. Since it is prohibited in Islam to award any rent to such capital, investment decision making will have to be based on expected rate of return on capital. However, it is to be noted that though an investment decision will have to be made on the basis of some expectation about the actual rate of return on capital, the capital will not be rewarded on the basis of the actual return on capital after it has been realized. Therefore, while making an investment decision, the decision maker will have to consider the expected rate of return with all the uncertainties attached to it.

The uncertainties associated with a rate of return are of two types: (a) uncertainties (risks) related to time; and (b) uncertainties (risks) unrelated to time. If we want to account for the time value of money, it will be captured by that expected rate of return which reflects a reward for time-related uncertainties only.

Islam allows earning a profit only through risk-bearing. If someone is willing to bear the loss arising out of the uncertainties of time, then he is also allowed to gain from the uncertainties of time. And if one is permitted to claim a reward for facing the uncertainties of the future, future cash flows can be discounted for the time element involved. Since longer time means higher uncertainty, it is only reasonable to discount a more remote future at a higher rate for the purpose of making inter-temporal comparisons.

Determination of Discount Rate in Islamic Perspective

The discount rate or the rate of time preference, even in the conventional framework is not directly observable. Since a rational consumer is assumed to equate his rate of time preference with the time value of his money at the margin, the time value of money can represent the rate of time preference and hence the discount rate. But as explained earlier, the time value of money can be determined only *ex post,* whereas discount rate must be known *ex ante* in order to make investment decisions. Conventional economics has an easy solution to this problem. If we assume away any uncertainty, then the marginal productivity of capital, the time value of money and the interest rate all coincide. Hence interest rate which is fixed and predetermined can serve as the discount rate. In the Islamic framework, interest is not permitted, and there is no *ex ante* measure of the time value of money. What measure, then, should we use to represent the discount rate in an Islamic framework?

Before answering this question, it is worth remembering that even the rate of interest may fail to represent discount rate in several practical instances. For example, if there is disequilibrium in the market, which is a real situation in most economies, the interest rate does not represent discount rate. Consider the following situation:

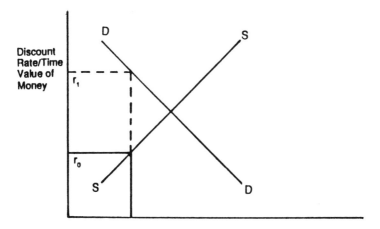

Supply and Demand of Investible Funds

SS is a supply curve of investible funds. It results from consumer's choice, i.e. from equality of his discount rate (d) with the time value of his money (r). All points on this curve, therefore, represent discount rates. The values on the X-axis corresponding to each point on this curve are the levels of savings if the time value of money is equal to the discount rate at that point.

DD is a demand curve for investible funds. It is determined by the equality of marginal productivity of capital and the time value of investible funds. At equilibrium, marginal productivity and discount rate are equal to the time-value of money which is called the interest rate (r).

Now suppose an economy chooses to have an artificially low rate of interest r_0. This will yield K_0 saving. But these savings do not have r_0 as their time value of money. The time value of money for these resources is r_1. However, r_1 is not observable *ex ante* in the market. Hence, even in the conventional framework, practical situations may not justify use of the interest rate as the discount rate. The point is that a rational consumer equates his discount rate with the time value of his money. On the other hand, a rational investor or the user of funds equates the rate of return with the cost of funds. The cost of funds is the time value of money that the supplier of investible funds will charge him.

Since, in an Islamic framework, the time value of money cannot be determined *ex ante,* some proxy for the expected time value of money will have to be used to make investment decisions. The time value of money can be approximated by the existing rate of return on capital. But the existing rate of return on capital will be different in different projects. These rates of return have two components: (a) rate of return due to bearing risks which are not related to time, and (b) rate of return due to bearing risks associated with time. It is the latter component that reflects time value and is required to be used for time discounting in investment decision making. But it is difficult to separate the former component from the latter for any existing project to determine the pure time value of money.

To approximate the pure time value of money we need to look for portfolios in which all risks are almost non-existent or negligible except purely time-related risks. The rate of return on such portfolios could represent the discount rate. It is commonly believed that portfolio diversification reduces risks. Therefore, the rate of return on capital which has been distributed over a large number of projects can provide a proxy for the time value of money since this rate of return will more closely reflect the reward for bearing the risks related to time-related uncertainties alone. The rate of return on deposits of Islamic banks can be considered to be such a rate. The bank distributes the collected deposits to different projects and pays the depositors a return out of the collective profits of all funds. Hence the rate of return of Islamic banks on deposits of different maturities will give an approximation of the time value of money for different periods of time. The Islamic banks do offer different rates of return on deposits of different maturities which is consistent with the hypothesis developed earlier that rate of time preference is expected to be different for different time-frames.

An alternative way of finding out the discount rate for time value may be to take projects of different duration already in operation and establish a relationship between profit and risk for projects of the same duration in different groups based on the extent of riskiness. This will give us a function of the following type:

$\pi_i = F(R^d_i)$

where π_i = rate of return in projects of ith group.
(Each group representing a different level of riskiness.)
(R^d_i) = risk, measured by standard deviation, for the projects of duration d in the ith group.

The limiting value of this function when $(R^d_i) \longrightarrow$ o will be taken as the time value of money and hence the discount rate for that duration.

$$\text{Hence, the discount rate} = R^d_i \overset{\text{Lim}}{\longrightarrow} o \ F(R^d_i).$$

This rate of discount is different from that suggested by Zarqa (5). He proposed that the rate of return in projects of comparable risk may be taken as the discount rate. Such a rate of return may be a valid basis for discounting some private sector projects but this may not be an appropriate rate for general investment decision making. This is particularly not appropriate in case of public sector projects since these need to be discounted for pure time value of money. In such projects, other risks do not have much significance because they are distributed over a large number of tax-payers. In this way they are minimized and hence do not need to be accounted for.

Summary and Conclusions

This discussion has addressed the following questions:

1. What is the concept of the time value of money in an Islamic perspective which prohibits interest?

2. What implications does this concept have for discounting for time in project evaluation.

The answers to these questions, in brief, are the following:

(a) Islam does not have anything against realizing time value of money but it cannot be claimed as a predetermined value.

(b) There is also nothing against having a positive time preference. It is, however, more reasonable to think of it as a function of time rather than treating it as fixed and independent of the time-frame under consideration.

(c) *Ex post* rate of return on capital is the only source for identifying the pure time value of money. Since the rate of return is also a function of the time-frame of the project, it is justifiable to use this rate to approximate the rate of time preference.

(d) Since the *ex post* rate of return is a result of two types of risk-bearing, one related to the time element alone and the other unrelated to the time element, the pure time value of money and hence pure rate of time preference would be reflected in the rate of return due only to time-related risk-bearing.

(e) The expected rates of return on the deposits of Islamic banks of different maturities can be treated as close proxies for the rates of time preference for the purpose of discounting projects of different maturities.

To conclude, economic agents in an Islamic economy will have positive time preferences and there will be indicators available in the economy to approximate the rate of those preferences. There is no justification for assuming, as has been done in many studies on investment behaviour in an Islamic perspective, a zero rate of time preference in an Islamic economy.

Notes

1. Sale on deferred payment basis, i.e. the goods are delivered now but the price is to be paid in future. The price in such a contract may be different from the prevailing market price.

2. Sale on advanced payment basis, i.e. the price is paid now and the goods are to be delivered in future. The price in such a contract is permitted to be different from the spot price.

3. See for example, Rafiq al-Masri (4) and Kauthar Abdul Fattah al-Abji (1).

References

1. Al-Abji, Kauthar Abdul Fattah, 'Feasibility Study in Islamic Perspective'. Paper presented at the International Seminar on Fiscal Policy and Development Planning, held in Islamabad, 1986.

2. Azhar, Rauf A., 'A Theory of Optimal Investment Decisions in an Islamic Economy', Islamabad, International Institute of Islamic Economics, 1986.

3. Hirschleifer, J., *Investment Interest and Capital,* Englewood Cliffs, NJ, Prentice Hall, 1970.

4. Al-Masri, Rafiq, 'Time Discounting in Islam' (Arabic). Paper presented in the Conference on Islamic Economics, Sokoto University, Sokoto, Nigeria, 1986.

5. Zarqa, M.A., 'Project Evaluation in Islamic Perspective', in Z. Ahmad et al. (eds.), *Fiscal Policy and Resource Allocation in Islam,* Islamabad, Institute of Policy Studies, 1983.

CHAPTER 9

Aversion to Risk, Moral Hazards and Policy for Islamizing the Financial System

A question that assumes particular importance in the context of policy making is whether abolition of interest-based finance is harmful to the supply process in the financial markets and hence to real growth targets in economic development. As Tag-el-din (5) rightly pointed out, this question is likely to arise because of two particular apprehensions:

(a)   That abolition of interest-based debt may depress prosperity, especially of lenders likely to be averse to risk, and this depression of prosperity would be a deadweight loss to the society.

(b)   That the possibility of moral hazards would make Islamization of the financial system a costly policy on account of information cost which would be a deadweight loss to the society.

Though Tag-el-din made a rigorous effort to critically evaluate the analytical basis of these apprehensions, he did not, I believe, succeed in removing these apprehensions. I should like to add the following comments and argument to his analysis.

The Aversion to Risk Theory

The apprehensions arising out of the aversion to risk have also been pointed out by Rafi Khan (3). It is worthwhile to briefly review the argument:

In the presence of interest-based debt financing the supplier of investible funds is assumed to operate in the following framework (as elaborated by Tag-el-din (5), p. 51).

(1)   There is an investment opportunity set constructed from the

knowledge of expected returns, and variance/convergence parameters of the marketable securities. This set determines an efficiency frontier as shown by the EF curve in Fig. 1.
(2)   There is a set of mean-variance indifference curves as shown by I_1 and I_2.
(3)   A capital market line as shown by the line CML in Fig. 1.

The equilibrium position is shown by the tangency of CML with EF frontier and the indifference curves. In this framework, the prosperity of investors is then shown to worsen, if the debt institution is abolished. This happens, the argument goes, because CML disappears from the scene and the tangency now has to be observed directly between indifference curve and the efficiency frontier. This tangency now occurs at a point where the indifference curve is at a lower level compared to where it was in the presence of interest (see Fig. 2). This reduction is treated as deadweight loss due to the elimination of interest-based debt finance.

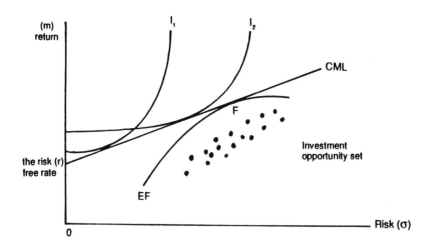

Fig. 1.   Equilibrium in Financial Capital Market

174

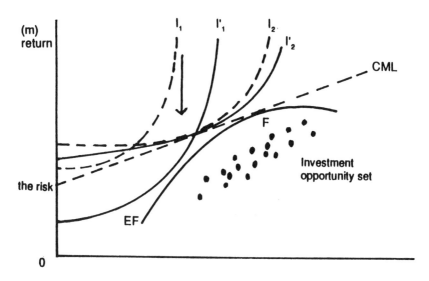

Fig. 2.   Welfare Losses due to Removal of CML

Tag-el-din takes the line that the above conclusion results from the convexity of indifference curves, and that the convexity of indifference curves will occur under *very restricted* assumption, namely, that

(a)   investment returns are distributed normally, and
(b)   investment returns are (pairwise) perfectly correlated.

This line of argument does not help much, particularly as regards Islamization of the financial system. The policy maker still remains in a dilemma. How can he establish that the indifference curves of investors in the economy are not convex?

The following points are to be noted in this context:

First, even if we accept that in an Islamic economy, the *restrictive* assumptions mentioned above will not be valid, the argument still does not establish that the tangency point shown in Fig. 2 will cease to lie below the point in an interest-based economy.

Second, the question of reduction in the prosperity of the investor should not cause alarm at least in the above framework. When we are talking of deadweight loss to the society, we have to weigh the reduction in the investor's welfare against the gains of other sections of the society.

175

What happens to the borrower's welfare? Though Tag-el-din did not discuss this, Rafi Khan (3) showed that the answer could not be determined in such a framework. If a borrower gains (and there are reasons to believe that borrowers would), it means he will be prepared to pay a higher price for the capital he uses and so push the efficiency frontier EF upward, and hence there may not be any deadweight loss to the society.

To my mind, a more appropriate line of argument would be this:

First, as already mentioned, if we take a more general equilibrium approach, we have every reason to believe that the gains to users of investment funds, i.e. to entrepreneurs, will push the EF upward. The greater diversity in the deployment of investible funds will also reduce risk which also will push EF upward. Both borrowers and lenders will be on higher indifference curves, and hence there are no *a priori* reasons to worry on this account.

Second, and more importantly, it is not correct to assume that, in the Islamic financial system, the CML line will disappear. Tag-el-din and others are perhaps unable to visualize the presence of such a line in the absence of interest, but there is no reason why absence of interest should eliminate the CML. We assume that financial intermediaries will continue to exist in an Islamic economy, except that they will not be paying interest on deposits and will instead be sharing their profits with depositors. Given the ability of Islamic financial intermediaries to sufficiently diversify their portfolio on the asset side, we may safely assume that they will be able to minimize risk to a negligible level. Islamic financial intermediaries can thus offer an expected return with almost zero risk. On the other hand, suppliers will have a choice to diversify their own portfolio utilizing the available securities outside financial intermediaries. (Financial intermediaries themselves may also offer different risk-return packages as well as a minimum risk-return package for small savers.) Hence, in a developed Islamic financial market, the suppliers' investible funds will not be void of a CML. Whether this CML will be lower or higher than that of an interest-based system is essentially an empirical question. There is no *a priori* reason for the CML to be lower in the absence of interest. There are, however, several *a priori* reasons for believing that, in a growing economy, the CML will be higher in a profit-sharing financial system than in an interest-based one. This is because in a growing economy they will be receiving, and so distributing, more profit.

In terms of Fig. 1 or Fig. 2, the only difference that we can point to is that the CML cannot start from the Y axis. It will start very close to the Y axis (where π may be approaching zero) and it will remain above the interest-based CML throughout the rest of the m, σ space. (With the contemporary failures of interest-based banking in the most advanced nations with the most advanced financial markets, that CML can start with an intercept on the Y axis is only a theoretical possibility. Following Moshin Khan's (2) argument, it can be easily concluded that CML in a profit-sharing based system can start from a point closer to the Y axis than it can start in the interest-based system.) There is a *a priori* case for saying that the prosperity of suppliers of investible funds may increase with Islamization of the financial system. Certainly, there is no *a priori* basis to show otherwise, and hence nothing for the policy makers to worry about on *a priori* grounds.

The Moral Hazard Thesis

Tag-el-din's attempt to remove the apprehension that moral hazards will impose an information cost and hence a deadweight loss to the society, again does not help the policy maker much. It is true that the moral hazard thesis may not have much relevance for the modern large-scale corporate sector which accounts for the bulk of investment activity. But the question is – yes, moral hazards may not be of much significance but, if the profit-sharing system is better than the interest-based system then why does it not prevail over the interest-based system and drive the interest-based system out of practice? There must be something wrong somewhere and a policy maker would like to know before he acts. The question still remains unanswered even if we prove that there are analytical flaws in Waqar Khan's (4) moral hazard thesis.

A more appropriate line of argument with respect to the above question would be the following:

The superiority of the profit-sharing system has always been established when it is considered as an alternative to the interest-based system, and when its benefits accrue only after elimination and replacement of the interest-based system. If profit-sharing is introduced alongside the interest-based system, the latter option will drive out the profit/loss-sharing option on the pattern of Gresham's Law of bad money driving out good. There are several reasons that need to be rigorously presented to prove that this must be so. Here, it is sufficient to mention only the following intuitive argument:

If the interest-based option is permissible, the demand for investible funds will tend to be mainly for projects which are low return or more risky, with entrepreneurs financing high return or low-risk projects from their own funds. Suppliers of funds, aware of this tendency, will find it easier to charge interest rather than make the effort of finding or selecting the more profitable projects, then closely monitoring their performance throughout the period of investment. These tendencies would eventually eliminate the profit-sharing based transactions from the bulk of the financial market.

Only when the option of interest-based financing has been totally abolished will the profit-sharing based system be able to prove all its merits described in the literature. The lesson for the policy maker, then, is if the profit-sharing based system is to be introduced and all its benefits realized, the interest option must be eliminated totally from the system. Once this is done the moral hazard thesis will lose its significance for the reasons presented by Tag-el-din (5) and Waqar Khan (4).

References

1. Khan, M. Fahim, *Islamic Financial System and Human Resource Mobilization,* Jeddah, Saudi Arabia, Islamic Research and Training Institute, Islamic Development Bank, 1991.

2. Khan, S. Mohsin, 'Islamic Interest Free Banking: A Theoretical Analysis', in Mohsin S. Khan and Abbas Mirakhor (eds.), *Theoretical Studies in Islamic Banking and Finance,* Houston, Texas, USA, The Institute for Research and Islamic Studies, 1989.

3. Khan, S.R. Rafi, 'An Economic Analysis of a PLS Model for the Financial Sector', *Pakistan Journal of Applied Economics,* Vol. 3 (1989), pp. 89–105.

4. Khan, Waqar M., 'Towards an Interest-Free Islamic Economic System', *Journal of King Abdul Aziz University: Islamic Economics* (Jeddah, Saudi Arabia), Vol. 1 (1989), pp. 3–37.

5. Tag-el-din, S., 'Risk Aversion, Moral Hazard and Financial Islamization Policy', *Review of Islamic Economics,* Vol. 1, No. 1 (1991), pp. 49–99.

CHAPTER 10

Investment Demand Function in a Profit/Loss-Sharing Based System*

Introduction

Substantial theoretical literature has appeared over the last two decades on the economics of a profit/loss-sharing (PLS) based financial system as an alternative to the interest-based system. Several Ph.D. dissertations have been written on the subject in Western universities.[1]

Investment demand has been one of the major topics subjected to rigorous analysis. The analyses, however, have been lacking in one way or another. The objective of the present chapter is to point out some of the deficiencies and suggest an alternative formulation for understanding investment demand in the PLS system.

The Issue

The theory of Islamic banking, offering PLS as an alternative to interest, defines the concept of PLS in the following terms:

The *investor* refers to the party who seeks funds for investment in an enterprise. If the investor does not contribute funds himself to the enterprise, he is referred to as *muḍārib*.

The *capital-supplier* refers to the party who supplies funds to the investor for investment in the enterprise.

Both parties agree to share the profit arising out of the investment according to any pre-agreed ratio.

---

*This chapter is adapted from a paper presented in the Seminar on Islamic Banking and Resource Mobilization in an Islamic Framework, jointly organized by the International Institute of Islamic Thought and Catholic University of America, in Washington, in December 1990, and published in the proceedings of the Seminar.

In the event of loss, the loss is to be shared by the two parties in exactly the ratio of their respective capital in the total investment of the enterprise. The *muḍārib*'s share of the loss, since he did not invest his own funds, is zero.

How will the demand for investment funds (by the investor) be determined in this framework?

Will the Investment Level be Higher under PLS?

Several writers have argued that under PLS the level of investment will increase because elimination of interest will allow firms to invest up to a level where marginal product of investment becomes equal to one.[2] Their argument is the following:

We have a production function $Y = F(L, I)$ where L and I represent labour and investment respectively. We define profit in the interest-based system as

$$P = F(L, I) - I - wL - rI$$
$$= F(L, I) - wL - (1 + r)I \qquad [1]$$

where w is price for labour, r the interest rate on capital, and P the profit.

Profit-maximizing conditions require that the marginal productivity of investment be equal to $(1 + r)$.

$$\frac{dF}{dI} = 1 + r \qquad [2]$$

Correspondingly, we define profit in the PLS system as

$$P = F(L, I) - I - wL - k[F(L, I) - I\ wL]$$
or
$$P = \{1 - k\}[F(L, I) - I - wL] \qquad [3]$$

where k is the ratio in which profit is to be shared by the capital-supplier.

Profit-maximizing conditions require that

$$\frac{dF}{dI} = 1 \qquad [4]$$

i.e. the marginal productivity of the investment be equal to unity. Comparison of equation [4] with equation [2] is used to directly imply that investment in PLS will be higher than in the interest-based system because $(1 + r) > 1.0$. And lower marginal productivity of investment implies higher level of investment.

The above analysis, though rigorous, fails to recognize the supply constraint. Marginal productivity of investment being equal to unity implies that the opportunity cost of capital is zero. This is a naive assumption. Islam has nothing against having positive time preference. Besides, there is risk-bearing involved in all investments. These two factors may not allow the capital-supplier to supply funds unless he finds it quite likely that he will realize a certain minimum rate of return. This capital-owner's reservation rate of return may occur above or below or equal to the interest rate r. Hence in the above framework, it is not *a priori* clear whether the investment demand will be lower or higher in the PLS system. As far as the investment demand function is concerned, equations [1] and [4] do not help us. Some alternative formulation is needed.

Infinitely Elastic Demand for Investment under PLS?

Some authors have argued that PLS implies an infinitely elastic demand for investment funds.[3] Their argument is the following:

The investor's stake in the enterprise is fixed at the extent of his own investment in the form of capital (physical, human or financial capital). The more investment funds he gets from the capital-supplier, the more of the liability for any loss will go to the capital-supplier. But the investor will be sharing any additional profit that may come as a result of more investment. In other words, the investor has nothing to lose by demanding more and more investment funds, especially as his gains are likely to increase with the level of investment in the project.

This argument too is naive. It assumes that:

(a)   the profit-sharing ratio is exogenously given and remains constant irrespective of the level of demand for and supply of investment funds; and that

(b)   the opportunity cost of capital is zero.

The problem arises because the above formulation assumes k to be independent of the level of investment demand.

It is, however, unrealistic to assume k to be independent of I (the level of investment demanded by the investor). There are objective reasons to assume that the higher the I, the higher k will be demanded by the capital-supplier to compensate for the risk of putting all his eggs in one basket. (This will be further discussed in the next section.)

If k is a function of I, then in terms of equation [3], the profit maximization would require $\dfrac{dF}{dI}$ to be greater than unity.

Equation [3] says:

$P = [1 - k] [F(L, I) - I - W]$ where $W = wL$

If $k = F(I)$ such that $k^{\backprime} > 0$

then $\dfrac{dP}{dI} = [I - k] [\dfrac{dF}{dI} - 1] + [F(L, I) - I - W] (-k^{\backprime}) = 0$

or $k^{\backprime} [F(L, I) - I - W] = (1 - k) \dfrac{dF}{dI} - (1 - k)$

or $\dfrac{k^{\backprime} P + (1-k)}{1 - k} = \dfrac{dF}{dI}$

or $\dfrac{dF}{dI} = 1 + \dfrac{k^{\backprime} P}{1-k}$

Two things are immediately clear:

(i) Whether the investment level will be higher in PLS is not certain. It may or may not be, depending on

    (a) the level of profit sharing (k)

    (b) $k^{\backprime}$, the rate at which k increases with increase in invest-ment

    (c) the level of profit of the enterprise (P).

Capital has an opportunity cost. Its productivity cannot be less than its opportunity cost and hence whether investment level will be higher or lower is either an empirical question or has to be answered in a general equilibrium framework.

(ii) There is no question of infinitely elastic demand for investment funds. The investor will demand the investment funds only up to the level where marginal productivity of capital becomes equal to $1 + k^{\backprime}$ P/1-k. Hence demand for investment will not, even theoretically, be allowed up to the level where its marginal productivity becomes unity. Hence there is no question of unlimited demand for investment funds.

Alternative Formulation

Demand for investment, supply of investment funds, and profit-sharing ratio, will be determined simultaneously. Supply of capital will not be infinitely elastic at a constant profit-sharing ratio. Beyond a certain level of investments, a capital-supplier may be inclined to increase the profit-sharing ratio (even at an increasing rate) in order to increase the supply of his capital. This may be due to the fact that the risks of giving higher amounts to a single investor may increase at an increasing rate, because the entrepreneurial abilities of the investor are fixed and his marginal productivity (in producing profits) may start to decline after a certain level

On the other hand, investment demand will depend on the profit-sharing ratio and the productivity of capital. The investor will not demand investment funds as soon as the profit-sharing ratio implies payment of a share in profit higher than the marginal contribution of the capital. A reduction in the profit-sharing ratio may thus increase demand for investment funds and vice versa.

Consider an investor demanding funds for an enterprise. With Y as output/income, I as capital and L as labour. We write the production function as

$$Y = F(L, I) \tag{5}$$

(Since labour and capital are sharing the income of the project and hence do not impose fixed costs, this production function also represents a net income function for the project.)

Assuming the labour component as fixed, we can write the production function as:

$$Y = F(L, I) \tag{6}$$

$$\text{or} \quad Y = F(I) \tag{7}$$

As a typical production function, we assume that it has a declining marginal productivity of capital, i.e. $F'(I) > 0$, $F''(I) < 0$.

Now, the provider of capital expects to receive a certain return on his capital. His expected return, of course, will be directly related to the total amount he invests. In the very simplest form, this relationship can be a linear one of the type:

$$C = rK \tag{8}$$

where C is the total return that the provider of capital expects to earn on

183

his capital I, and r is based on his own utility function or on the opportunity cost of capital.

In the interest-based framework, the provider of capital demands a fixed r from the user of his capital. In the Islamic framework, the provider of capital cannot demand a fixed r. He can only fix a share in the income or profit of the project. Call this share k. Since income, i.e. Y is not fixed and varies at different levels of I, the profit-sharing ratio therefore becomes a function of the amount of capital. At different levels of I, the changing productivity of capital will require the supplier of capital to adjust the profit-sharing ratio k so that his rate of return r remains unchanged.

Using equations [7] and [8], we can write:

$$k = \frac{C}{Y} = \frac{rK}{F(I)} \qquad [9]$$

This equation shows that the profit-sharing ratio will vary as more and more capital is invested, because C is increasing at a constant rate and Y is increasing at a declining rate. This can be more clearly seen in the following diagrams:

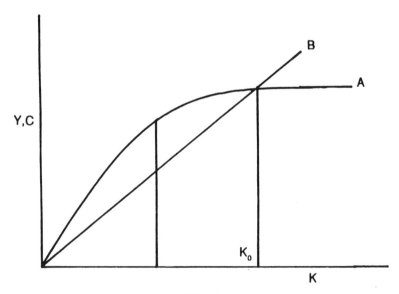

Fig. 1

184

Curve A is the production function representing equation [7]. Line B shows the total return expected by the capital-owner at different amounts of capital to be provided by him. This is a straight line representing equation [8].

Investment Demand Function

Two things should be clear from Fig. 1. First, the profit-sharing ratio k is different at different levels of I. The value of k can be observed at any level of I as a ratio of the corresponding value at line B to the ratio of the corresponding value at curve A.

It can be noted that beyond a certain level of I, the profit-sharing ratio starts increasing until it reaches a level equal to 1.0. This occurs at I_0.

Second, it will not be in the interest of the investor to demand any amount of capital from the capital-owner. A profit-maximizing investor will demand only as much capital from the capital-owner as will allow him to retain maximum profit. In terms of Fig. 1, he would demand that amount of capital against which the distance between curve A and line B is maximum. (The distance between curve A and line B measures the income to be retained by the investor after paying the capital-supplier's share of the income of the enterprise.)

Hence, again, the assertion that under PLS there will be infinite demand for capital is not valid. The argument can be taken a step further.

Under PLS, the supply schedule for capital funds may not be a linear function as shown by equation [8]. Since the capital-owner is subject to losses up to the full extent of his capital, he will not be inclined to supply as much capital as demanded by the investor at a constant rate of return r. Giving all his money to one investor would mean putting all his eggs in one basket. He will prefer to spread his investment among different enterprises unless a *muḍārib* is willing to offer a return higher than r – high enough to offset the risk of putting more capital in one enterprise.

Thus a higher supply of capital for the same investor would mean a higher income-sharing ratio, with that investor. In other words, we must re-write equation [8] as follows:

$$C = g\,(I) \qquad\qquad\qquad [10]$$
$$\text{with } g'\,(I) > 0$$
$$g''\,(I) > 0$$

The profit-maximizing investor then faces the following profit function:

$$P = Y - C$$
$$P = F (I) - g (I)$$

Optimum demand for capital by the investor will be for that level of k where

$$F' (I) = g' (I)$$

This can also be represented in a diagram (Fig. 2):

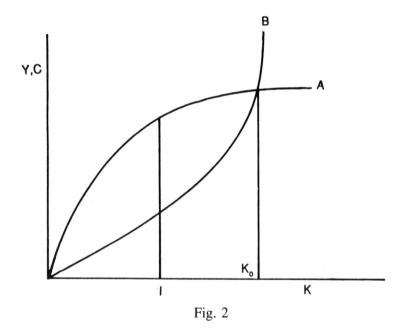

Fig. 2

Curve A represents the production function as shown by equation [7]. Curve B represents the capital supply schedule of the capital-owner as shown by equation [10].

A profit-maximizing investor will demand İ where the distance between A curve and B curve is maximum, reflecting the maximum profit left with the *muḍārib* after paying out the share of the capital-supplier. This again demonstrates that the demand for *muḍāra-bah* capital will not be infinite when $F'' (I) < 0$ and $g'' (I) > 0$.

Keeping in view the conclusion of Fig. 1 and Fig. 2, we can define a relationship between I (the effectively demanded level of investment) and k (the profit-sharing ratio) as below (Fig. 3):

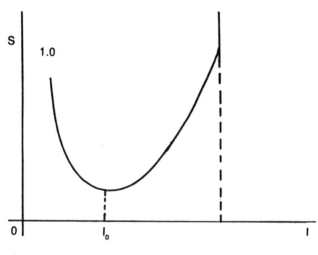

Fig. 3

Between zero and I_0 level of investment for this project, the effective relationship between I and k is negative. Beyond I_0, the portion of the curve is irrelevant from the point of view of demand for investment as the investor will have no reason to demand any investment beyond k_0.

Within the range of 0 to I_0, we observe I = I (k) with $\Gamma < 0$.

Market Demand for Investment

One more dimension needs to be added when discussing market demand for investment and that is the riskiness of the enterprises for which investments are intended. Coming back to Fig. 2, the position of the supply schedule B will depend on how risky the project is. The more uncertain the productivity/profitability of the project (curve A), the higher will be the B curve to compensate for the higher risk being borne.

The following diagram explains the point:

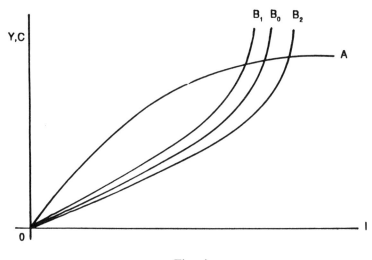

Fig. 4

B_0 is the supply schedule of the capital-owner with respect to a certain riskiness of the project involved in curve A. The supply schedule would have been higher than B_0 (say, at B_1) if the project was more risky and the supply schedule would have been lower than B_0 (say, at B_2) if the project was less risky. (The schedules B_0, B_1, and B_2 may not be referring to the same person.) The economy may have projects of varying riskiness, as well as capital-owners with varying degrees of aversion to risk.

We assume that there are m sets of projects having different levels of riskiness $\sigma_1, \sigma_2, \sigma_3 \ldots\ldots \sigma_n$. The demand from these sets of projects and the supply of funds available for each determines the respective equilibrium level of k (i.e. profit-sharing ratio) for each set of projects. In the economy, there will therefore be n sets of k. Let us see the market demand for the ith set of projects that corresponds to σ_i level of riskiness.

The k value in the market of a particular set of projects will determine the market demand for investment for that set of projects. The market demand will decline as the k in the market of a particular set of projects goes up, and go up as the k value goes down. Suppose a marginal project is yielding a return C and hence yielding kC as the share of the funds-owner in the return. If k increases, the marginal project would be compelled to reduce its demand for investment (as explained in Fig. 4

188

and Fig. 2) because it would mean a shifting up of the supply schedule (curve B). If k goes down, not only may existing projects increase their demand for investment (because decline in k means downward shifting of supply schedule) but also some projects previously not feasible from the investor's point of view may become feasible.

We thus draw the conclusion that the market demand for investible funds will be negatively related to the profit-sharing ratio k. This relationship, we may express as

$$I = I (k) \quad I < 0 \qquad\qquad [11]$$

This will be referred to as the investment demand function.

Properties of k

1. k varies between 0 and 1.

It is possible for k to become zero.

k = 0 implies that the owner of funds supplies his funds to the investor with no share in profit. This also implies that he will also not share or bear any loss and the investor is obliged to return the full amount at some time in the future. It is thus possible that the owners of funds may supply their funds at k = 0. This may come about for a number of reasons:

(i)   Expected profits are too low and risk of loss is considered too high to be compensated for by the share in the expected profits.

(ii)   The religious imperative to help a poor investor and allow him to keep all the profits till his enterprise is developed to the extent that it can afford to pay a sizeable share in the profit.

These two factors become particularly important when there is also an incentive to avoid the penalty, z, on money balances (*zakāh* at the rate of 2.5 per cent), and when there is also a religious commitment to helping the needy.

2.   It is possible that there may be a lower limit on k which may refer to a value below which k may not decline except to become zero. This will happen when the equilibrium value of k happens to be the value that generates a low expected return for the owners of funds which they find not worth accepting because of the larger risks involved. In such a situation, an owner of funds rather prefers to advance his funds at k = 0 for reasons already explained.

3. It is not possible for k to become unity or more than unity though it may approach unity. This is because k = 1 implies that the owner of funds will take all the profits that the investor is making. This will not be a rational situation from the investor's point of view, and so he may cease to effectively demand any amount of investible funds. k may be approaching unity if the profitability of investment or productivity of capital is very large and/or supply of investible funds is very scarce.

Bank's Demand for Investment Fund: Case for Infinitely Elastic Demand

It is worthwhile to consider a bank as an investor that demands investible funds from depositors.

A bank is able to diversify its portfolios and hence ensure with negligible risk a certain return, R, on its investment. Competent diversification of investments in a large and/or open economy can enable a bank to reduce risks to almost (though not exactly) zero and still earn a substantial return. A bank can therefore offer an opportunity to those owners of funds, typically small savers, who do not want to take substantial risks but are looking to earn some return on their funds. It follows that a bank or a financial intermediary may have an infinitely elastic demand for the investible funds of small savers. This may occur because:

(1) The risks associated with investment do not increase with increased investment.

(2) There are large numbers of suppliers of capital so that no one holds a significant portion of the total supply of capital and hence is not able to influence the profit-sharing ratio.

(3) The investor (the bank) has access to and enjoys credibility in the large number of suppliers available.

(4) There are a large number of feasible projects available to the investor (the bank).

(5) The bank is able to adequately diversify its investment over such a large number of projects that the risk is reduced to an almost negligible level.

Based on past records, banks can offer a profit-sharing ratio to attract sufficient funds from the suppliers. They will not need to change the profit-sharing ratio as long as they are attracting deposits from large numbers of small savers. They will thus have an infinitely elastic demand for deposits on a fixed and predetermined profit-sharing ratio as long as capital is scarce in the economy and there is no dearth of viable projects.

Discounting for Time Value of Money

As already explained in detail in Chapter 8, discounting for time value of money for the purpose of investment decision making poses no special problem in a PLS system. The appropriate discount rate will still be the opportunity cost of capital which, for a particular investor in a particular project, will be the expected rate of return on his capital that he expects by supplying his capital on a PLS basis in projects of similar riskiness. This is also the conclusion drawn by Zarqa.[4] Thus the expected rate of return on capital in the marginal project in each class of projects of similar riskiness will serve as a discount rate for that class of projects. There is nothing new about using expected rate of return on capital as the discount rate in investment decision making. The actual practice, in fact, uses R rate of return on capital rather than interest rate as the discount rate.[5]

The discount rate R contains two elements of the opportunity cost of capital:

(a) A compensation for the pure time value of money or the pure time preference reflecting uncertainties associated with time alone.

(b) A compensation for bearing risks other than those attributable to time alone.

In public sector projects, the consideration for type b risks may be negligible as risk is distributed over large numbers of taxpayers. These projects, therefore, need to be discounted for pure time preference alone. The most representative discount rate reflecting pure time preference alone will be the expected rate of return on deposits of the banks. The average rate of return on such deposits paid in the past would be a close estimation of the expected rate of return and hence of the discount rate.[6]

Notes

1. See, for example, Waqar M. Khan (18); Nadir Habibi (8); Shah Rukh Rafi Khan (16).

191

2. See, for example, Waqar M. Khan (18, 19), Nadeemul Haq and Abbas Mirakhor (23).

3. See, for example, Nadir Habibi (8).

4. See M. Anas Zarqa (28).

5. For more arguments on this, see M. Anas Zarqa (28).

6. *Ibid.*

References

1. Ahmad, Ausaf, *Development and Problems of Islamic Banks,* Jeddah, Islamic Research and Training Institute, Islamic Development Bank, 1987.

2. Ahmad, Ziauddin, Munawar Iqbal and M. Fahim Khan (eds.), *Money and Banking in Islam,* Jeddah, Centre for Research in Islamic Economics, King Abdul Aziz University, 1983.

3. Ahmad, Ziauddin, *Concept and Models of Islamic Banking: An Assessment,* Islamabad, International Institute of Islamic Economics, 1985.

4. ———, *The Present State of Islamic Finance Movement,* Islamabad, International Institute of Islamic Economics, 1985.

5. Akerlof, G.A., 'The Market for Lemons: Quality, Uncertainty and Market Mechanisms', *Quarterly Journal of Economics* (August 1970).

6. Chapra, M. Umer, *Towards a Just Monetary System,* Leicester, UK, The Islamic Foundation, 1985.

7. Council of Islamic Ideology, 'Elimination of Interest from Economy', in Ziauddin Ahmad, et al. (eds.), *Money and Banking in Islam* (28).

8. Habibi, Nadir, *The Economic Consequences of the Interest-Free Islamic Banking System,* unpublished Ph.D. Dissertation, USA, Michigan State University, 1987.

9. Heal, G., 'Do Bad Products Drive Out Good?', in *Quarterly Journal of Economics* (August 1976).

10. Ismail, Abdul Halim, 'Sources and Uses of Funds: A Case Study of Bank Islam Malaysia Berhad'. Proceedings of seminar on 'Developing a System of Islamic Financial Instruments', Kuala Lumpur, 1986.

11. Khan, M.A. Jabbar, 'Non-Interest Banking in Pakistan: A Case Study'. Proceedings of seminar on 'Developing a System of Islamic Financial Instruments', Kuala Lumpur, 1986.

12. Khan, M. Fahim, 'Comparative Economics of Some Islamic Financing Techniques' (Mimeograph), Jeddah, Islamic Research and Training Institute, Islamic Development Bank, February 1989.

13. ———, 'Contemporary Practice of Islamic Banking: Lesson from the Market for Lemons'. Lecture delivered in the monthly cultural meeting of Islamic Development Bank, Jeddah, 1990.

14.   Khan, Mohsin, 'Islamic Interest-Free Banking: A Theoretical Analysis', in Khan and Mirakhor (15).

15.   ——— and Abbas Mirakhor, *Theoretical Studies in Islamic Banking and Finance,* Houston, Texas, USA, The Institute for Research and Islamic Studies, 1987.

16.   Khan, Shah Rukh Rafi, 'An Analysis of a PLS Model of the Financial Sector', *Pakistan Journal of Applied Economics,* Vol. 3 (1984), pp. 89–105.

17.   ———, *Profit and Loss Sharing: An Economic Experiment in Finance and Banking,* Karachi, Oxford University Press, 1987.

18.   Khan, Waqar M., *Towards an Interest Free Economic System,* Leicester, UK, The Islamic Foundation, 1985.

19.   ———, 'Savings and Investments in an Interest-Free Economy'. *Proceedings of the Islamic Economics Seminar for University Teachers of Muslim Countries,* Jeddah, Islamic Research and Training Institute, Islamic Development Bank, 1986.

20.   Mannan, M.A., *Islamic Economics: Theory and Practice,* revised edition, Hodder & Stoughton, The Islamic Academy, Cambridge, 1984.

21.   ———, 'Mobilizing Muḍārabah's Other Half', *Arabia* (London), (July 1984).

22.   Mirakhor, Abbas and Iqbal Zaidi, *Stabilization and Growth in an Open Economy: IMF Working Paper,* Washington, IMF, 1988. Also in the proceedings of the International Institute of Islamic Economics, Islamabad, and the Islamic Research and Training Institute of Islamic Development Bank, Jeddah.

23.   Mirakhor, Abbas and N. Haq, 'Optimal Profit-sharing Contracts and Investment in an Interest-Free Economy', in Khan and Mirakhor (15).

24.   Modigliani, F. and M.H. Miller, 'The Cost of Capital, Corporate Finance and the Theory of Investment', in A. Abdel (ed.), *The Theory of Finance and Other Essays,* Vol. 3, Cambridge, USA, The MIT Press, 1980.

25.   Siddiqi, M.N., *Banking Without Interest,* Lahore, Islamic Publications, 1973.

26.   ———, *Issues in Islamic Banking,* Leicester, UK, The Islamic Foundation, 1983.

27.   ———, 'Islamic Banking in Theory and Practice', in M. Ariff (ed.), *The Muslims of South-East Asia,* Singapore, South-East Asian Studies Centre, 1988.

28.   Zarqa, M.A, 'Project Evaluation in Islamic Framework', in Ziauddin Ahmad, et al., *Money and Banking in Islam,* Jeddah, Centre for Research in Islamic Economics, and Islamabad, Institute of Policy Studies, 1983.

29.   ———, 'Stability in an Interest-Free Islamic Economy', *Pakistan Journal of Applied Economics* (Winter 1983).

PART IV

GROWTH AND DEVELOPMENT

195

CHAPTER 11

Development Strategy in an Islamic Framework With Reference to Labour-Abundant Economies*

Introduction

A conventional strategy for the development of a labour-surplus economy, as adopted in several developing countries in the recent past, is based on the following elements:

1. The problem is abundance of surplus labour and wages at minimum subsistence level.

2. Development requires creating enough job opportunities in the modern organized sector to absorb the entire labour surplus, and bring the country to a point where the economy is set to move on a self-sustained path of development.

3. The employment of human resources requires capital accumulation which in turn requires mobilization of savings.

4. Capitalists can save and invest better than the labour class. The profits in the economy should, therefore, be raised to encourage investment out of these profits.

5. Profits of the capitalists can be increased by various fiscal and monetary incentives as well as by keeping wage levels in the economy at the minimum. (Since labour is abundant, it will be willing to take whatever wage is offered, even if it is merely a subsistence wage.)

6. Continued investment out of the capitalists' surplus will bring the economy to a stage when all the surplus labour gets absorbed and it becomes impossible for the capitalists to keep wages at subsistence

---

*Adapted from a paper presented at the International Seminar on Fiscal Policy and Development Planning, held in Islamabad, 6–10 July, 1986, under the auspices of the International Institute of Islamic Economics, International Islamic University, Islamabad.

level. Supply pressures force wages to go up. This will be the turning point for the economy.

7. After this turning point, the economy is set on a path of self-sustained growth which raises employment as well as wages in the economy.

The focus of this strategy is to expand job opportunities at an accelerated rate to absorb the labour supply. Such a strategy cannot succeed in reaching the hoped-for turning point. The failure of this strategy has been witnessed in several countries, e.g. India, Pakistan, Bangladesh, Indonesia, etc. The problem is simple.

The problem of absorbing the surplus human resources, in fact, can be tackled in two ways:

(i)   Creating fixed-wage job opportunities.
(ii)   Creating entrepreneurial opportunities.

Development strategies in the conventional framework have been focusing only on the former, that is, trying to create fixed-wage job opportunities for labour. This obviously requires the capitalists to invest and create jobs. Not much attention has been paid to the second solution which is to provide entrepreneurial opportunities to all human resources that have potential to obtain entrepreneurial opportunities. The capitalist framework on its own generally discourages human resources to get involved in entrepreneurial activities.

It may be argued that human resources in the developing countries is illiterate and that entrepreneurial management cannot be expected from them. But providing entrepreneurial opportunities does not mean providing a large factory or big store to manage. It means providing such business opportunities as they can handle on their own. It means opportunities for street vendors, for those with elementary skills: carpenters, masons, blacksmiths, etc., to set up a small manufacturing unit employing a couple of persons who may be family members. Several illiterate and uneducated persons have been found running small businesses successfully – businesses which can earn them at least what they could earn as hired labour. A lot of emphasis has been put, in recent literature, on the development of small-scale industry. I am talking here of even smaller small-scale.

In a labour-abundant economy, say Pakistan or Indonesia, people do not work because they do not want to work, but because they do not find

198

work around that they can do. With per capita incomes as low as in Pakistan or Indonesia, it is not fair to assume that these people do not want to increase their income and that they prefer to stay poor rather than try to avail some economic opportunity. The problem is that there is no one to offer them a job. And they are unable to have or run their own business. Why? Because in order to have one's own work or business one needs capital. In a labour-abundant economy, the bulk of the human resources does not have capital. They must borrow capital if they are to have their own work or business.

Promoting entrepreneurial opportunities for the human resources requires the following:

(i)   Making the necessary capital available to them to help them initiate their business.

(ii)   Having a system that ensures equitable sharing of business risks between the financier and the entrepreneur.

(iii)   Having a system of social security which guarantees at least subsistence, that entrepreneurs may rely upon until they succeed in their entrepreneurial endeavours (as they lacked resources for subsistence).

The interest-based non-Islamic system ensures none of these requirements, particularly in a labour-abundant developing country. As we shall see in more detail below, an interest-based system will first of all not provide a potential entrepreneur with the required capital and, if it does, there is so much at stake for him that he will prefer to wait for a fixed-wage job rather than risk a business opportunity. By contrast, an Islamic system has the potential to meet the above-mentioned requirements and expand entrepreneurial opportunities so that the individuals concerned can choose whether to opt for a fixed-wage job or a business opportunity.

In an Islamic economy with surplus labour, development is simply creating an appropriate demand for that surplus. It is with this in mind that an Islamic strategy of development is presented here.

Labour Supply Situation in a Labour-Abundant Economy of an Islamic Country

Under-development in our framework is defined as mass unemployment or underemployment of some of the economic resources. In the case of a labour-abundant country, under-development means that a large part of the able-bodied population is either out of the labour market or in it at a very low wage level. The problem is to employ the entire stock of human resources to earn a better living for themselves and to contribute to self-sustained growth in the economy. The explanation in the conventional economic theory as to why the problem persists, can be seen in any treatise on economic development.[1] We define the problem as below:

The abundance of human resources relative to other productive resources keeps wages at a very low level. The scarcity of other productive resources does not allow enough jobs to be created for all those willing to work even for a low wage. Besides, there is a large stock of human resources that does not find it worthwhile to offer themselves at this low wage. The situation is shown in the following figure.[2]

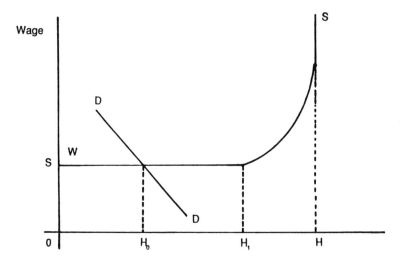

Fig. 1.   Supply of Labour

SS is the labour supply curve. DD shows demand for labour in the organized sector. H is the total stock of people of working age with productive capacity. H_1 is that part of the total stock of labour (H) that is willing to be employed on wage W which is the minimum reservation wage in the society below which no-one is willing to work on a wage basis in the organized sector.[3] Out of H_1, only H_0 get employed at wage

W. The $H_0 H_1$ is the pool of labour that is willing to work at wage W but unable to get a job. Let us call them unemployed. The $H_1 H$ is the pool of labour that is not willing to work at wage W. They will be willing to take employment only when the wage level rises to match their supply price. This stock of human resources in conventional economic terminology is called 'out-of-labour-force'.[4]

It should be noted that several labour-abundant under-developed countries may fail to report a significant amount of $H_0 H_1$ in their statistics. This happens because, when the survey question is put to them, 'Are you looking for a job?', they most probably reply 'No'. $H_0 H_1$ are then classified as 'out-of-labour-force' whereas in fact they are 'unemployed'. The fact is that these people report themselves not looking for a job because they believe there is no job around for them at their minimum reservation wage.[5] The bulk of these people are in rural areas where the assumption is justified. They cannot honestly report themselves as 'looking for a job'. Most women reported as out-of-labour-force in several developing countries also reflect this phenomenon. Women's participation in the labour force increases as soon as labour demand increases, otherwise they report themselves as 'out-of-labour-force'.

In an Islamic framework we must include even $H_0 H_1$ in 'surplus labour' because, in an Islamic perspective, no human resource can be assumed to be sitting idle or voluntarily unemployed. Idleness is discouraged in Islam for any resource, whether land, labour or capital. The Prophet (peace be upon him) is reported to have said that Allah hates persons of sound body and mind who sit idle. Also, begging as a profession is prohibited and dependence on others is disliked. To remain in poverty is regarded as undesirable because it weakens religion and destroys one's sense of dignity. Thus, in the religious framework of Islam, it is imperative that every individual person looks for an economic activity of his own because:

(i) he is not encouraged to remain as an idle resource;
(ii) he is required to support himself and his family and not be dependent on others for his or his family's living;
(iii) he is required to support the have-nots of the society;
(iv) he is required to spare resources for spreading the message of Islam.

This framework is, therefore, assumed to persuade all able-bodied people of working age to look for an appropriate economic activity to be involved in. This is what leads us to count the entire $H_0 H_1$ stock as 'surplus labour'.

This surplus of human resources must either seek a wage-paying job or seek involvement in entrepreneurial activity.[6] With demand for labour at DD, we can regard all the $H_0 H_1$ as human resources potentially looking for entrepreneurial activities as they have no other practical option until enough job opportunities are available to employ each one of them at or above their reservation wage.

The aim of 'development' should be to generate opportunities that can start absorbing surplus human resources and to lead to a turning point,[7] after which the remaining surplus human resources become absorbed into the system through endogenous forces.

Consider a human resource beyond H_0. His reservation wage or supply price is W. He is unable to get a job at this wage. He wants to work. If a wage-paid job is not available to him he may think of initiating a project of his own that could yield him an expected profit equal to or greater than W. In other words, he is a potential entrepreneur looking for a project

With $E(R_i P_i) \geq W$

Where R   = the set of different values of anticipated profits or losses likely to arise out of the project.

P_i = the set of probabilities corresponding to respective anticipated profit/loss values.

If he succeeds in obtaining an entrepreneurial opportunity (with the above condition), he will not only be employing himself, he may also be creating a demand for other human resources to join him, either as partners or on the basis of rent (wage).

Development Process in an Islamic Economy

Growth of Entrepreneurship in the Economy

The institutional framework of an Islamic economy has a very clear bias towards creating and encouraging entrepreneurial activities in the economy. The following elements of the institutional framework point towards this end.

First, Islamic injunctions do not allow resources (whether human or physical) to be kept idle. There are several institutional arrangements (besides moral norms) that will achieve these objectives in the Islamic economy.

The traditions of the Prophet (peace be upon him) also clearly indicate that resources are required to be productively utilized. One such tradition concerns a poor man who came to the Prophet (peace be upon him) asking for alms. Instead of giving the man alms, the Prophet arranged for the man to be provided with an axe and a rope, and asked him to cut wood and sell it in the market. After a few days, the man reported that he was economically better off and did not need alms. This teaches us two things:

(i)   An able-bodied person is required to work rather than sit idle and live on alms. (It was not difficult for the Prophet (peace be upon him) to have arranged alms for him.)

(ii)   An unemployed person was asked to get involved in an entrepreneurial activity rather than in a fixed-wage job. (It was not difficult for the Prophet (peace be upon him) to have asked some affluent member of the community to employ him. He judged it more correct to get the unemployed man involved in entrepreneurial activity than to arrange a job for him.)

Second, there are institutional arrangements which force one of the scarce resources in an economy to go for entrepreneurial activities rather than earning a rent. This scarce resource is financial capital. Financial capital has been strictly forbidden to earn rent, i.e. interest. The only way for financial capital to earn income is to get involved in entrepreneurial activity where profit will be earned only in return for bearing a productive risk of loss. The option for financial capital of remaining idle is also difficult as the *zakāh* levy will soon deplete the resources if they are not employed in productive activities.

Third, the compulsion for financial resources to get involved in entrepreneurial activities creates a demand for complementary resources to work on an entrepreneurial basis with the financial capital. Financial capital cannot produce anything on its own. It needs complementary resources, of which the best are human resources, especially when they are in such abundance that capital can negotiate better profit-sharing ratios.

Thus, the institutional arrangements in Islam not only force financial resources to be entrepreneurial but also create a demand for human entrepreneurial resources.

Fourth, the institutional arrangements for social security and the absence of interest on financial capital encourage human resources in an Islamic economy to look for an entrepreneurial activity rather than a fixed-wage job.

Entrepreneurial activities provide more chances of growth in income compared to fixed-wage jobs. Human beings motivated to maximize their present as well as future income are, therefore, likely to prefer entrepreneurial activities to fixed-wage jobs if the stake in the former does not outweigh the expected income. The following are at stake in an entrepreneurial activity *vis-à-vis* a fixed-wage job in an interest-based economy:

(1) The whole of the human effort invested.
(2) The whole of the financial capital invested.
(3) The interest accrued on the financial capital (irrespective of whether the capital is owned or borrowed because financial capital can always earn fixed interest rate).

In case of a loss, an individual entrepreneur with no capital of his own, not only faces the unbearable liability of having to return the borrowed capital with interest, but also faces starvation for himself and his family. In the face of such risk, a fixed-wage job that ensures at least subsistence will always be preferable. Compared to this, in the Islamic economic system, which guarantees minimum living needs through various institutional arrangements, private as well as public, and which prohibits interest, the individual faces a risk that is far less serious. Moreover, whatever the risk, it is shared between the human resources and the owner of the financial capital. The financial risk is borne wholly by the owners of the financial capital. In case of loss, there is no liability for the return of capital; all that is at stake for the human resources is their effort. In case of loss, there is also no fear of starvation as the community assures subsistence. In such an environment, it is likely that human resources will look for entrepreneurial activities rather than fixed-wage jobs. They will have a fixed-wage job until they can find the financial capital needed to initiate an entrepreneurial activity.

In short, close examination of the institutional and ethical framework of an Islamic economy leads us to conclude that it promotes enterprise rather than fixed-wage rent for labour. The system creates supply of, as well as demand for, entrepreneurs in the economy.

The more enterprise is promoted, the more productive risks are distributed, and the more economic activity accelerates in the economy.

Capital Accumulation

There is no reason to believe that capital accumulation would be retarded in an Islamic economy compared to an interest-based one. Rather, there are several reasons for believing that capital accumulation may be higher. Several recent research papers have argued this point.

(i) There are no inhibitions on earning income as long as it is being earned through permitted sources. The need to spend in the cause of Allah provides an additional motivation not available in other economies. Verse 39 of *Sūrah al-Rūm* is but one example of such motivation. It clearly indicates that it is not interest but *zakāh* (spending in the cause of Allah) that raises the wealth of the people.

(ii) There are several restrictions on consumption, particularly on the conspicuous consumption currently so integral a part of the consumption pattern of contemporary societies.

(iii) The fact that there will be more entrepreneurs in the economy suggests that there will be higher savings/reinvestment of incomes/profits than in the interest-based economy. In an Islamic economy, entrepreneurs have the opportunity to best utilize their savings to satisfy their urge to become bigger and wealthier and they, therefore, will have enough incentive to save as much as they can. In the interest-based economy, there are only a few entrepreneurs and a very large number of wage/rent earners. There is not as much incentive to save among wage-earners as among entrepreneurs. A rate of interest on their savings obviously cannot give them enough incentive particularly when there is an equal or higher rate of inflation in the economy. A human resource once employed as wage-paid labour is likely to remain so no matter how much he saves. An entrepreneur has a wider horizon before him, inducing him to save more.

(iv) As already explained, all savings will be directed to income-earning capital accumulation, or face depletion annually by the *zakāh* levy at 2.5 per cent.

Comparison with the Interest-Based System

The basic process of development in an Islamic economy, therefore, should be through generating entrepreneurs. The supply of capital to prospective entrepreneurs on a profit/loss-sharing basis is a part of this process, part of the built-in mechanism to generate entrepreneurs in the economy. Compared to this, the development process in an interest-based economy comes basically through capital accumulation. Capital accumulation, therefore, is not designed to generate entrepreneurs. Those who already have capital are assumed to be capable of accumulating more. There is no built-in mechanism in the system that can ensure generation of capital accumulation for growth. A protective environment is a necessary requirement for capital accumulation in the system.

Consider the problem of under-development in a labour-abundant economy with a capitalist institutional framework. The situation is as shown in Fig. 1. The stock of labour is surplus. H_1 H will enter the labour force only after the entire H_0 H_1 has been absorbed into the wage-paid sector and wage-levels start rising.

H_0 H_1 as well as H_1 H, are referred to as 'out-of-the-labour-force'. These human resources generally own no other factors of production except their own human capital. There is no institutional framework in the system to provide them with the complementary resources (financial or physical) to initiate work of their own. (There can hardly be enough entrepreneurial opportunities in the economy that can be initiated with human efforts alone – such as gathering wood from the jungle and selling it in the market.)

There will be no entrepreneurial supply of physical assets and financial resources unless the profits on investment, higher than the interest, are ensured with enough certainty. Thus a person needing financial resources to initiate a project will have to pay a fixed interest irrespective of whether he makes profits or losses. The stake in this case is too much, as already mentioned:

(a)   He loses all his human effort invested in the project.

(b)   He will have to make up the loss of financial resources to return the full amount of finances borrowed.

(c)   He will have to pay the interest.

Whereas he can bear risk (a), perhaps by starving, he has no way to bear risks (b) and (c) – except by further borrowing on the same conditions. Some of these potential entrepreneurs may have access to interest-free loans from relatives or friends but will still face the unbearable risk (b). Excess supply of human resources thus waits for a paid job as there is little hope of obtaining an entrepreneurial opportunity.

The institutional arrangement is such that only the capitalist can become an entrepreneur. The banking system that generates financial resources offers these resources to those who already have capital. The more capital an individual owns, the more financial resources he can get from the banks. Thus the banking system too is biased against supporting the excess human resource supply to look for a productive activity of their own. Individual savers, i.e. individuals with financial resources, prefer to give it to the bank to earn a fixed rent than to utilize it in their own entrepreneurial activity or to participate with their resources in someone else's entrepreneurial activity – unless they are sure of a profit higher than the interest rate.

The process of development in an Islamic economy, as described above, may be constrained if the following factors are not dealt with.

(1) First of all, of course, the development of the Islamic institutional framework: particularly the replacement of interest by a profit/loss-sharing system in its true spirit, and social security to guarantee provision of minimum needs to all.

(2) In the economies where one resource is in extreme abundance (such as human resources), and other resources are in extreme shortage (such as physical or financial capital), the scarce resources will obviously earn high rents. In such a situation, even if financial resources are strictly prohibited to earn interest, they will find it more profitable to convert their financial resources into physical capital than seek profits by joining the entrepreneurial activities of human resources. It will be a very long time before the flow of financial resources into physical capital reduces the rent to a level where it becomes profitable to join the entrepreneurial activities of the human resources. It may be desirable, therefore, for the government to intervene to keep the rent of physical capital (including real estate, etc.) from rising beyond the level determined by the profitability of capital in entrepreneurial activities.

Lesson for Development Strategy

The primary lesson for the development strategy for an Islamic economy is clear. Make the necessary institutional arrangements to directly involve people in their own entrepreneurial activities rather than pampering capitalists to create fixed-wage job opportunities in the labour market. The Islamic economy has a built-in mechanism to support this strategy. In addition to what was suggested in 'Development Process in an Islamic Economy' above, this built-in mechanism can be further reinforced by taking the following steps:

(1)   Entrepreneurial ability is human capital which can be greatly boosted by appropriate education. Widespread planned education can also contribute a lot to reducing the entrepreneurial risk by improving what has been called the 'social climate', as well as 'awareness of the rules of the game'. This requires imparting, at economy-wide level, not only commercial education to enable people to understand 'the rules of the game', but also Islamic education to improve the business and social climate and the ethical and moral fibre of the society.

(2)   Expansion of financial accommodation through the banking system can serve as an effective tool to raise finances for entrepreneurial human resources. The efficiency of the banking system in providing such finances within an Islamic framework requires substantial reforms not only in the existing banking structure but in the entire fiscal and monetary sector. In an Islamic framework, banks and financial institutions should be required to offer financial accommodation only to entrepreneurs. Consumption loans from the commercial banking system will be nearly negligible as these loans must be *qard hasan* (i.e. loans with no interest or profit-sharing).

(3)   The Islamic institution of the *Hisbah* must be revived to oversee effectively the norms of socio-economic justice in the economy. Prices, rents, means of production, production structures, wage-structures, the market and its functions, etc., all fall within the purview of this institution.

Notes

1.   For example, W.A. Lewis, 'Economic Development with Unlimited Surplus Labour', Manchester School of Economics and Social Studies (May 1954).

2.   This figure is meant to reflect all those economies where human resources are abundant relative to physical capital and financial capital resources, and where a very large proportion of the population of working age are treated as out-of-the-labour-force.

3.   This minimum wage reservation will depend on the economic conditions of the family from which the labour is generated, and the extent to which the family can provide support to their members if they are unable to get a job of their own choice. For more details see Khan (2).

4. It is because of this reason that the neo-classical type labour supply curve is not applicable in analyzing the unemployment of labour-abundant countries.

5. Henry Bruton (1).

6. An individual would become an entrepreneur in the sense that he would be on the look-out for a productive opportunity and be willing to bear the risks associated with undertaking it.

7. This turning point has been a target for several 'labour surplus' countries. The experiences of these countries including Pakistan, which pursued the Lewis model and planned rapid industrial and urban development suggests that, despite economic planning for more than thirty years, these countries have been unable to reach the turning point, which seems always to move away into the future.

References

1. Bruton, Henry J., 'Unemployment Problems and Policies in Less Developed Countries', in *Unemployment in Comparative Perspective,* American Economic Association, May 1978.

2. Khan, M. Fahim, 'A Study into the Causes of Fluctuations in the Real Wages in the Labour Surplus Economy of Pakistan', Ph.D. Dissertation (unpublished), Boston University, 1978.

CHAPTER 12

A Simple Model of Income Determination, Growth and Economic Development in the Perspective of an Interest-Free Economy

Introduction

Several attempts have been made to develop macro economic models for an Islamic economy. Usually, these models, being income-determination models, have been developed primarily to study the stability aspect of an Islamic economy, as for any macro economic model developed in the secular framework. No attempt has so far been made to describe the macro economic framework of an Islamic economy in the context of growth and development, although such macro models have been presented in the secular framework. For example, Keynes related a macro model with growth through the concept of full employment equilibrium, suggesting that manipulation of aggregate demand might improve fuller utilization of productive capacity and hence generate growth in the economy; Leif Johansen discussed the macro economic framework in relation to growth in the economy by explaining the impact of prices in the model and hence showing that casual demand encourages growth by increasing the profitability implicit in a rise in price levels. For an Islamic economy, no comparable attempt, though much needed, has so far been made.

The secular attempts referred to above related macro economic models to growth and development through manipulation of aggregate demand. I feel that an Islamic economy will potentially have a macro model in which growth and development can be affected through manipulation on the supply side.

In the previous chapter, relating to Development Strategy in an

Islamic Framework, it was emphasized that growth in the Islamic economy can be manipulated on the supply side by mobilizing human resources through the peculiar nature of the Islamic financial system. However, no formal macro model was presented in this respect. In this chapter the aim is to develop a macro model to show that the Islamic financial system generates an implicit macro framework that leads the economy towards full employment and then sustains it to further growth and development. The conventional ISLM framework will be used to link a simple income-determination model to growth in the economy, but the framework will be developed under the assumptions of an Islamic economy. It will particularly highlight the investment and money demand functions in an Islamic economy, and then link this to the process of economic development.

The Model

We assume an economy with unemployed resources so that supply of output is perfectly or almost perfectly elastic and all prices remain constant. The aggregate supply curve for output is horizontal and so is the labour supply curve (at least a very big chunk of the total labour stock).

We assume an Arthur Lewis-type economy.[1] There is surplus labour available with an almost infinitely elastic supply at a constant wage,[2] say W.

The economically active population can be divided into two categories: (a) those who work as 'entrepreneurs', that is, for themselves for profit, and (b) those who work as 'labour', that is, for someone else for a wage or salary. We thus write the human resources equation as

$$H = E + L \qquad [1]$$

where H is stock of economically active human resources;
E is that proportion of H who are active as entrepreneurs,[3]
i.e. working for (uncertain) profits.
L includes all those who are either working for someone else for a wage in a modern sector, or are 'disguised unemployed' in the subsistence sector.

There are two types of L: (a) those employed in the modern sector (call these L_1), and (b) those employed in thesubsistence or traditional sector (call these L_2). The bulk of L_2 are disguised unemployed in the sense that their removal from the traditional sector would not affect its output.

The output that L_2 shares in the traditional sector is a sort of average product in that sector. This average product determines a floor for the minimum wage that L_1 will demand in the modern sector.[4] We may call this W which is assumed to remain constant as long as there is a stock of surplus labour in the traditional sector.

The employment of labour in the modern sector (L_1) is generated by the demand for labour from the entrepreneurs (E), which, in turn, depends on the following:

(i)   Marginal productivity of labour.
(ii)   Reservation wage W referred to above.

The recruitment of human resources (H) into E depends on the following:

(i)   Available opportunities to work for themselves.
(ii)   Expected profits (P) from entrepreneurial activities.
(iii) Availability of the capital required for the activity.
(iv)   Their willingness and ability to avail themselves of an entrepreneurial opportunity yielding a certain expected return (P) by bearing certain risks.

Since W is assured in the subsistence sector, the human resources will take up entrepreneurial work only if it assures them a certain minimum profit (P). The reservation for expected profits is a function of W.

$$P = F (W) \qquad\qquad [2]$$

Expected profits (P) from possible entrepreneurial opportunities motivate resources to organize profitable enterprises which, once initiated, may also generate demand for labour (L_1).

There may also be a minimum capital requirement to generate minimum reservation of expected profits P. However, the more capital is available to an entrepreneur, the more profits (P) he expects to make.

A typical entrepreneur may perceive a potential entrepreneurial activity as below:

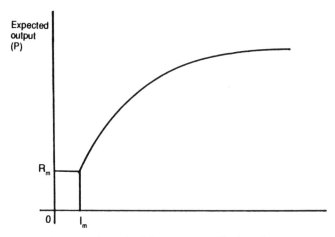

Fig. 1.   Level of Investment Undertaken

R_m = Minimum expected output that may motivate a typical human resource to take up an entrepreneurial activity.

I_m = Minimum level of investment required to generate R_m profit in the activity.

The curve implies diminishing marginal output on investments as more and more funds are used by the same entrepreneur.

We further assume the following:

(a)   Savers and entrepreneurs are different agents. Savers are owners and suppliers of investible funds and entrepreneurs are users of these funds.

(b)   There is no cost charged or profits made by institutions for financial intermediation. (This is only for simplifying the analysis. The assumption can be withdrawn without affecting conclusions.)

(c)   There are no funds available on an interest basis.

(d)   Owners of funds can supply funds to entrepreneurs only on a profit/loss-sharing basis. Under this arrangement owners of funds agree to share the actual profits according to a pre-agreed ratio and to share the losses (if any) in the proportion of their funds in the total investment of the enterprise. (If the entrepreneur has no investment of his own, all losses will have to be borne by the supplier of the funds.)

(e)   There is a tax (Z) on the ownership of money balances or on defined assets capable of investment or growth or of generating income.

The tax is lifted in the initial stages of development if the money or
assets are loaned to a potential or a low income earning entrepreneur.
(As the economy grows even the loans to entrepreneurs may become
taxable.)

(f)   Growth in GNP comes from motivating human resources to take
up entrepreneurial activities when wage-paid jobs are not available.
Supply of finance on a profit/loss-sharing basis provides the necessary
motivation. The entrepreneurial sector competes with the wage-earning
sector and an equilibrium is simultaneously achieved in the wage-earning labour market and in the entrepreneurial labour market.

(g)   The entrepreneurial sector serves as a catalyst for growth in the
economy. When it moves it makes the other sector (the wage-earning
paid sector) move also.

This model of growth in GNP has two basic elements:

(i)   There is no interest in the economy.

(ii) All finances/investments are available on a profit/loss-sharing
system.

What type of macro framework will result in the economy if the above
strategy is implemented, and what implications such a framework will
have for growth, are discussed in the rest of the chapter.

The above-mentioned elements are primarily expected to affect
investment demand and money demand. The reformulation of the macro
framework therefore concentrates on reformulation of these two sectors
only.

Investment Demand

*Determination of Profit-Sharing Ratio and Demand for
Funds at Micro Level*

An entrepreneur, intending to avail himself of a particular entrepreneurial opportunity, generates demand for investible funds. The
effective demand of the entrepreneur for investment funds depends on
expected profits (P) that he can earn from the potential entrepreneurial
activity. This P, in turn, depends on

(i)   Total profits (R) expected from the entrepreneurial activity.

(ii) Share in the profits claimed by the owner of funds.

215

The profits that the supplier of funds will expect to receive on his investment may increase at a constant rate, implying constant expected rate of return on his funds, or it may increase at an increasing rate because the risk may increase for the supplier of funds as he supplies more and more funds to the same entrepreneur. There may be a limit beyond which the supplier of funds may not be willing to supply the funds irrespective of the expected profits. This limit may depend on various factors including the human capital of the entrepreneur seeking the funds.[5]

On the other hand, the entrepreneur may expect certain profits from his enterprise at different levels of investment, as shown above in Fig. 1.

The expectations of profits for both entrepreneur and supplier of funds are shown together in the following diagram:

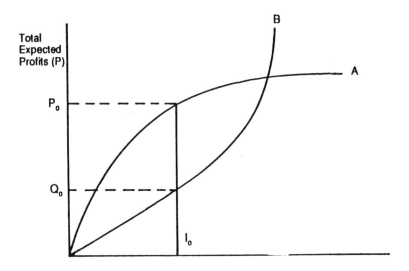

Fig. 2.   Level of Investment

Curve A shows the total expected profits that the entrepreneur expects to make from his enterprise with different levels of investment.

Curve B shows the expected profits that the supplier of funds wants to claim for his investment in the enterprise. The ratio of expected profits at each point of curve B to the expected profits at the corresponding points on curve A would be referred to as the profit-sharing ratio for the corresponding levels of investment.

The entrepreneur will effectively demand that amount of investment funds which leaves him maximum expected profit after paying the share of the supplier of funds. In the above diagram the effective demand would be I_0. At this level of investment, the enterprise is expected to make a total profit P_0 out of which the supplier of funds expects to claim Q_0. The ratio of Q_0 to R_0 at I_0 is a_0. This is an optimum point for both parties and becomes a basis for entering into a mutual contract. The contract between the parties will then be made to include the following:

(1) The supplier of funds will supply an amount I_0 to the entrepreneur to invest.

(2) The supplier of funds shares in the actual profits. That share will be determined according to the pre-agreed ratio a_0.

(3) If the entrepreneur has made no investment of his own, all losses will be adjusted against the investment made by the supplier of funds.

Investment Demand Function at Micro Level

The 'a' value is agreed upon *ex ante* and determines the planned level of investment. The changes in 'a' will affect the effective demand of investment funds from the entrepreneur. The changes in 'a' may occur as a result of shifts in A or B or both.

Curve A may shift up or down depending on the shifts in the level of human capital, technology available to human resources, and various environmental factors, affecting the entrepreneurial productivity of human resources.

Curve B may shift up or down depending on various factors such as the availability of more investible funds, improved credibility of the users of funds, reduced risks due to improved political and economic climate, etc.

An upward shift in curve A (other things remaining the same) means reduction in 'a' as the ratio Q_0/R_0 goes down at all levels of investment. This may lead to an increase in the entrepreneurs' effective demand for investment funds. An upward shift in curve B, on the other hand, means increase in 'a' at all levels of investment and hence may lead entrepreneurs to reduce their effective demand for investment. It should

217

be noted that curve A and curve B are determined independently of each other.

The equilibrium point for an entrepreneur to enter into a contract with an owner of the funds will occur when the marginal productivity of investment in the enterprise becomes equal to incremental increase in the expected profits claimed by the owner of the funds. (For further elaboration see Appendix.)

We thus draw the conclusion that the entrepreneurial demand for investible funds will be negatively related to the profit-sharing ratio 'a'. This relationship, we may express as

$$I = F (a) \ Fa < 0 \qquad [3]$$

This will be referred to as the investment demand function.

'a' varies between 0 and 1. It is possible for 'a' to become zero. $a = 0$ implies that the owner of funds supplies his funds to the entrepreneur with no share in profit. This also implies that he will not share or bear any losses either, and the entrepreneur is obliged to return the full amount at some time in the future. The possibility that the owner of funds may supply funds at $a = 0$ may occur for several reasons:

(1) Expected profits are too low and risk of loss is considered too high to be compensated for by the share in the expected profits.

(2) Goodwill – helping a poor entrepreneur by allowing him to keep all the profits until his enterprise is developed to the extent that it can afford to pay a share in the profit.

(3) To avoid the tax penalty (Z) on money balances as already mentioned.

It is possible that there may be a lower limit on 'a' which we may refer to as 'a' below which 'a_m' may not decline except to become zero. This will happen when optimum value of 'a' happens to be the value that generates such a low expected return for the owner of funds that he judges it not worth accepting because of the larger risks involved. In such a situation the owner of funds may prefer to advance funds at $a = 0$, for reasons already explained.

It is not possible for 'a' to become unity though it may approach unity. This is because $a = 1$ implies that the owner of funds will take all the profits that the entrepreneur makes which is not a rational situation from the entrepreneur's point of view, and he may cease to effectively demand investible funds. 'a' may be approaching unity if R is very large and/or supply of investible funds is very scarce.

Investment Funds Market: Macro Perspective

At this stage it is important to recognize that there may be projects in the economy of varying riskiness. Equally there may also be owners of funds with varying degrees of aversion to risk. In other words, there will be 'n' sets of projects of different levels of riskiness σ_1, σ_2 —— σ_n. The demand for these sets of projects and supply of funds available for each determines the respective equilibrium level of 'a' for each. In the economy overall, there will thus be 'n' sets of 'a'. To keep the analysis simple we assume homogeneity with respect to riskiness and hence we can get rid of the third dimension to reflect σ_1.

We assume a large number of entrepreneurs and a large number of suppliers of funds. An entrepreneur chooses a supplier whose return-risk preferences (curve B) enable him to agree upon an optimum value of 'a' yielding him maximum expected profit (P).

In this process of search, it is possible to enter into a contract jointly with more than one supplier, in order to arrive at the optimum investment to profit-sharing ratio package. We will, therefore, refer to the supply of investible funds in terms of units of investment funds (rather than owner of investment funds) available at different levels of 'a'. At macro level, curve B is thus replaced by an upward supply curve, as shown below:

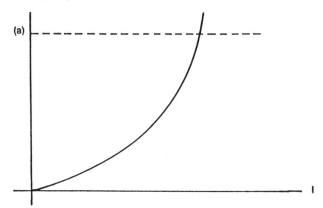

Fig. 3. Supply of Units of Investment Funds

On the other hand, the available investment funds look for more productive entrepreneurs so that they are able to claim more profit. The most productive entrepreneur believed to be offering the highest return (R) at all levels of investment would be chosen first. At this stage we may not distinguish between entrepreneur and enterprise. In the presence of a surplus of human resources, we assume that each entrepreneur represents a single enterprise. Hence we need not distinguish between profitability of an enterprise and productivity of an entrepreneur. Competitive conditions can be assumed to ensure that profitability of enterprises is equalized over all enterprises in the economy. The investment funds market, thus, will determine:

(i) Profitability of marginal enterprise in the economy (R).
(ii) Investment level in the economy (I).
(iii) Profit-sharing ratio (a) for the owner of the investment funds.

Because of the assumption of a large number of enterprises/entrepreneurs in the economy, we can also assume that the profitability (R) of the enterprises in the economy at the margin will not be affected by the changes in the level of investment (I) and profit-sharing ratio (a).

Hence at macro level, while the investment will continue to be negatively related to the 'a' value, as shown in equation [3] the (total) profits per enterprise (R) will remain fixed in the background in a short-term perspective.

Goods Market Equilibrium

Let us take the simplest model of the goods market:

$$Y = C + I + G \tag{4}$$

where C = private consumption
I = investment demand
G = government expenditure
and Y = aggregate demand (equal to aggregate supply)

$$C = b_0 + b(1-t)Y \tag{5}$$
$$I = i_0 - ia \tag{6}$$
$$G = G \text{ (exogenously given)}$$
$$Y = b_0 + b(1-t)Y + i_0 - ia + G$$
$$Y = A_0 - A_1 a \tag{7}$$

where $A_0 = \dfrac{b_0 + i_0 + G}{1 - b(1-t)}$

220

$$A_1 = \frac{i}{1-b\,(1-t)}$$

Equation [7] shows a negative relationship between 'a' and Y. This is an IS curve in our framework with positive slope.

Money Demand

Money Demand Function

Demand for real money balances depends on the level of real income and the expected return on financial assets. This is so because individuals hold on to money to finance their expenditures which in turn depend on their income.

$$L = by \qquad [8A]$$

The demand for money depends also on the expected return on financial assets. The higher the expected return on the financial assets the less worthwhile it is to just hold on to money.

This part of the demand for money may not be a directly speculative demand. In an Islamic environment it has the following elements:

Besides the transaction demand for money, there is a demand for meeting the short-term borrowing needs of others. With the importance attached to *qard hasan* and with the embarrassment attached to not helping a brother in need, the Islamic environment would motivate everyone to keep some cash to meet the short-term borrowing needs of others. The money demand for such motives will, however, depend on the cost of holding on to money which, of course, is the expected rate of return on investment. The lower the rate of return the higher the demand for this purpose. The demand for money motivated by altruistic considerations in fact will be a function of both income (Y) and rate of return (Q). While it will be positively related to Y, it will be negatively related to Q. This part of the demand for money for altruistic purposes can be written as

$$A = a_2\, Y - hQ \qquad [8B]$$

The equations [8A] and [8B] can be combined to write:

$$LA = ky - hQ \qquad [8]$$

As far as speculative demand for money is concerned, theoretically it

221

can exist on the same basis as it exists in the interest-based economy. The expected rate of return will be more volatile than the fixed interest rate and hence give rise to a greater urge to speculate. Though speculation will always be on expected rate of return, it can always be translated into the profit-sharing ratio prevailing in the market. Thus, the higher the profit-sharing ratio, the lower the speculative demand for money and vice versa.

There is generally an impression given by Islamic economists that speculative demand for money cannot exist in an Islamic economy because of the prohibition of gambling.

Since there will be a natural urge to hold on to money in periods of low expected return, in order to be able to invest in periods of high expected return, and since such an urge cannot be institutionally controllable, some speculative demand for money is inevitable. It can, however, be said that the speculative demand for money will be overshadowed by the altruistic demand for money. In periods of low expected return on investment the urge to hold on to money for altruistic purposes will be greater than in periods of high expected return. There is some institutional control on speculative demand for money in the form of *zakāh*. That will only reinforce the altruistic motive for holding on to money. The speculative motive can be expected to remain, however, and the presence will, therefore, keep the form of the demand function the same as shown in equation [8].

Hence, the demand for real money balances increases with the level of real income and decreases with the expected rate of return on financial assets. We can write the demand for money function as:

$$LA = kY - hQ \quad k > 0 \quad h > 0 \qquad [8]$$
$$L = \text{demand for money}$$
$$Q = \text{expected profits on financial assets for the owner of the assets.}$$

But we know that $Q = aR$

Since R is exogenously given to money holders as far as money demand is concerned, we can write equation [8] as

$$LA = kY - haR$$
or $$LA = kY - h'a$$
where $h' = hR$ \qquad [9]

Money Market Equilibrium

Assuming a fixed money supply (M) and a constant price level (P) implying fixed real money balances $\dfrac{M}{P}$, we write money market equilibrium as:

$$kY - h'a = \frac{M}{P} \tag{10}$$

This gives a relationship between a and Y as below:

$$a = \frac{1}{h'} \left(kY - \frac{M}{P}\right) \tag{11}$$

This is the equation which will be referred to as the LAM curve in order to distinguish it from the LM curve that represents interest-based speculative demand for liquidity. The LAM curve is based on the demand for liquidity that is motivated by profit-cum-altruistic considerations.

Income Determination – Islamic Framework

The IS and LAM curves determine equilibrium level of income as usual, except that we have profit-sharing ratio 'a' instead of interest rate, as shown below:

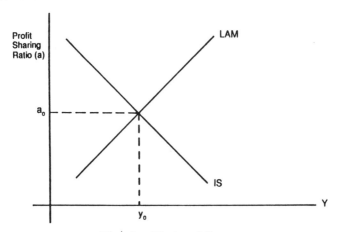

Fig. 4. National Income

223

Slope of LAM Curve

The LAM curve is represented by the equation

$$= \frac{1}{h'} (ky - \frac{M}{P}) \qquad [12]$$

Is there a vertical section in the LM curve?

The answer depends on whether h' can be zero, i.e. whether demand for money can be insensitive to changes in 'a'. (Equation for money demand is $M = ky - h'a$.)

'a' may cease to have any effect on demand for money when Q (the expected rate of return for the owners of the financial assets) is very low. At very low Q, the owners of financial assets may not be inclined to invest at positive 'a' as a consequence of aversion to risk. Positive 'a' means also the responsibility for carrying losses. Low Q may not attract the financial assets owner to bear the responsibility of loss implied in this Q. On the other hand, there is a cost in holding on to money. The holders pay Z on the amount held by them. In such a situation, holders of money, being disinclined to invest it on a PLS basis, while wishing also to avoid the penalty of Z, may prefer to lend the money to those who need it. Money lent, in the Islamic framework, does not share any profit because it is returnable in full at some future date. This may also be referred to as investment with a = 0 (i.e. neither earning profit nor bearing any loss).

The money demand will remain insensitive to 'a' until Q reaches a certain level beyond which owners of financial assets become responsive to changes in 'a'. With R (expected total return on investment) as given, this implies that there is a corresponding 'a' well below which $h'a$ is zero.

Hence it is possible to have a vertical section below a certain 'a'. There may not be any vertical section, if R is not low.

Is there a horizontal section in the LAM curve? The answer depends on whether it is possible for money demand and financial assets to be perfect substitutes for each other. In terms of lower Q, we have already discussed that it is not possible that any addition to money supply will add to the money demand because of the existence of a cost (Z) for holding on to money.

Thus, the LAM curve cannot be horizontal at lower values of Q. It may be vertical up to a certain level of 'a' and after that it will have a positive slope. However, there is a limit to the value of 'a' as it cannot be equal to or greater than unity. If R is very high, there is scarcity of capital and excess supply of human resources willing to undertake entrepreneurial activities, the 'a' may rise to a very high level, still leaving enough P (expected return for the entrepreneur from the investment) to induce the entrepreneur to remain in the entrepreneurial activity. As 'a' approaches unity, the LAM curve will become flatter and flatter. At higher levels of 'a', with R being very high, Q will also become very high which enables money-holders to demand more money as they can afford to pay Z on their money balances out of the Q earned on the finances already invested. Hence the bulk of any addition to money supply at this stage may simply add to the money demand. A horizontal section in the LAM curve is therefore possible at very high (close to unity) levels of 'a'. Such a horizontal section may not occur at very low levels of R because, even a very high 'a' at very low level of R may mean that P is less than P_m (a threshold point for entrepreneurial human resources remaining in entrepreneurial activities).

We can therefore observe two extreme positions:

1.   When Q is very low due to lower values of R, the LAM curve may be vertical below a certain level of 'a'.

2.   When Q is high because of higher R, the LAM curve will be horizontal as 'a' approaches unity.

In between these two extreme situations, the slope of the LAM curve will depend on the slope of money demand functions which is an empirical question.

In this framework, it is important to recognize that the slope of the LAM curve will be different at different stages of economic development. Whereas a vertical LM curve will occur at initial stages, the horizontal section of the curve will occur at advanced stages of economic development.

Slope of IS Curve

Can the IS curve have any horizontal section? To see this, let us reconsider the IS equation, viz.

$$Y = A_0 - A_1 a \qquad\qquad [12]$$

or $$a = A - A' Y \qquad\qquad [13]$$

225

$$\text{where } A' = \frac{1 - b\,(1-t)}{i} \tag{14}$$

b = marginal propensity to consume
t = rate of income tax
i = responsiveness of effective demand of investment funds to the profit ratio

IS can be horizontal if A_1 is infinity or A' is zero. This can be possible either when i is infinity or when b(1-t) is equal to unity. For i to be infinite, implies that more and more investment funds can be offered by the owner of funds without any change in 'a' and the entrepreneurial human resources are available to utilize the increased supply of financial resources without a change in i.

For b(1-t) to be equal to unity implies that there are no taxes on income and the marginal propensity to consume is equal to unity. Let us consider under what circumstances either of these two conditions may hold good:

It may be convenient to start by considering investment demand as a function of Q (the expected return on investment to be paid by the entrepreneur to the owner of the funds). We ask the question: Is there any level of Q at which investment may continue to be made without any decline in Q? In our framework this can occur as below:

(i)   For a given R on investment, for the entrepreneur there will be a level of Q which leaves just that amount of P which is the threshold point for human resources to stay in entrepreneurial activity.

(ii)   There is surplus stock of human resources, which implies an infinitely elastic supply curve of entrepreneurs at P_m. The surplus stock cannot compete to raise Q because that would mean a return for them below P.

(iii)   Any additional supply of financial assets in this situation does not have to offer a lower Q to secure deployment with an entrepreneur.

(iv)   Investment can therefore continue to take place at Q because of the surplus supply of human resources. It is not necessary that new entrepreneurs always have to come from the surplus stock in the subsistence sector. Labour already employed in the modern sector can take entrepreneurial jobs, thus vacating wage-paid jobs in the modern sector to be filled by the surplus labour in the subsistence sector. The investment function may then have a horizontal section.

An infinitely elastic portion in the investment curve may occur without the presence of the surplus stock of labour. This may occur in a situation where R and P are such that they leave Q which is not acceptable to the owner of funds. Accepting Q (expected return for owners) also means responsibility of bearing the loss, if any. The risks may be too high to be compensated by Q. But the owner of investible funds cannot keep the funds idle in view of the existence of the tax Z. An easy alternative would be to give his financial resources temporarily to an entrepreneur with a = 0 (i.e. neither sharing profit nor bearing losses). Besides avoiding tax Z, the various considerations may also comple-ment the motivation for advancing funds on a = 0, when R, P and Q are too low. (These considerations were elaborated in 'Investment Demand Function at Micro Level' above.)

In this case a horizontal section in the investment curve will occur at a = 0, as shown below:

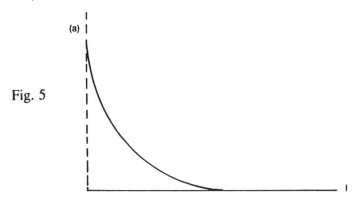

Fig. 5

Now we come to consider the conditions when l-b(l-t) may approach zero and hence cause the IS curve to have a horizontal section. The expression l-b(l-t) can approach zero only if b approaches unity and t approaches zero. This can occur, generally, at very low levels of personal income. We can safely say that in the initial stages of development when R is very low, l-b(l-t) may approach zero. This is because when R is low, P and Q will also be low, and P will not be low if W is not low. Hence low P, Q and W imply low personal incomes in the economy which in turn may make l-b(l-t) approach zero.

The conclusion from the above is that the slope of the IS curve may be horizontal at some low level of R if the economy is in the initial stages of development.

Since R is given per entrepreneur, the investment function expressed in (a, I) space will be as below:

Fig. 6

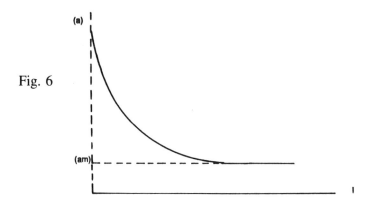

This in turn implies that there can be a horizontal section in the IS curve in the initial stages of development when there is a surplus of human resources and the return on investment is quite low.

At advanced stages of economic development when surplus labour has been absorbed and R is not too low, the IS curve will have a negative slope as shown in equation [13] where the magnitude of slope will depend on the values of marginal propensity to save and the responsiveness of investment to the values of 'a'.

Is there a vertical section in the IS curve? We again revert to equation [13], viz.

$$a = A - A` Y \qquad [13]$$

The question then is whether it is possible to have A` at infinity. We look at the determinants of A` in equation [14] which is

$$A` = \frac{1 - b(1-t)}{i} \qquad [14]$$

A` will be infinite only if i = 0

Equality of i to zero implies that investment of investible funds is insensitive to changes in 'a'. It has already been discussed that the money demand function becomes horizontal at very high levels of 'a' which in turn may be possible if R is very high. The same is true for the investment function, as already discussed.

The above discussion can be represented in summary form, in following three shapes of the IS curve at three different stages of development:

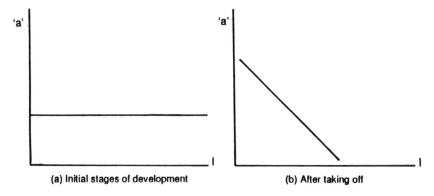

(a) Initial stages of development   (b) After taking off

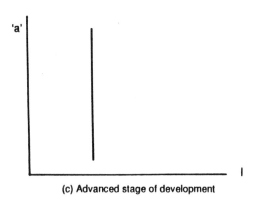

(c) Advanced stage of development

Fig. 7

Liquidity Trap

The liquidity trap occurs when the LAM curve becomes horizontal. This can happen when people are willing to hold on to more and more money at the same ratio 'a'. As explained above, this may occur when 'a' is close to unity and (total) return on investment (R) is very high. Hence monetary policy may become ineffective only at higher levels of national income when the owners of financial assets are receiving high rates of return on their investment.

Economic Development and the Macro Framework

Efficacy of Monetary Policy vis-à-vis Fiscal Policy

The LAM curve has been shown to be vertical or to have a steep slope when 'a' is very low and rates of return (Q and P) are also lower. In such cases fiscal policy will be ineffective whereas monetary policy will have full impact on GNP. When returns (Q and P) are higher and 'a' is also closer to unity, the LAM curve has been shown to be flatter. Monetary policy, in this case, will cease to be very effective and government spending (preferably to help improve the productivity of human resources) will produce more effective results on growth and employment.

This means that, in our framewotk, the government will have to rely more on monetary policy when the economy is in the initial stages of development. But as the economy grows, the government may use both policies. Ultimately, when the country has developed sufficiently, the government may need to rely only on fiscal policy.

This appeals to common sense. In the initial stages of development (meaning low income for capital, for labour, and for entrepreneurs), the lack of taxable capacity may substantially limit government spending. Monetary policy may be the better alternative. When the country has developed sufficiently, people own a lot of financial assets and they are earning high rates of return on them, pumping in more money may not be as helpful to the economy as government spending which may achieve certain social goals as well, at the same time expanding GNP.

Process of Economic Development

We start with the following situation:
The economy is at a very low stage of development. There is a stock of surplus labour.
R is very low and so are W, P and Q.
This implies a horizontal IS curve.

The government has to rely on monetary policy. It decides to increase money supply, and instructs the monetary authority to purchase government shares in private enterprises. The monetary authority selects suitable enterprises and purchases shares at 'a' from the owners of the funds in these enterprises. This increases money supply in the economy.

Increased money supply looks for new entrepreneurs. (No portion of the
increased supply can be held because of the tax Z.) New entrepreneurs
with new investment opportunities are generated, thus absorbing some
of the surplus labour from the subsistence sector. Output and
employment in the modern sector increases without affecting the output
of the traditional sector because of the presence of surplus labour. The
aggregate demand and hence output increases with the full effect of the
new investment. As more and more money is injected, not only do
employment and output increase but entrepreneurial productivity
improves through learning by doing and through the competition that
newly entering entrepreneurs pose to the existing ones. In the process R
improves. This in turn raises Q as well as P. This means demand for
money goes down. The IS curve becomes horizontal at a higher level of
'a'. The above process continues with the IS curve shifting in horizontal
jumps till all surplus labour is absorbed. Now, as R is at a higher level
than from where we started and there is no surplus, 'a' has to be reduced
to attract human resources to employ the additional supply of investible
resources. But reduced 'a' will also affect money demand. A choice has
to be made between monetary policy and fiscal policy depending on
which of the two will be more powerful, given various parameters. R
keeps on improving till we reach a stage where the IS curve becomes
vertical. Monetary policy loses its significance. Fiscal policy becomes
important. Now it is time for the government to take up big development
projects of its own. This will further increase R forcing 'a' to come
down, and once again, we are on a downward sloping IS curve and
upward sloping LAM. The process continues till a stage where the
government's role in the economy diminishes considerably, and
self-sustaining growth can take place.

Low Income Trap

In the horizontal section of the IS curve, it is possible that even money
supply may not be effective if demand for investible funds from the
entrepreneurial human resources ceases to exist. This may happen when
the entrepreneurial abilities of human resources are extremely limited
due to illiteracy or extremely bad infrastructure (absence of roads, etc.)
or extreme political instability, etc.

In such a case, mere injection of money supply may not be enough. It
will have to be supplemented by measures conducive to generating
entrepreneurial demand for investible resources.

Notes

1. See Arthur Lewis (6).

2. This may be a subsistence wage, as assumed by Arthur Lewis, or a market-cum-reservation wage for labour in a labour surplus economy, as in Khan's framework (2).

3. This includes those self-employed.

4. For further elaboration of this hypothesis see Fahim Khan (2). The theory basically is that of Arthur Lewis (6).

5. For more discussion, see Khan (4).

References

1. Ahmad, Ausaf, *Income Determination in an Islamic Economy,* Jeddah, Scientific Publishing Centre, King Abdul Aziz University, 1987.

2. Khan, M. Fahim, 'A Study into the Causes of Fluctuations in the Real Wages in the Labour Surplus Economy of Pakistan'. Ph.D. Dissertation (unpublished), Boston University, 1978.

3. ———, 'Development Strategy for a Labour Abundant Economy: An Islamic Perspective'. Paper presented at the Third International Conference on Islamic Economics, held in Islamabad under the auspices of the International Institute of Islamic Economics, 1986.

4. ———, 'Comparative Economics of Islamic Financing Techniques', Mimeograph, Jeddah, Islamic Research and Training Institute, Islamic Development Bank, 1989.

5. ———, 'Investment Demand Function in Islamic Framework'. Paper presented at the Conference on Resource Mobilization and Islamic Banking, organized by the International Institute of Islamic Thought, Washington, 1990.

6. Lewis, Arthur, 'Economic Development with Unlimited Supply of Labour'. Manchester School of Economics and Social Studies, Vol. 22, 1954.

7. Metwally, M.M., 'al-Tawazan al-Aam al-Siyasat at-Iqtisadiyyah al-Kulliyah fī Iqtessade al-Islam' (General Equilibrium and Macroeconomic Policies in an Islamic Economy), *Journal for Research in Islamic Economics,* Jeddah, King Abdul Aziz University, 1981.

APPENDIX: DEMAND FOR PROFIT-SHARING CAPITAL

Consider an entrepreneur demanding capital for an enterprise. With Y as output/income, K as capital and L as labour, we write the production function as

$$Y = F (K, L) \qquad [1]$$

Since labour and capital are sharing the income of the project and hence do not impose fixed costs, this production function also represents the net income function for the project.

Assuming that the entrepreneur is the only labour in the project and hence the labour component is fixed, we can write the production function as:

$$Y = F (K) \qquad [2]$$

As a typical production function we assume that this production function has a declining marginal productivity of capital, i.e. $F'(k) > 0$, $F''(k) < 0$. The function, in other words, has the following form:

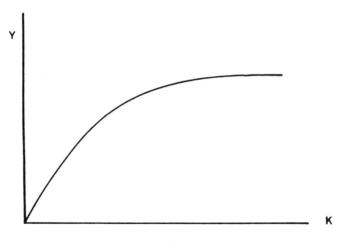

Fig. 1

On the other hand, the provider of capital expects to receive a certain return on his capital. His expected return, of course, will be directly related to the total amount he invests. In the very simplest form, this relationship can be a linear relationship of the type:

$$C = rK \qquad [3]$$

where C is total return that the provider of capital expects to earn on his capital K whereas r is based on his own utility function.

In the interest-based framework, the provider of capital demands r from the user of his capital. In the Islamic framework, the provider of capital cannot demand r. He can only fix a share in the income or profit of the project. Let this share be called 'a'. Since income, i.e. Y, is not fixed and varies at different levels of K, the profit-sharing ratio becomes a function of the amount of capital. Using equations [3] and [2] we can write:

$$a = \frac{C}{Y} = \frac{rK}{F(K)} \qquad [4]$$

This equation shows, that the profit-sharing ratio will vary as more and more capital is invested because C is increasing at a constant rate and Y is increasing at a declining rate. This can be more clearly seen in the following diagram.

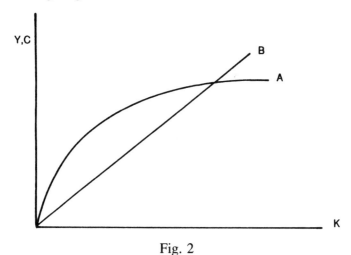

Fig. 2

Curve A is the production function representing equation [2]. Line B shows the total return expected by the capital-owner at different amounts of capital provided by him. This is a straight line representing equation [3].

Two things are clear from Fig. 2.

First, the income-sharing ratio 'a' is different at different levels of K. The value of 'a' can be observed at any level of K as a ratio of the corresponding value at line B to the corresponding value of curve A.

It can be noted that beyond a certain level of K, the income-sharing ratio starts increasing until it reaches a level equal to 1. This will occur at K_0.

Second, it will not be in the interest of the entrepreneur to demand any amount of capital from the capital-owner. A profit-maximizing entrepreneur will demand only that much capital from the capital-owner that will allow him to retain maximum profit. In terms of Fig. 2, he would demand that amount of capital against which the distance between curve A and line B is maximum. (That distance between curve A and line B measures the income of the entrepreneur after paying the share of the capital-owner from the total income of the enterprise.)

Hence, the assertion made by several scholars that under the profit-sharing system, there will be an infinite demand for capital is not valid *per se*.

The argument can be taken a step further.

Under the profit-sharing arrangement, the supply schedule for capital funds may not be a linear function as shown by equation [3]. Since the capital-owner bears all losses of an enterprise, he will not be inclined to invest as much capital as demanded by the entrepreneur at a constant rate of return r. Giving all his money to one entrepreneur would mean putting all his eggs in one basket. He will prefer to spread his investment among different enterprises unless an entrepreneur is willing to offer a higher than r return; high enough to compensate for the risk of putting more capital into one enterprise.

Thus a higher supply of capital for the same entrepreneur would mean a higher income-sharing ratio with the same entrepreneur. In other words, we must rewrite equation [3] as:

$$C = g(K) \qquad\qquad [4]$$
$$\text{with } g'(K) > 0$$
$$g''(K) > 0$$

The profit-maximizing entrepreneur then faces the following profit function:

R = Y - C
R = F (K) - g(K)

Optimum demand for capital from entrepreneurs will be for that level of K where

F´ (K) = g´ (K)

This can be shown in diagram form as well:

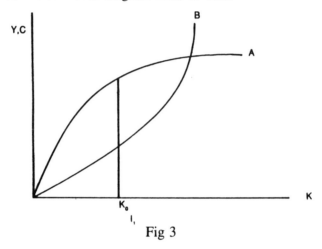

Fig 3

Curve A represents the production function as shown by equation [2].

Curve B represents the capital supply schedule of the capital-owner as shown by equation [4].

The profit-maximizing entrepreneur will demand K, where the distance between curve A and curve B is greatest, reflecting the greatest profit-share for the entrepreneur after the capital-owner's profit-share has been paid out.

PART V

SOME PUBLIC POLICY ASPECTS

Chapter 13: Practical Considerations Regarding the Introduction of Profit/Loss-Sharing (PLS) Based Financial System

CHAPTER 13

Practical Considerations Regarding the Introduction of Profit/Loss-Sharing (PLS) Based Financial System

Introduction

The discussion in previous chapters has been on purely theoretical grounds. In theory, PLS financing has been shown, in Chapters 4 to 6, to be generally superior to other modes of financing for virtually all dimensions of the economy. But what is good in theory does not necessarily find a way into practice, as the contemporary operations of Islamic banking clearly show. Despite theoretical claims that in an Islamic framework *mushārakah* and *muḍārabah* will be better modes for utilizing resources in the financial sector, the Islamic banks have found mark-up based financing to be the most suitable for the practice of Islamic banking on their asset side. Chapter 5 elaborated on how, in the initial formative stage, mark-up based financing might suit the commercial banks but that, in the long run, they would find PLS more attractive. Nevertheless fifteen years of practice has not so far shown any significant movement from mark-up to PLS-based financing. The superiority of PLS-based techniques, discussed in Chapters 4 to 6, may not be very meaningful, therefore, if we do not also discuss the practical considerations in the application of these techniques.

Islamic economists are, in general, neglecting the question of what practical considerations there are that inhibit the application of PLS and what can be done about it. Indeed, some Islamic economists who had initially likened mark-up to interest and recommended that it be used only exceptionally, are now finding themselves compelled to change their stand and find justifications for wider use of mark-up instead of PLS, in view of various practical considerations in the way of applying PLS techniques.

239

Waqar M. Khan (1) first raised this question in a comparison of PLS with the interest-based system. After establishing the superiority of the former for lenders as well as borrowers, he asked why the interest-based system exists in competitive societies where economic efficiency is the sole motivation for economic activities, a question that applies equally to the contemporary practice of Islamic banks. If for Islamic banks PLS is better than mark-up in the long run (see Chapter 5), why do Islamic banks continue to prefer mark-up based techniques and show so little inclination to shift towards the PLS-based system? Waqar Khan answered the question in terms of the problems and costs of informational asymmetry involved in PLS techniques. He argued that (interest-based) debt minimizes the information cost. PLS techniques with high information cost turn out to be inefficient as compared to interest-based debt servicing. This answer is not only far from being sufficient, it also fails to get to the root of the problem.

The Informational Asymmetry Argument

To begin with, there is no such thing as minimization of information cost in debt financing. Debt financing, in fact, by-passes the need for information by requiring collateral and creditworthiness to ensure repayment of principal plus fixed, predetermined interest. The issue of information cost is an issue for the PLS system only, and has to be judged within that system by comparing the benefits of collecting information with the costs associated with it.

The issue of information cost, in fact, has been greatly exaggerated by Waqar Khan. In a bank-client relationship, finance is sought and provided for business and commercial enterprise: it is hardly likely that the client will be thinking of a one-off deal with the bank (and hence be tempted to cheat the bank by withholding the correct information about his business). When there is likely to be more than a one-off relationship, and when there is competition in the market for scarce (and risk-bearing) capital, the problem for the bank of losing on account of informational asymmetry cannot be so great as Waqar Khan makes out. The issue of informational asymmetry is present in all market transactions, but the market can take care of such asymmetries in almost all cases. Some deadweight loss can be ascribed to some degrees of informational asymmetry involved in the transactions, but the transactions exist in the market because of the benefits to be derived from them. Attributing the absence of PLS from the market to informational asymmetry might be convincing if Waqar Khan had shown that the information cost in PLS outweighs the benefits from the superiority of the system that Waqar Khan himself established. In the context of the need for a continued bank-client relationship for commercial purposes, and of a competitive demand for bank finances, the problem of informational asymmetry is much less than in the marketing of several other goods. The fact that a market exists at all for used cars should be enough to show that informational asymmetry alone cannot be the hindrance to the existence of PLS techniques in the financial market.

Several conventions and instructions in a market will always be present to limit the domain for fraud arising from informational asymmetry, particularly when credit-rating and client relations become important in repeat transactions. Institutions and conventions can be developed, if they do not already exist, to restrict gains from fraud. There is also the possibility of developing an appropriate incentive system to induce the agent to disclose information. Furthermore, there are sectors that have a quite developed market and where information asymmetry is almost non-existent. The corporate sector in developed economies is an example.

Why the PLS system with all its superiorities over debt financing, explained and rigorously proved by Waqar Khan himself, could not find its way in these sectors still remains to be explained, even if Khan's thesis of information asymmetry were to be accepted. There is, thus, a need to find an explanation beyond the issue of informational asymmetry.

Financial and Fiscal Structure

One explanation may lie in the economic structure which may have a bias in favour of the interest-based system rather than a PLS-based one. The tax structure is often described as a hindrance to PLS techniques. Since interest payments are deductible expenses the replacement of interest-based financing by PLS-based financing will increase the tax liabilities for the capital-user. Since most capital-users in the contemporary banking system are big entrepreneurs whose income bracket for tax purposes may imply a very high tax rate, making interest payments rather than claiming a share in profit saves a lot of income tax. Modigliani and Miller (2) have shown that the only advantage of debt financing *vis-à-vis* equity financing is the tax savings generated by the deductibility of interest from taxable income.

The International Institute of Islamic Economics, Islamabad, initiated an investigation into the structural changes in the economy required to promote the use of PLS techniques in Pakistan's Islamized banking structure. A working group consisting of economists, bankers, chartered accountants, lawyers and tax consultants of the country was formed to study the issue. The group commissioned experts to prepare studies on issues relating to the country's tax structure, financial laws and auditing practices, and point out the structural reforms needed to promote PLS. The group also interviewed renowned businessmen of the country. The report of this working group has not yet been published. As a member of this working group, I can report that its deliberations clearly showed that unless fundamental changes are brought about in the financial, fiscal and legal structure, there will neither be a desire nor an incentive on either side (the finance-provider and finance-user) for the use of PLS techniques.

The existing economic structure of contemporary societies may thus be the basic hurdle in the adoption of PLS techniques in place of the interest-based system, or in making PLS preferable to mark-up based techniques.

The fundamental question, however, remains unanswered. If PLS is best for all parties concerned, how can an economic structure have come about and persisted that militates against PLS, even in the developed Western countries where efficiency is the sole concern?

Bad Products Driving Out Good Products

Another explanation may lie in the well-known phenomenon of bad products driving out good ones. The existence of an inferior product and absence of a superior product is possible on various non-economic grounds, including short-sightedness, that makes economic agents unable to see fully the economics of a phenomenon under consideration. Some of the considerations that may have driven out the more efficient PLS financing techniques are:

The Convenience or Aversion to Effort Argument

First, convenience may outweigh economics. The PLS system puts on every capital-owner the following burdens:

(i)   look for a viable and feasible project for investment;
(ii) be vigilant over the operations of the project;
(iii) bear the financial loss, if any should arise.

If an option to rent capital out on interest is available, the capital-owner may choose this option even if carrying those PLS burdens would mean more profit. This is an argument beyond aversion to risk, it is rather a sort of aversion to effort.

The scarcity of capital makes it possible to take the convenient option. There are always entrepreneurs willing to undertake interest payments rather than share profits or responsibility for their operations with someone else. Since there are capital-owners who can afford to forego possible advantages for the sake of convenience and capital-users who can afford to bear all the risk of loss, if any, the interest rate is bound to drive out the PLS option. The same argument applies to the preference for mark-up over PLS-based techniques: the convenience of the former would drive out PLS.

Since all Islamic financing techniques require some effort on the part of the capital-owner, these techniques cannot be brought into practice until the option of interest is eliminated. Within the Islamic financing techniques, PLS cannot be put into practice as long as the option of mark-up based techniques is available.

Security of Scarce Commodity

Capital is scarce and storable whereas human resources are not scarce nor storable. There is therefore a tendency to reserve capital away from risk as far as possible, and expose human resources to risk instead, in entrepreneurial activities. This may happen even at the cost of a lower return on capital than would be possible in PLS techniques. (Interestingly enough, even if entrepreneurs become scarce relative to capital, they too may prefer to use capital on interest, i.e. a fixed charge, than to share growing profits.) As long as the option of interest is available, PLS techniques will remain in the background. The same is true of mark-up based techniques. Mark-up based techniques provide relatively more security to capital than any other techniques and hence will be preferred over PLS techniques as long as the option is available.

Demand for Consumption Loan

Demand for consumption loans is perhaps the most powerful argument for the existence of the interest-based system and for rejecting the PLS-based system.

There is always a demand for consumption loans as well as productive loans in a society. There can be no sharing of profits/losses in consumption loan. Consumption, however, can be financed through interest-based loans. The interest or interest-based loans will be determined by the utility functions of consumers.

The possibility of earning interest on consumption loans prevents capital-owners from seeking profit/loss-sharing ventures with investors. The expected rate of return that they would get from investors will involve a certain amount of risk whereas a comparable return can be obtained from consumers without bearing any risk, as the market will not sustain different rates of return on financing for different purposes. The modes suitable for consumption financing, being more convenient, thus drive out the modes suitable for production financing.

The superiority of PLS, as established by Waqar Khan, has been proved under the assumption that there is no income on consumption loans. The Islamic financial system of PLS-financing has to be associated with *qarḍ ḥasan* for consumption loans. The superiority of PLS, its potential appeal in the market, rests on the assumption that consumption loans are prohibited to earn an income. In other words, as long as the option of interest is available, though only for consumption loans, capital-owners will prefer their capital goes to consumption loans unless commercial loans can offer the same return with the same security as consumption loans can. Gresham's Law will prevail: the bad money (interest on consumption loans) will drive out the good money (income through PLS techniques).

The Corporate Sector Dilemma

The corporate sector dilemma, in the words of Modigliani and Miller, is:

If the owners of a firm discovered a major investment opportunity which they felt would yield much more than RK, they might well prefer not to finance it via common stock at the then ruling price, because this price may fail to capitalize the new venture. A better course would be a pre-emptive issue of stock (and in this connection, it should be remembered that the stock holders are free to borrow and buy). Another possibility would be to finance the project initially with debt. Once the project had reflected itself in increased actual earnings, the debt could be retired either with an equity issue at much better prices or through retained earnings. Still another possibility along the same lines might be to combine the two steps by means of a convertible debenture or preferred stock, perhaps with a progressively declining conversion rate.

In fact, Modigliani and Miller themselves are in a dilemma about how to explain the existence of debt financing when their own research shows that interest rate plays no role in investment decision making in the corporate sector. The passage quoted above shows clearly that the dilemma arises because the option of interest-based debt financing is available. If the option were eliminated, the corporate sector would not be worse off, and would possibly be better off.

Conclusion

The conclusion, therefore, is that as long as interest is allowed to prevail in the economy, an Islamic financing technique based on PLS cannot prevail.

As already noted, the Qur'ān uses the word *maḥaq* (elimination by the very roots) for interest, so that no sign of it should be seen in the society. If that is done, an Islamic financing technique will be the only choice and will make all the economic agents better off as well as bringing improved social welfare at an economy-wide level. The same argument applies to various techniques within the Islamic financial system. The PLS techniques are more efficient for most of the operations in the economy but these techniques may remain in the background as long as the option of mark-up based techniques is available to capital-providers.

Mark-up based techniques do have a root in the *Sharī'ah*. They cannot therefore be eradicated as interest must be. The option will have to be left open to the economic agents in the economy. What can be done, however, is that since commercial banks are institutions of financial intermediation only, they should be prohibited from getting involved in the trading, leasing type activities (as is the case with non-Islamic banks), which in practice would mean they would be prohibited from doing mark-up based financing. The banks, will, thus, have no option but to deal in PLS techniques. There may, however, be trading banks and leasing banks which are permitted to finance trading and leasing on the basis of mark-up and leasing-based techniques. The commercial banks may have their own independent trade subsidiaries or leasing subsidiaries whose activities may be financed by commercial banks on a PLS basis. This, however, is recommended only as a long-term policy objective. In the interim period, mark-up may continue if it is required for the survival of the institution of financial intermediation. A gradual but consistent effort will be required to ultimately disallow banks the mark-up option. Without such efforts, the PLS-based system will never be enforced. PLS techniques will remain in use only to the extent to which equity participation is in use in the activities of interest-based banking. Continued permission to use mark-up may lead the banks to a situation where they would be doing all trading on paper and their financing will be the same as interest-based financing with the addition of a few more documents to be filled in.

In the long-term perspective there are no services that mark-up based financing can provide that PLS cannot. Hence, in the long run, PLS will come to be generally preferred over mark-up because of the advantages of PLS techniques.

The situation is not so clear-cut with regard to leasing-based financing which offers services that are not as easily provided by the PLS system. These services particularly relate to the formation of capital (through production of capital goods and infra-structural development in the economy), and mobilization of capital-owners to actively participate in the increasing production of goods in the economy (rather than be sleeping partners through PLS, or do some trading through trading-based financing techniques).

There is, however, a possibility of combining the advantages of PLS and leasing in a single financing technique which involves profit/loss-sharing through investment of fixed assets. Under this technique, the capital-owner offers the services of a fixed asset on a *mushārakah* or *mudārabah* basis for investment in the enterprises of entrepreneurs who need financing. For example, a bank may offer a tractor to a farmer on the basis of *mushārakah*. This *mushārakah* will be between the rental value of the tractor and rental value of the land. Sharing of profits (after paying all other inputs) will be based on these rental values. In the event of no output, both parties lose the rental value of their asset. This technique has not been much discussed in the literature but has a lot of potential because it combines the advantages of two (otherwise) mutually exclusive financing techniques.

It is thus possible that, in the long run, PLS financing techniques will be able to take care of all financing needs of the economy. Comparative study of the economics of Islamic financing techniques requires investigation into two basic elements:

(a)   What will be the rate of return on capital for the capital-owner, and the cost of capital for the capital-user, and how will these be determined under each technique?

(b)   What conditions are associated with deriving a higher rate of return under one technique compared to the rate of return under another technique?

A rigorous study of these two questions can provide several policy-oriented conclusions and guidance to planners and policy-makers in Islamic banks as well as in countries which have Islamized the financial structure or intend to do so. The success of Islamic financing techniques has more to do with implementation than with a theoretical understanding of their economics. The theory of Islamic financing techniques is not only simple but well known in general economic theory, albeit not necessarily under the rubric of Islamic financing techniques. It is implementation that needs the immediate attention of scholars. Our policy conclusion is that, first, the option of interest must be eradicated from the economy, and then, that the mark-up based techniques be limited in commercial financing. The implementation of this conclusion, however, will require certain institutional reforms to be made in the economic structure of the society. The nature of these reforms will differ from economy to economy but, in the light of the discussion in 'Fiscal and Financial Structure' above, two areas in particular need proper study before Islamic financing techniques can be confidently introduced and implemented:

1.   What changes in the fiscal, financial and legal structure of the economy are needed to make it conducive to the use of suitable Islamic financing techniques? The research efforts of the International Institute of Islamic Economics (IIIE), already mentioned, can be benefited from.

2.   What institutions are needed to meet the needs that were met by the interest-based system and which also need to be met in an Islamic system? One subject for consideration in this respect is consumption loans. *Qarḍ ḥasan* is the only financing technique that can cater to this need but is not one that can be used by commercial institutions. Some special institutions will have to be set up. Similarly, there is the problem

of that class of the population who do need some income on their small financial assets but are unable to use Islamic financing techniques, or unable to afford to take the risks involved in these techniques. Some institutional arrangements will have to be designed to meet this situation.

References

1. Khan, Waqar M., *Towards an Interest-Free Economic System,* The Islamic Foundation and International Association for Islamic Economics, Leicester, UK, 1985.

2. Modigliani, F. and M.H. Miller, 'The Cost of Capital, Corporate Finance and the Theory of Investment', in A. Abdel (ed.), *The Theory of Finance and Other Essays,* Vol. 3, The MIT Press, Cambridge, USA, 1980.

Index

ACCION, 20
Al-'adl, 23
Africa, 42
Agriculture, 83, 139, 144
Allah, 10, 31, 39, 41, 47–50, 52, 60–2, 64, 66, 68–9, 72, 77, 79, 158, 201
'Aql (reason), 12, 39
al-'Arabī, Muḥammad ibn 'Abdullāh ibn, 78
Asia, 42
Assets, 61, 79, 90, 118, 123–4, 162, 206, 215; financial, 85; fixed, 14, 16; price, 83; productive, 82; profit from, 87; purchasing, 104; rent on, 93, 120; service provided by, 118; total life of, 93

Bangladesh, 20, 198
Bank(s), 2, 12, 84, 102–3, 109, 121, 207; commercial, 87, 105–6, 121–2, 239; interest-based, 122–3, 127, 129–30, 177; intermediation, 105, 108n; Islamic, 13, 16–17, 89, 98, 117, 121–2, 127, 168–70, 179, 239–40; leasing, 87; liquidity of, 106; modern day, 117, 241; non-Islamic, 245; profitability, 104; 'reserve account', 123; trading, 87, 110
Bay' mu'ajjal, 102, 159, 161, 163
Bay' murābaḥah bi Thaman ājil, 83, 86
Bay' al-salam, 83, 86, 89–95, 98, 105, 106, 159, 161
Borrower(s), 121, 160, 176, 240; credit-worthiness of, 127; exploitation of, 106; welfare, 176
Borrowing, 19, 21, 79–80, 126, 199, 206; absence of, 63; public, 85; short-term, 221

Business(es), 160, 198–9, 240; investment in, 126, opportunities, 198; risks, 199

Capital, 14–16, 18–19, 62, 84, 87, 91, 94–6, 99, 121, 127, 129–30, 136, 199, 233, 235, 246; accumulation, 45, 197, 205–6; allocation of, 128–9; cost of, 94–6, 98–9, 101–2, 128; financial, 12, 81, 84–5, 203; fixed, 16; human, 81, 100, 208, 216; interest-bearing, 131; investment, 82, 91; malleable, 118–19, 160; marginal productivity, 101, 233; opportunity cost of, 18–19, 181–2, 184, 191; owner, 80–1, 99–100, 103, 127, 181, 185–6, 188, 234–6, 242–3, 246; price of, 14, 99, 118–19, 122, 129, 176; productivity of, 109n; provider, 81, 95, 100, 128–9, 179, 181–3, 190–1, 233–4; rate of return on, 14, 18, 83, 92–4, 102, 128, 130, 164, 166, 168, 233, 247; repayment, 98; risk-bearing, 16, 85, 131, 154; scarcity of, 103–4, 225; supply of, 18, 100, 131, 146, 183; user, 80, 98–101, 103, 128–9, 243, 247
Capitalist(s), 30–2, 198, 207; institutional framework, 206; society, 62
Collateral, 240
Compensation, 79, 84
Consumer(s), 5, 30–2, 37, 41, 45, 52, 56–7, 60, 65, 84, 107n, 108n, 166, 226, 244; behaviour, 5, 8, 10–11, 29, 31, 39–40, 42–3, 46–7, 50, 55; choice, 40; decision making, 8, 11, 46; Islamic, 6–7, 47, 50, 52; secular, 51, 53, 55, 64, 66, 71; time prefer-ence, 160

Index

Partner(ship), 146–50, 154, 202; sleeping, 246
Portfolio(s): diversification, 17, 97, 168, 176, 190
Poverty, 13, 19–20, 23–4, 201; reduction in, 131
Price(s): fluctuations, 104, speculation over, 106; spot, 159, 170
Principal, 20, 79
Private sector, 22–3, 71, 87, 106, 169
Production, 2, 5, 12, 14–15, 23, 38, 204; cost of, 155; factors of, 14–16, 117, 183; financing, 244; methods of, 19
Profit/loss, 90, 103, 119, 125
Profit/loss-sharing (PLS), 17–22, 85–6, 89, 99, 106–7, 107n, 108n 110n, 122–4, 128, 148, 177, 179–82, 185, 191, 205, 214–15, 239–47
Profit(s), 15, 18, 84, 103, 105, 120, 124, 132, 139, 181, 197, 213, 215; expected, 216; predetermined, 120
Profit-sharing, 18–19, 89, 97, 177–8; ratio, 18–19, 81, 97, 100, 129–30, 147, 189–91, 203, 217, 219–20; techniques, 98–9, 101
Project(s), 189, 191, 233; evaluation, 160; high return, 178; investment for, 243, 245; long-term, 164; low return, 178; low risk, 178, 190; public sector, 191; rate of return in, 169; risky, 178; short-term, 164
Property, 51
Property rights, 2, 24
Prophet, the, 33, 48–51, 80, 143, 203
Public sector, 22–3, 71, 85, 87, 106, 169

Qarḍ ḥasan (free loan), 52, 78, 80, 86, 107n, 221, 244, 247

Rabb al-Māl, 103
Reform(s), 1, 71; institutional, 23, 247
Rent, 14–16, 80, 82–3, 87, 93, 119–20, 137, 140, 162, 203
Resources, 7, 13, 29, 39, 99, 119, 140, 239; abundant, 150; allocation of, 37;

disposable, 34; efficiency with, 102; hired, 155; human, 15, 19, 21, 131, 141, 145, 150, 152, 156, 197–200, 202, 205, 208, 212–13, 215, 220, 225–6, 230, 243; idle, 201, 212; misallocation of, 143; mobilizing of, 13, 19, 70; monetary, 121, 141, 148–9; scarce, 37–8; time value of, 117, 119; transfer of, 9–10
Reward, 16, 79
Ribā, 77–8, 117–18; nature of, 121; prohibition of, 117, 120, 125
Risk, 13, 84, 188, 244; aversion to, 173, 185, 219, 224, 243
Risk-bearing, 12, 15–16, 78, 85, 91, 170

Ṣadaqah, 150
Saver(s), 9, 108, 121, 176, 190–1, 207, 214
Savings, 7–11, 23–4, 32–3, 45–6, 51–3, 58, 63, 73, 156, 205; behaviour, 11; long run, 70; mobilization of, 102, 197; motives for, 18; propensity of, 67–9; return on, 33, 97, 205; short term, 64–6; tax disincentive to, 11; *zakāh* on, 33
Say's Law, 154
Securities, 85
Self-employment, 19–20
Sharīʿah, 6, 13, 23–4, 34, 38, 41–2, 104, 110n, 245
Shāṭibī, 34–5
Social security, 150, 154, 199, 204, 207
Speculation, 132n, 222
Spending, 6, 51–2, 60; charitable, 7; patterns, 153
Spot sale, 91
Sudan, 1, 22

Taḥsīniyyāt, 12, 37, 39–42
Taqwā (God-consciousness), 48
Tax(ation), 43, 45, 71, 214–15, 218, 226, 230, 241–2
Time preference: concept, 164; positive, 181

253